Battleground Bodies

RECONFIGURING IDENTITIES IN THE PORTUGUESE-SPEAKING WORLD

Edited by

Paulo de Medeiros and Cláudia Pazos-Alonso

VOL. 7

PETER LANG

Oxford • Bern • Berlin • Bruxelles • Frankfurt am Main • New York • Wien

Eleanor K. Jones

Battleground Bodies

Gender and Sexuality in
Mozambican Literature

PETER LANG

Oxford • Bern • Berlin • Bruxelles • Frankfurt am Main • New York • Wien

Bibliographic information published by Die Deutsche Nationalbibliothek.
Die Deutsche Nationalbibliothek lists this publication in the Deutsche National-
bibliografie; detailed bibliographic data is available on the Internet at
http://dnb.d-nb.de.

A catalogue record for this book is available from the British Library.

Library of Congress Control Number: 2017934184

Cover image: The ground at Catembe, on the margins of Maputo: birthplace of Noémia de
Sousa, and site of cultural encounter, national myth-making, and resistance. Photograph
taken by the author.

Cover design: Peter Lang Ltd.

ISSN 2235-0144
ISBN 978-1-78707-317-3 (print) • ISBN 978-1-78707-597-9 (ePDF)
ISBN 978-1-78707-598-6 (ePub) • ISBN 978-1-78707-599-3 (mobi)

Published by Peter Lang Ltd, International Academic Publishers,
52 St Giles, Oxford, OX1 3LU, United Kingdom
oxford@peterlang.com, www.peterlang.com

This publication has been peer reviewed.

Contents

Acknowledgements

This book began its official life as a PhD thesis, completed at the University of Manchester. The inspiration for it, however, began to emerge the moment I entered the undergrad classroom of one Professor Hilary Owen, whose teaching first introduced me to the histories and cultures that would ultimately shape my career. For this, and for her inimitable intellectual and moral support through eight years of study and beyond, I give her my greatest thanks. My thanks also go to Lúcia Sá and Chris Perriam, both of whom were invaluable sources of encouragement, enthusiasm and evaluation throughout the PhD process.

Warm thanks to Rhian Atkin, who showed me that research was my path, convinced me I had something to contribute, and has supported me to do just that ever since – through degrees, submissions, peer reviews, job interviews and the pitfalls of early career research, and sometimes just through a bottle of wine. I must likewise thank David Frier, Carmen Ramos-Villar and Mark Sabine, all of whom have been endlessly generous with time, advice and opportunities, and my Portuguesistas-in-arms, Anneliese Hatton, Emanuelle Santos and Deborah Madden. For their meticulous review of the manuscript and for offering to publish the book as part of their series with Peter Lang, many thanks indeed to Paulo de Medeiros and Cláudia Pazos-Alonso.

In the summer of 2014 I was lucky enough to travel to Maputo for four weeks to rifle through archives and libraries and to purchase my bodyweight in books, a trip financed by the AHRC and the University of Manchester School of Arts, Languages and Cultures. Professor Nataniel Ngomane of the Universidade Eduardo Mondlane offered fantastic guidance on navigating the city before and during the trip, and the technicians at the Arquivo Histórico truly went above and beyond to help me find what I needed – walking me halfway across the city to find one dusty 1985 copy of *Notícias* was a particular highlight. For helping me to scratch under the surface of this beautiful city, thank you all.

I completed this book during the first year of a lectureship at the University of Southampton, where I have been generously supported by my colleagues; in particular, I wish to thank Sophie Holmes-Elliott, Dan Finch-Race, Mimie Morin, Jaine Beswick, Tony Campbell, Marion Demossier, Scott Soo, Aude Campmas and Vivienne Orchard, and honorary department member Lucy Holmes-Elliott.

For the company, gossip, lunch breaks and celebrations, many thanks to the extended family of the Ellen Wilkinson building – especially, in no particular order, Joe, Kaya, Janek, Nikki, Jess, Gwynne, Lynda, Joaquín and Lucía. Also responsible for keeping me sane, with (variously) cats, wine, sitcoms, visits, phone calls and Travelodge trips, are Lou, Simon, Ellie, Zoë, Katherine, Jules and Wadoud.

Thanks to all at Peter Lang Oxford for making the publication of the book such a smooth process.

Finally, I must thank my wonderful family – Sal, George and Max – for their unconditional love, support and motivation.

This book is dedicated to my favourite *bruxas*, Mary Farrelly and Maria Montt. Thank you for everything.

An Iron House: Approaching Gender and Sexuality in Mozambique

In the heart of urban Maputo, halfway between the modern skyline of downtown and the uphill sprawl of residential neighbourhoods, stands an unusual building. At odds with the colonial grandeur, Soviet minimalism or capitalist gleam that characterize the bulk of the city's architecture, the building is unique, made not from stone, concrete or weatherboard, but of neatly stacked geometric iron panels. The popular legend behind Maputo's 'Casa de Ferro' [Iron House], repeated *ad libitum* by tourist guides online and in print, is that it was designed by Gustave Eiffel himself, and commissioned in the early 1890s by Mozambique's Governor General to serve as his place of residence in the city, then known as Lourenço Marques. Having never set foot in Mozambique, however, Eiffel had failed to take the country's tropical climate into account, and the newly constructed Iron House turned out to be too hot inside to inhabit (Briggs n.d.; Fitzpatrick et al. 2013: 149; Slater 2013: 39).

The House's official history is both more complex and less certain. An 1895 study by Eduardo de Noronha, tasked with organizing the district's governmental archive in 1880, states that the House was indeed commissioned by the Portuguese colonial government as a place of residence (108). The reason for choosing the design, Noronha affirms, was one of fashionable caprice, inspired by the craze for Belgian-manufactured prefabricated iron houses in the Congo (108). It was brought in pieces from Belgium to Mozambique, along with two construction workers to put it together (108). Eiffel, meanwhile, is nowhere to be seen. He is similarly absent from the 1966 account of Lourenço Marques's historical buildings authored by historian and travel writer Alfredo Pereira de Lima, who concurs with Noronha's implication that the House, once built, was rejected as a governmental residence on the basis of aesthetics rather than pragmatics (59); neither account mentions the climate as a deciding factor.

Following its abandonment as a place of residence, both sources agree that in 1893 the Governor-General, Rafael de Andrade, donated the unwanted building to the Bishop of Mozambique António Barroso, who repurposed it as a girls' school run by missionary nuns: the Instituto de Ensinho Rainha D. Amélia. Noronha waxes lyrical about the institution, lauding the nuns for their 'affectuoso trato, que não conhece raças nem distingue cores' [affectionate demeanour, which knows neither race nor colour] and for saving their young charges from a hitherto inevitable lifetime of 'boçal ignorância' [rude ignorance], transforming them into 'seres aproveitáveis, que serão um dia mães, e que ensinarão aos filhos o amor por nós, amor que lhes foi inoculado pela catequese sensata e meiga das caritativas senhoras' [productive beings, who will one day be mothers, and who will teach their children love for us, a love instilled in them through the sensible and kindly catechism of these charitable ladies] (167).[1]

Upon entering the school, Noronha describes with some enthusiasm the diverse ethnicities of its pupils, whose faces appear as 'um tapete matizado das mais caprichosas cores; ali uma pretinha retinta, aqui uma mulata, acolá uma mestiça, alem uma india, mais perto uma chineza' [a carpet dotted with the most whimsical of colours; there a little dark black girl, here a mulatta, over there a *mestiça*, over yonder an Indian girl, nearby a Chinese girl] (167). He experiences 'uma recordação vaga da familia, uma saudade intensa das caricias que nos fizeram a pequenos' [a foggy memory of family, an intense nostalgia for the caresses that are given to us as children] (167), and leaves the school convinced that the women in charge, 'tendo por norma o progresso, por bordão a crença, por alvo a civilisação, valem mais do que todo um exercito' [having progress as their rule, faith their tool, and civilization their aim, have more worth than an entire army] (168).

This saccharine vision of racial harmony is where the story of the Iron House ends for Noronha. Thanks to Lima, we learn that following the fall of the Portuguese monarchy in 1910, the school was shut down and

---

1   Unless otherwise stated, all translations from Portuguese throughout this study are my own.

passed over to the Sociedade de Instrução e Beneficiência 1º de Janeiro, who reopened it as a mixed-sex school (1966: 65), a point confirmed by a 1911 photograph of the House marked with the school's name, held by the Instituto de Investigação Científica Tropical (see Figure 1). In 1912 the school moved buildings, and in a later volume, first published in 1968, Lima notes that its erstwhile home now belongs to the government's Geography and Mapping Department (67). An unpublished doctoral thesis by Pedro Guedes includes a photograph of the House, taken in 1972, still in its original location. By 1987, the date given for another photograph appearing in a 1997 Nelson Saúte text commemorating Portuguese expansionism (39), the House has been dismantled and moved to where it stands today: within sight of the colossal statue of Samora Machel that looks out on downtown Maputo, and just off the busy avenue that bears his name. It houses some archival material, and serves as a tourist curio.

Figure 1: Children standing in front of the Iron House, which by now (1911) housed a mixed-sex school known as the 'Sociedade Instrução e Beneficiência 1.º Janeiro'. Author unknown; held by the Instituto de Investigação Científica Tropical, Lisbon.

The story of the Iron House functions as an unexpected yet rich starting point for approaching the role of gender and sexuality in the history and cultural output of late colonial and post-independence Mozambique. On a pragmatic level, it underscores the necessity, for those wishing to understand recent Mozambican history, to return to a broad patchwork of primary sources, to interrogate historical narrative, and to pay attention to silence and absence. From a perspective of cultural history, Noronha's account in particular provides vital insights into the romanticization of the Portuguese colonial presence in Mozambique by those who upheld it. His portrayals of the pupils at the Instituto de Ensinho Rainha D. Amélia additionally exemplify the enduring colonial fantasy of the female body as the site of regenerative national unity, which itself anticipated the racialized permutations of that vision that would emerge following the Portuguese government's espousal of Lusotropicalism five decades later.

In a more symbolic vein, the House itself can be imagined as a figurative representation of Mozambican colonial, anticolonial and post-independence gender discourses: like those discourses, the House has functioned as a palimpsest of Portuguese late colonial endeavour and its post-independence aftermath, while its true story and provenance have remained obfuscated by propaganda and exoticizing mythology from various quarters. Interpellated into a liminal space between the public and private spheres, it has been dismantled and rebuilt, but its essential components remain intact, identical. Imagining colonial and anticolonial gender discourse as symbolized by the Iron House, then, ensures that we do not limit ourselves to simple deconstruction, but that we also examine individual segments, the materials and processes that form them, and the ways they fit together.

This study examines and compares the ways in which six Mozambican authors have approached gender, sexuality and the body in and through their work. In doing so, it aims to shed light on those discourses themselves, exploring their constituent parts from new angles using new or unfamiliar tools, and highlighting the productive value for Mozambican literary studies of a flexible, dynamic use of critical theory that engages frameworks from a range of geographical and disciplinary origins. In addition to surveying the representation of gender and sexual constructs and ideologies in the selected works, the study seeks too to identify the ways that the authors utilize and interrogate sexed and gendered bodies and modalities. These literary analyses are intended to demonstrate that the sexed body, by virtue of its homogeneous position at the heart of meaning-making, can be imagined as a battleground, figuring as a place in and through which oppression is produced, enacted and violently enforced – but also as a site with the unique potential to generate contestation, resistance and revolution.

The authors to be studied are poets José Craveirinha (1922–2003) and Noémia de Sousa (1926–2002), and prose fiction writers Lília Momplé (1935–), Paulina Chiziane (1955–), Ungulani Ba Ka Khosa (1957–) and Suleiman Cassamo (1962–), all six of whom were born either black or *mestiço/a* in Mozambique under the Portuguese colonial regime. Despite this superficially similar status, there is a diversity of experience to be found between the former three, who lived through the nascent stages of the authoritarian dictatorship that would dominate Portugal and its colonies for nearly half a century, and the latter three, who were born amid the waves of liberation struggle and decolonization that swept over Africa following World War II, and during the heyday of the Civil Rights Movement in the USA. A related sense of difference is evident too between, on one hand, Craveirinha and de Sousa, both of whom were writing and disseminating their poetry long before independence and under the grind of colonial state censorship, and Momplé, Chiziane, Khosa and Cassamo, all of whom began to publish in the distinct turbulence of the post-independence late 1980s. Though evidently at very different stages of their lives, then, five out of these six writers were at least partially resident in the country through the anticolonial struggle, witnessing the achievement of independence in 1975, the gruelling seventeen-year conflict that followed, and the country's move toward a Western model of democracy in the 1990s; the exception is de Sousa, who left Mozambique for Lisbon in 1951 in response to heavy New State scrutiny (Chabal 1994: 118–19) and remained resident in Europe until her death in 2002.

The breadth of temporal experience represented by these writers means that the selected texts collectively span a little over half a century, with the earliest – de Sousa's poetry – written under Portuguese New State authoritarianism between 1948 and 1951, and the most recent – the novels *O Sétimo Juramento* by Chiziane and *Palestra para um Morto* by Cassamo

– first published post-democratization in 2000. This wide span allows for critical analysis that confronts the *longue durée* of gendered discourse in Mozambique, in addition to the sociopolitical and ideological 'flash points' that have constituted it. This objective has also come to bear on the study's structure, which divides the writers into pairs along intergenerational lines; the resulting comparative approach serves to encourage – and indeed makes necessary – a flexible use of critical theory, while acknowledging historical and literary motifs and patterns.

Common Ground

This book builds on an important and growing, but as of yet still small, body of existing work on the role of gender and the gendered body in Mozambican literature, in addition to related work in the arena of Mozambican and Lusophone African studies more broadly. Since 2004, Hilary Owen, Ana Margarida Martins and Phillip Rothwell have each published groundbreaking monographs – along with numerous articles, book chapters and edited volumes between them – that speak directly to the presentation and role of sexuality and gender in Mozambican texts, rooting their analyses firmly in the complexities of the country's recent history. Owen's *Mother Africa, Father Marx* (2007a), a text that remains unique in its depth and scope, provides an insightful analysis of gendered discourse in late colonial and post-independence Mozambique as the backdrop to its literary studies of exclusively women authors. In so doing, the text reveals the pivotal role of gender in shaping both Portuguese New State colonial policy and anticolonial rhetoric and praxis.

The literary studies included in Owen's text are each dedicated to one of four Mozambican women writers, three of whom are included in the present volume: Noémia de Sousa, Lília Momplé, Paulina Chiziane and Lina Magaia. Owen makes extensive use of postcolonial and psychoanalytical feminist theories to interpret gendered meanings both within the works themselves and in the authors' respective locations within national literary hierarchies. In the process, she opens such theories up to critical interrogation, evaluating their usefulness for understanding Mozambican constructs of femininity and the lived realities of the women behind them. Her chapter on de Sousa, for example, utilizes Homi Bhabha's theories of hybridity and mimicry to deconstruct tropes of black and *mestiça* femininity in the light of the poet's imposed role as 'Mother of the Mozambican canon and founding mother of Moçambicanidade' (45), while at the same time revealing the limits of Bhabha's theories for meaningful gendered analysis in the specific context of Mozambique (43–76). This symbiotic deconstruction of both primary text and theory is an approach the present study seeks to incorporate as part of its employment of a diverse range of critical frameworks, ensuring the development of new perspectives that will enter into dialogue with the foundational work laid here by Owen.

Aside from this important monograph, Owen's body of work includes two shorter pieces that contribute to the foundation of this study by virtue of their comparative approach. The first compares 'Maria Pedra no Cruzar dos Caminhos' [Maria Pedra at the Crossroads], a short story by Mozambique's best-known contemporary writer Mia Couto, with Chiziane's story 'As Cicatrizes do Amor' [The Scars of Love], examining the authors' respective representations of the tension between oral and written cultures in terms of their distinct racial and gendered subject positions (2007b). The article concludes that whereas the idiolectic codeswitching espoused by Couto – the white Mozambican son of Portuguese settlers – is read by critics as an example of pioneering postcolonial innovation, Chiziane's engagement with linguistic hybridities is interpreted as a deficient mastery of 'standard' Portuguese (488).

The second of these comparative pieces by Owen, a chapter in her co-edited volume *Narrating the Postcolonial Nation* (2014), compares Khosa's first novel, *Ualalapi*, and Chiziane's short story collection *As Andorinhas* [*The Swallows*], exploring the authors' representations of the legacy of late nineteenth-century indigenous Nguni chief Ngungunhane. Making use of Julia Kristeva's theory of abjection, the article argues that both Khosa and Chiziane utilize abject corporealities and gender blurring to express discontent with the post-independence Mozambican nation-building process, and in Chiziane's case to cleave open the latent hierarchy of sexual difference

underpinning Frelimo ideology as well as the Nguni and Portuguese imperial projects. The comparative methodology Owen employs in these two
articles, bringing male and female authors into a critical dialogue that
deconstructs their presentations and uses of gendered discourses with their
relative subjective positions in mind, remains an unconventional framework
in the field of Mozambican literary criticism; yet, as the articles demonstrate, it has the potential to bring vital critical and metacritical connections between gender, power and authorship to the fore. It is this potential
that the present study seeks to harness by carrying Owen's comparative
precedent forward, using subject positionalities both as contextualizing
lenses and as points for analysis in themselves.

By putting Chiziane's work into conversation with that of Portuguese
author Lídia Jorge, Martins's 2012 monograph *Magic Stones and Flying
Snakes* brings this comparative approach to Chiziane to a transnational
level. With reference to the influential theory of Portugal's imperial 'semipe-
ripherality' first proposed by Boaventura de Sousa Santos (2002), Martins's
work examines the means by which Chiziane and Jorge navigate this 'Luso-
limbo' in terms of their respective positions at the intersection of race
and gender, making strategic use of exotic tropes and scenarios in order to
'reconcil[e] a wide target audience with otherwise sophisticated subversive-
ness' (4). Engaging Anglophone postcolonialist Graham Huggan's concept
of the 'postcolonial exotic' with Santos's theory, Martins, like Owen, opens
these frameworks up to interrogation, underscoring the theorists' shared
disregard of gender as a pivotal complicating element in the negotiation
of identity and subversive strategy. By comparing the interrelated but distinct literary spheres of Mozambique and Portugal through the figures of
Chiziane and Jorge, Martins's text is furthermore able to imbricate questions of identity and subversion in the Lusophone world with ones of
canonicity and author discourse, a conceptual area hitherto largely unexplored with reference to Lusophone Africa. Martins's insight into the ways
in which women authors might achieve a refraction of exoticizing tropes
by strategically exploiting their own locations on the axes of race, gender
and nationality is one the present study aims to develop in the chapters
on both Chiziane and de Sousa, carrying it forward by introducing male
subjectivities and masculinities into its analytical frame.

This study of gender in male-authored works, and indeed of masculinities themselves, is for the most part absent from the field of Mozambican
literary criticism, as Chapter 2 will explore. An important exception to
this relative silence among scholars is Phillip Rothwell, whose monograph
A Postmodern Nationalist (2004) provides extensive insight into the work of
Mia Couto, a writer whose very existence as simultaneously Mozambican,
white, anticolonial and antifascist, and the best-known and most widely
translated author Mozambique has ever seen calls into question the rigid
social binaries enforced during colonialism and partially upheld by the post-
independence regime.[2] Underpinned by a broadly postmodernist theoretical framework, Rothwell's chapter 'Playing Gam(et)es with Gender' begins
with a brief but significant rereading of both Portuguese and indigenous
Mozambican belief systems through the lens of blurred gender boundaries,
a unique take on these interrelated cultural spheres that sets a precedent
for analyses of Mozambican cultural expression that acknowledge the
contingency of gender, sex and sexuality (136–9).

Rothwell's subsequent close readings focus on Couto's depiction and
utilization of gendered and sexual crossings and transgressions, seen to work
hand-in-hand with Couto's deconstructions of racial and ethnic hierarchical
distinctions and to '[trouble] any reading of his work that seeks to position
him as proposing a simplistic restoration of an African tradition' (2004:
152). For Rothwell, Couto employs ludic strategies of gender-bending as
a means of troubling other socio-taxonomical constructs, affirming that
'[b]y liquefying the most sacred of frontiers, [Couto] disavows the innate
legitimacy of all boundaries' (156). Despite having been published more
than a decade ago, Rothwell's text remains unique in its use of postmodernism as the conceptual lens for its exploration of Mozambican themes,
including gender, and in its acknowledgement of masculinity as a vital

2   During the writing of this study, Couto became the first Lusophone writer to be
     nominated for the Man Booker International Prize (M. Lopes 2015), a prize awarded
     on the basis of a writer's entire body of work. Couto lost the prize to the Hungarian
     László Krasznahorkai; nonetheless, the nomination alone is an accolade that cements
     his status both as Mozambique's best-known writer and as an international repre-
     sentative of Lusophone literature as a whole.

point of critical analysis. Couto is not among the writers studied in this volume; nonetheless, Rothwell's insights into the potential of gender and sexual transgressions to symbolically destabilize power structures more broadly have influenced several of my analytical threads, particularly those followed with reference to Khosa in Chapter 3 and to Momplé and Cassamo in Chapter 4.

Aside from their own monographs, Owen and Rothwell are the editors of the 2004 volume *Sexual/Textual Empires*, which includes four essays that have contributed to the study of gender and sexuality in Mozambican – or, in the case of Ana Sofia Ganho's piece, Angolan – literature and that have thus informed the present volume. Mark Sabine's chapter 'Gender, Race, and Violence in Luís Bernardo Honwana's *Nós Matámos o Cão-Tinhoso*' (23–44) explores the role of masculinity and emasculation in the titular 1964 collection of short stories by Honwana. Through his analysis of Honwana's text, Sabine articulates important ideas regarding the role of masculinities in the Lusotropicalist fantasy of New State colonialism, particularly the regime's 'brutal imposition on black men of the label of inadequate or aberrant masculinity' (25). Honwana's stories are interpreted as seeking to revindicate the 'noble values of African masculinity' (30) lost to colonial aggression. Nonetheless, as Sabine suggests in the final pages of his essay, Honwana's assertion of black masculine resistance in the face of colonial emasculation often hinges on a tacit acceptance of the subjugation of women (42–3). In the present study this predication of masculine reconsolidation on the subjugation of women will be examined in further detail as a key element of early anticolonial Mozambican cultural expression with reference to early work by Craveirinha, whose first collection of poetry, *Xigubo*, was published in 1964, the same year as *Nós Matámos o Cão-Tinhoso*.[3]

While Ganho's contribution to the volume (2004: 155–75) focuses on the cultural output of Angola, rather than Mozambique, it is nonetheless an important precedent for the present study thanks to its comparative discussion of corporeal gendered and sexual tropes in one female poet,

---

3   The first edition of *Nós Matámos o Cão-Tinhoso* was also dedicated to Craveirinha (Pazos-Alonso 2007: 67).

Paula Tavares, and one male, João A. S. Lopito Feijóo. Ganho argues that both writers make use of sexual modalities in their work in order to subvert the sexualized symbologies of the early anticolonial literary generation in Angola, interpreted by Ganho as reproducing hierarchical gender structures that 'are evident remnants of a colonial ideology' (157). Feijóo is shown to enact this poetic reappropriation through an ambiguous, polymorphous portrayal of sexuality, itself intertwined with reference points and images from Western, Islamic and indigenous Angolan practices and mythologies (158–64). Ganho furthermore reads Feijóo's use of intersex characters and veiled references to homosexuality as evidence of engagement with an aesthetics of abjection that troubles the erasure of internal differences that characterized Angolan cultural nationalism (164–7).

Paula Tavares, meanwhile, is shown to make use of the nature imagery characteristic of early anticolonial poetry, recasting it in a way that 'celebrates sexuality while partly dissociating it from maternity, in a pure engagement of multisensuality' (Ganho 2004: 169). The poet is additionally shown to play with subject positionalities, suggesting that certain elements of her work render the naturalization of the nationalist male–female/subject–object equivalence problematic (172–5). Both poets, then, make use of 'powerful, liminal representations [that] continue to occur in the shadow of the nation, while nevertheless performing it' (175). Ganho's suggestion that the shrewd poetic use of sexual images, characteristic of the aesthetics of both late Portuguese colonialism and Angolan anticolonial nationalism, can function to subvert the ideological implications of images themselves is a concept that the present study explores in its discussions of Chiziane and de Sousa in Chapters 2 and 3, respectively.

Claire Williams's piece in the same volume, entitled 'Maidens, Matriarchs and Martyrs' (2004: 117–35), discusses the presentation of women characters in the works of Lília Momplé, one of the subjects of the present study's third chapter. Williams makes use of the Caribbean and African feminist frameworks of literary criticism developed by Carole Boyce Davies, Buchi Emecheta and Molara Ogundipe-Leslie to examine Momplé's critique of the 'double yoke' of oppression imposed on Mozambican women, constituted by both colonial and precolonial gender ideologies. Momplé is shown to free her women characters from the two-dimensional caricatures that often represent black women in African literatures, ensuring their identities are delineated in terms other than ones relative to men (119). Williams's chapter suggests that by foregrounding the stories and interiorities of women, Momplé is able to orchestrate a gynocentric counternarrative of Mozambican recent history, underlining both the exploitation and abuse of women under colonialism and their resourceful and persistent acts of resistance to imperial and neoimperial brutality.

These marginalized gestures of resistance by women to gendered oppression, and to colonial violence as a whole, are further explored in the following chapter by Sandra Campos (2004: 137–54). Using French feminism's exhortation to women to 'write the body' as a starting point, Campos examines Paulina Chiziane's presentation of female corporealities, and in the process challenges the gender essentialism underpinning the exhortation itself (138–9). Women characters in Chiziane's novels are ultimately shown to enact various multivalent subversions of the corporeal and sexual abuse meted out on black women in the colonial era and during its aftermath, rediscovering their own bodies as sites of regenerative resistance (153–4). With these two very different approaches to the work of Mozambican women writers, Williams and Campos both shore up the need for a feminist critique to recognize the literary representation of the manifold and often concealed or silent ways in which Mozambican women have negotiated agency and resistance from beneath the 'double yoke' of bilateral oppression, an obligation the present study seeks to engage with throughout.

The focus on women's writing as counternarrative featured in the cited texts by both Williams and Campos is a recurrent theme in the work of Laura Cavalcante Padilha. Padilha's corpus mostly does not deal with Mozambique specifically, instead taking a more transnational approach by including other Lusophone African literatures; nonetheless, it forms part of a significant body of scholarship that has informed or influenced the present volume despite differences in focus or even discipline. The first part of her essay 'Silêncios Rompidos' (1999) discusses women's contributions to two early Lusophone African literary journals that share the same name, *Mensagem*: one published by the Casa dos Estudantes do Império in Lisbon between 1948 and 1964, and one published only once, in Luanda in 1951 (64–5). Here, Padilha charts the fluctuating ways in which women contributors to the journals – among them Noémia de Sousa – give voice to their perceptions and experiences of the colonial regime and their respective countries' statuses as 'overseas provinces' of Portugal.

The second part of Padilha's study focuses on de Sousa's *Sangue Negro* collection specifically, examining the desire reflected in her poetry to speak with and for 'os seres vitimados de sua terra, os torturados corpos marcados "pelos chicotes da escravatura" dentro e fora da África, enfim, os negros de todo o mundo' [the victimized inhabitants of her homeland, the tortured bodies marked 'by the whips of slavery' within and outside of Africa: in sum, black people the world over] (75). Padilha furthermore explores de Sousa's transposition of the female body onto the Mozambican nation, suggesting that both woman and nation 'têm a ligá-las o desejo de estabelecer um outro sentido para suas fronteiras, atravessando-as' [are linked by their desire to establish another meaning for their borders, thereby crossing over them] (75). These uses of multivocality and female corporeality, identified by Padilha as central to *Sangue Negro*, are two areas that this study seeks to examine in further detail in its third chapter.

Luís Madureira's work also offers a more transnational outlook on the study of Lusophone Africa, focusing on analysis of Portuguese colonial discourse and responses to it. His monograph *Imaginary Geographies in Portuguese and Lusophone African Literature* (2006) charts the evolving narratives of Portuguese expansionism and empire, beginning with the fifteenth- and sixteenth-century chronicles and dramatizations of the Portuguese 'discoveries' and ending with the postcolonial 'writing back' of Mia Couto. Though gender is not an explicit point of analysis in this particular text, Madureira's understanding of the Portuguese imperial project as principally defined by a profound sense of anxiety and instability, tied to its semiperipheral status, speaks to the possibility of exploring gender as a constituent element of this affective precariousness. Indeed, in an earlier essay (1994), Madureira makes this link between gender, sexuality and the marginality of Portuguese imperialism explicit, arguing that the mid-twentieth-century reframing of Portuguese colonialism 'as a sexual conquest of the tropics' was intended 'to conceal Portugal's semiperipheral status' (162). This understanding of the New State's espousal of Lusotropicalist ideology as the essentially gendered manifestation of the anxieties that defined Portuguese colonial discourse from its earliest days is one that underpins the present study, and one that will be revisited and developed throughout.

While academic work dealing directly with the multifaceted presentations of gender and sexuality in Mozambican and Lusophone African literatures sets the clearest precedent for this study, it builds additionally on the work of several scholars from the fields of history and the social sciences. Kathleen Sheldon's *Pounders of Grain* (2002) provides a unique historical and ethnographic insight into the changing societal roles of women through the last two centuries of Mozambican life, revealing the heterogeneous and sometimes contradictory implications for women of Mozambique's palimpsestic cultural shifts. In addition to informing the present study in contextual terms, the text also outlines several concepts that will be examined in literary terms in the present study, including the nineteenth-century anthropological trend of using indigenous women's characteristics as 'a way of marking ethnic boundaries' (3), thus casting women in the role of bearers of culture, and the intimate connections between the specific gendered abuses suffered by black women under colonialism, their assumed roles as wives, mothers and cultivators of food, and their means of resistance (52–5).

Sociologist Signe Arnfred's comprehensive monograph *Sexuality and Gender Politics in Mozambique* (2011), in contrast to the bulk of the above-cited texts, deals primarily with traditional indigenous systems of belief around gender and sex, with particular focus on those of the southern, patrilineal Tsonga (specifically Changaan) and northern, matrilineal Makhuwa societies. Her understandings of the encounters between traditional belief systems and colonial and anticolonial policies are heavily informed by this focus, offering a vital perspective on the role of gender in Mozambican recent history and current society that remains lacking in Mozambican cultural studies. Arnfred's text is furthermore invaluable for this study due to its evaluative studies of both Western and non-Western feminist theories against the Mozambican case, in which the author examines and interrogates the work of theorists as diverse as Simone de Beauvoir, Chandra Talpade Mohanty, Oyèrónké Oyěwùmí, Ifi Amadiume and Judith Butler.

A final social science text that has contributed to the foundations of this study despite its very different scope and focus is Carolyn Nordstrom's affecting work on the Mozambican post-independence conflict, *A Different Kind of War Story* (1997). Structured primarily as an ethnography of the conflict based on Nordstrom's fieldwork in rural Mozambique during the war's most violent years, the text incorporates case studies relating specific events, processes and motifs of the conflict to theoretical frameworks on the roles of violence, terror and (un)speakability in the formation of individual and collective identities. Nordstrom's insights into Mozambicans' negotiations of subjectivity in the face of violence have proved valuable throughout the study; in particular, however, her deconstructions of the specific brutalities of the post-independence conflict have revealed several conceptual topics developed further in Chapters 3 and 4.

Moving Forward

This survey of the literature that forms the basis of the current volume is by no means exhaustive, and further important texts will be introduced as it progresses. Nonetheless, this initial outline does reveal some of the areas for further development and examination that will be addressed during the course of the study. First, the field of published Mozambican literary criticism as it stands still contains very few works that analyse masculinities and male subjectivities, and even fewer that analyse them comparatively; some notable exceptions notwithstanding (Rothwell 2004; Sabine 2004), gendered studies have tended to focus on representations and uses of women and femininity. While the study of femininity is undoubtedly vital for the development of the field, a space remains for analysis in which masculinity and femininity are approached as constructs that are produced and maintained symbiotically, bringing to light the importance of studying them in tandem in order to reach a fuller understanding of both.

In a similar vein, the current field provides very few examples of works that explore issues of gender and sexuality in male-authored Mozambican texts, or that put male and female authors into extended dialogue on such themes; Owen's two short articles (2007b and 2014) appear to be the only published examples of the latter that pertain specifically to Mozambique. Comparative analysis of writers from different generations is also lacking, with pairings generally complying with chronological convention; for example, Chiziane with Couto (Owen 2007b), Khosa (Owen 2014) or Jorge (Martins 2012). The result of this lack of inter-gendered and inter-generational comparison is that existing work, while of groundbreaking critical value in itself, has the tendency to consciously eschew patriarchal literary conventions while nonetheless adhering to a broadly progressiv-ist and historically teleological literary outlook, which by its very nature favours an androcentric metanarrative wherein male writers are implicitly both originators and vanguardists while women writers remain tied to a tacitly mimetic 'other' category. The continuing development of frame-works that aim to understand the evolving ways that gender and sex have functioned in Mozambican literary discourses, and that question how political treatment of gender has been woven into literary metanarratives themselves, thus requires increased engagement with less conventional comparative pairings and analyses.

As illustrated by the critical precedents left open by Martins (2012), Campos (2004), Williams (2004) and Padilha (1999), the literary expres-sion of resistance to gendered power structures merits further analysis and development. In recent Mozambican history, as Sheldon (2002) affirms, women's expressions of resistance to gendered subjugation were often latent, concealed and inextricable from gestures of resistance to oppression more broadly. Despite this latter point, however, work on gendered resistance has so far mostly remained limited to envisaging it as an end in itself, rather than as a means of challenging wider power structures. With this in mind, the present study seeks to carry forward the valuable analyses presented by earlier work by identifying and understanding ways in which male and female writers display resistance in gendered terms, while locating those gestures in relation to broader oppressive and resistant practices.

Finally, the ongoing development of gendered frameworks for examin-ing Mozambican literature hinges on the incorporation of a wider range of critical theory texts into gendered analysis. While scholars such as Owen,

Rothwell, Martins and Williams in particular have worked to integrate a range of critical approaches into the field of Mozambican literary criticism, there are still many theoretical areas that have yet to be explored for analysis of the writers studied here. Work in the field so far has tended to favour theoretical outlooks that are more or less singular, and that correspond in broad terms to the chronological context and aesthetic tendencies of the primary texts in question. What remains open, then, is work that moves beyond theoretical categories such as postcolonialism, feminism or postmodernism in order to work in turn against categories of generation, gender, aesthetics and literary form: in other words, a flexible theoretical approach that enables an unconventional structure, and vice-versa. Producing innovative new perspectives on gender and sexuality in a field that remains under-studied demands this unconventional and dynamic drive. It is this gap that the present study seeks to fill, an aim that the following section will address.

Mozambique in Theory

Critical theory, as Achille Mbembe affirms, 'has always sought to legitimize itself by stressing its capacity to construct universal grammars' (2001: 9). When 'legitimate' theory is necessarily produced within the protected environs of the academy, itself coded almost exclusively as Western, these 'universal' theories have turned out to be anything but. Inevitably informed by the historicities and self-perceptions of the societies that produced them, such frameworks have failed to see Africa as anything other than the monolithic 'sign of a lack': interpretable only as 'incomprehensible, pathological, and abnormal' (Mbembe 2001: 8). They have thus fallen short of 'account[ing] for *time as lived*, not synchronically or diachronically, but in its multiplicity and simultaneities, its presence and absence' (9).

This fundamental inability of any one Western framework to account for African lived realities is at the foundation of contemporary postcolonial thought on the continent. Studying Lusophone Africa complicates

the issue of theory even further. Mbembe himself highlights this problematizing factor, albeit unintentionally, when he describes the limits of
Western theory on Africa as owing in part to 'some analysts, only reading
French, others only English, and few speaking local languages' (2001: 9).
Portuguese is here sidelined in much the same way as Portuguese (post)-
colonialism has been in postcolonial studies as a whole, with the frameworks that dominate the field inherited primarily from the Anglophone
and, to a lesser extent, the Francophone colonial experiences. Boaventura
de Sousa Santos's seminal essay 'Between Prospero and Caliban' (2002)
brings this marginality into focus, positing Portuguese colonialism as a
'subaltern colonialism' (9) radically distinct from that of other European
nations due to Portugal's status as a 'semiperipheral country' (9) and thus
outside of the productive reach of mainstream postcolonialism (16–17).

Santos's essay (2002) has been the subject of much due critique in
Portuguese studies (Ferreira 2007, 2012; Rothwell 2010), not least for its
superficial and reductive treatment of an axis of analysis that the present
study depends on: that of gender (Owen 2007a; Martins 2013). Owen
notes that within Santos's understanding of hybridity in the Portuguese
context as always-already embodied, and thus requiring articulation with
feminist theory, women 'remain tied to a predominantly abject narrative of
hybridity as a physical imposition on the female body' (2007a: 31). She asks
in response if 'recognizing Portugal's material histories of miscegenation
ha[s] to imply so total an exclusion of transcultural, psychoanalytical, and
metaphorical concepts of the hybrid?' (31). Indeed, as Anne McClintock
makes clear, gendered interpretation of (post)colonialism, including but
not limited to studies that foreground the experiences of women, has long
remained limited in postcolonial studies (1995: 9–17). Within this branch
of critical theory, McClintock explains, gender difference has either been
passed over completely, used as only an extended metaphor for (male) imperial relations, or examined solely in terms of a monolithic understanding of
'woman' (9–17); Santos's essay, as a key text of Portuguese postcolonialism,
is clearly no exception.

At the same time, Western feminist theory, in privileging gender difference as a point of analysis, has itself all too often fallen into a universalizing pattern wherein the experiences and theories of women of colour and

particularly women of colour in the 'Third World' are either elided into the 'universal' realities of white women or are subsumed under the single, monolithic heading of 'other'. The works of black and Chicana US women writers were among the first to begin to recognize and expose the implications of this tendency, albeit specifically for women of colour living in the US and attempting to work within mainstream US feminist movements. Audre Lorde, in a paper first delivered in 1980, identified within the US women's movement 'a pretense to homogeneity of experience covered by the word *sisterhood* that does not in fact exist' (1984: 116). In the iconoclastic 1981 anthology of essays and creative texts *This Bridge Called My Back* (2nd edn 1983), Gloria Anzaldúa – co-editor of the volume, along with Cherríe Moraga – carried Lorde's idea forward, affirming that the 'woman of color is invisible both in the white male mainstream world and in the white women's feminist world' (165). She further warns that followers of the mainstream feminist movement 'are notorious for "adopting" women of color as their "cause" while still expecting us to adapt to *their* expectations and *their* language' (167). Writing in the same year, black feminist bell hooks notes that 'the hierarchical pattern of sex-race relationships already established [in America] by white capitalist patriarchy merely assumed a different form under feminism' (1981: 190). The need was here established for feminist activism and scholarship to go beyond simply acknowledging the heterogeneity of women's experiences and modalities, working instead toward the development of frameworks radically based on that heterogeneity. The message of Chicana and black feminists was clear: that the discourse and practice of gender difference is fundamentally inseparable from oppression on the basis of race, ethnicity, class or sexual orientation.

The work of black and Chicana women during the 1980s was undeniably pioneering in terms of its exposure of the racism within US women's movements. Furthermore, it provided a theoretical starting point for the production of wider, transnational critique of Western feminism, including Chandra Talpade Monhanty's influential article 'Under Western Eyes' (1984). Mohanty's essay warned that Western feminist writing on women living in the 'Third World' was prone to treating its subjects as an undifferentiated, monolithic mass, and in doing so produced 'a composite, singular "Third World Woman" – an image which appears arbitrarily constructed,

but nevertheless carries with it the authorizing signature of Western human-
ist discourse' (335) Not only did such work fail to effectively communicate the lived material conditions of life in the 'Third World', then; it also
served to reproduce the representational privileges that partially uphold
the imperialist denomination of the 'Third World'.

In the later 1980s and 1990s, Nigerian feminists Oyèrónké Oyěwùmí
and Ifi Amadiume expanded upon Mohanty's critique of hegemonic feminisms by questioning the usefulness of a 'Third World' feminist movement
that spoke primarily to a singularly North American experience. In the
preface to Amadiume's monograph on Igbo gender systems (1987), after
laying out a damning indictment of the white ethnocentricity of mainstream feminism, the author goes on to criticize what she perceives as the
tendency among US black feminists to appropriate the experiences and
mythologies of black African women living in Africa (1–10). Of particular
concern to Amadiume is Lorde's use of the example of 'women-bonding' in
'African communities' to challenge black lesbophobia (Lorde 1984: 121–2),
which Amadiume decries as an indication that black lesbians are using
'prejudiced interpretations of African situations to justify their choices
of sexual alternatives which have roots and meaning in the West' (4). To
interpret examples of women-bonding given in Amadiume's own book as
indicating lesbian tendencies would 'be totally inappropriate, shocking
and offensive' (7) to the women in question, the author contends. While
Amadiume's words here carry with them at least a degree of lesbophobia
themselves, they do underscore the risk that a 'Third World' feminism
led by US women might display its own brand of racial essentialism and
cultural appropriation.

Oyěwùmí's work on gender systems among the Yorùbá people of south-
western Nigeria (1997) also questions the usefulness of feminist ideology for
indigenous African women, asserting that feminism simply consolidates a
Western somatocentric and biological determinist understanding of gender
and sex utterly at odds with precolonial Yorùbá social categories (xiii). Since
'there were no *women* – defined in strictly gendered terms – in [Yorùbá]
society' prior to British colonial occupation, such thinking becomes simply
another imperial imposition, and a redundant means of analysing Yorùbá
cultural output (15–16). Yet, as Agnes Atia Apusigah (2006) contends,

Oyěwùmí's work reflects a romanticization of the past that is itself prone to essentialism, and that forestalls productive and pluralistic discourse on African gender systems due to the author's rigid adherence to an uncritically relativist position. Indeed, while Oyěwùmí's text takes her critique of the imposition of Western social theory on African societies as its starting point, it frequently extrapolates her case study of the Yorùbá, and with it the specificities of British occupation, to the rest of Africa. We are thus led back, in circular fashion, to the all-too-familiar sidelining of Lusophone Africa within postcolonial theory and the imperial Anglocentricity it implies. Nevertheless, the work of Oyěwùmí, along with that of Amadiume, acts as an important warning against the uncritical or singular transposition of gender and sexual theories – whether 'mainstream' or 'marginal' – onto African social topographies.

Taking into account these complicating factors regarding the use of postcolonial and feminist theories for the analysis of African contexts, then, how can critical theory play a part in presenting new perspectives on gender and sexuality in texts produced in Mozambique, at the very intersection of marginality and elision? The present study aims to tackle this question by favouring a 'toolbox' methodology, engaging a diverse range of theories from various disciplines, backgrounds and theoretical schools as critical issues arise. While the study thus agrees with the assertions of Mbembe (2001), Amadiume (1987) and Oyěwùmí (1997) regarding the limits of uncritical use of Western-centric frameworks for analysis of Africa, and places emphasis on acknowledging and understanding the specificities of Mozambique, it also resists the suggestion that theories must speak directly to a given context in order to provide useful insight into the discourse and literature produced from within that context. Treating theories critically, as tools rather than as blueprints, can facilitate a dialectic and symbiotic relationship between literature and theory that situates the literary text within wider global discourses while at the same time interrogating and evaluating the theoretical framework. This fundamentally flexible and dynamic approach allows for fresh analysis of the polysemic and often contradictory roles that gender and sexuality have played throughout recent Mozambican history, while keeping the problematizing factors outlined above firmly in view.

With these objectives in mind, the study makes use of a range of frameworks chosen to address the critical issues it raises around gender, sexuality, race, (post)coloniality and the body from a standpoint that is both theoretically engaged and contextually grounded, including second- and third-wave, Chicana, African-American, and 'Third World' feminisms; poststructuralism; queer theory; psychoanalysis; pain and violence theories; and further schemata outside of the immediate remit of literature and cultural studies. As noted in the study's review of current secondary materials on Mozambican literature, this eclectic approach extends to the book's unconventional structure, which consists of three comparative analyses of one male and one female author each, with the pairings decided according to thematic or strategic affinities rather than along more traditional chronological or aesthetic lines. These consciously ahistorical pairings are intended to challenge analytical assumptions made on the basis of gender identity or historical context, emphasizing instead the reemergence, transformation and subversion of literary themes and strategies across the boundaries of time, age, gender and aesthetic. The comparison of male and female authors has remained a rarity in Mozambican cultural studies; intergenerational comparison, meanwhile, is all but entirely absent. By addressing these two gaps, the study aims to bring to light issues around subject positionality and thematic patterns that might otherwise go unexamined.

Notes on Terms

The use of a range of sometimes divergent theories necessitates a brief clarification of key terms used throughout the study. This is particularly true of the mobile terms 'gender' and 'sexuality', whose meanings have been rendered uncertain and problematic by decades of critical theorization. Rather than offering a fixed, stable definition of these terms and the relationship between them, the present study aims to take advantage of the fluidity they imply in order to in turn highlight the ambiguous and occasionally contradictory ways in which the selected authors have deployed gendered and sexual tropes. For this reason, a consciously discontinuous understanding of the terms, based loosely on the broadly poststructuralist theories first fully explicated by Judith Butler in her texts *Gender Trouble* (1990, repr. 2007) and *Bodies that Matter* (1993, repr. 2011), will be used as a key reference point for the historical and literary analyses that follow this Introduction.

Butler posits 'gender' as an unstable concatenation of constantly reiterated cultural meanings 'whose totality is permanently deferred, never fully what it is at any given juncture of time' (2007: 22). She proposes that the radical discursive split between gender and sex promoted by earlier feminist formulations like those of Simone de Beauvoir, wherein sex is a prediscursive biological fact and gender the cultural meanings the sexed body accrues, is something of a false construct since there is no prediscursive body; 'sex' is thus as constructed as gender, and is in fact 'itself a gendered category' (2007: 9–10). The same conclusion regarding the sex/gender split, as Arnfred points out (2011: 262), has been reached by Oyěwùmí (1997: 9), albeit from a very different starting point from that of Butler. While both gender and sex are performative social constructs, however, they are also deeply 'real', in the sense that cultures using a binary gender system inevitably depend upon that system for social coherence. This hierarchical structure of 'man' and 'woman' into which gender is largely reified is, for Butler, a disciplining mechanism that 'consolidate[s] and naturalize[s] the convergent power regimes of masculine and heterosexist oppression' (2007: 46).

Sexuality, meanwhile, is here understood as the embodied triangulation of sexual capacity, desire and practice; within a binary gender system, this triangulation is strictly regulated as a compulsory and naturalized heterosexuality (Butler 2007: 30–1). The internal coherence of binary gender categories requires this 'heterosexualization of desire' as a means of delineating and reinforcing the boundaries between what is 'male' and what is 'female' (Butler 2007: 24). In turn, the construct of gender difference produced by this 'heterosexual matrix' serves symbiotically to uphold that same matrix (Butler 2007: 24). It is this very contingency, however, that speaks to the fragility of binary categories of gender and compulsory heterosexuality. If, as Butler affirms, gender is nothing more than 'the repeated stylization of the body, a set of repeated acts [...] that congeal over time to produce the appearance of substance' (2007: 45–6), and enforced heterosexuality is a means of symbiotically regulating that performative illusion, then both can be seen as radically unstable, open to infinite disruptive possibilities.

Working from this understanding of gender and sexuality as at once inherently unstable and profoundly 'real', intrinsically linked but not interchangeable, enables the present study to engage with texts that treat both constructs as fixed, continuous, essential and biologically determined, and with others that refuse or challenge those characterizations. The suggestion that the constitution of the subject depends on the dynamic interplay of multiple axes of identification furthermore allows for the concept to be used in an auxiliary manner alongside theoretical frameworks that implicate other embodied categories in the production of gender and sexual constructs, including, perhaps most importantly for the purposes of this study, ones of race and ethnicity.

Along similar lines, Butler's understanding of gender and sexuality as being at once discursively chained to the body and at the same time hypothetically separate from it permits an equally fluid and flexible definition of identity, which in this study is used to capture both the network of prohibitions and permissions imposed by external entities on the individual or collective, and the articulations of corporeal and psychic selfhood formulated and expressed by that same individual or group. Finally, the openness of her framework to multiple, potentially untold strategies of disruption and destabilization facilitates the identification of subversive literary strategies that have hitherto gone unacknowledged, or that might remain concealed. The notions of 'subversion' and 'resistance', then, will be used to describe those literary gestures that offer a discursive 'pushback' against the naturalized, contextually specific normative triangulations of gender, sexuality and race that have emerged in Mozambican colonial, anticolonial and post-independence discourses and that will be described in the historical background provided by Chapter 1.

The study will thus begin, by way of establishing its discursive and historical backdrop, with a genealogical exploration of the ways gender and sexuality have figured in late Portuguese imperial and Mozambican anticolonial thought, structured as an examination of specific, often interrelated and overlapping, discursive moments and trends rather than as an exhaustive history. While the earliest literary texts studied in the subsequent chapters did not emerge until the late 1940s, this framing will take in a longer period, spanning the century between the aftermath of the Berlin Conference in the final decade of the nineteenth century, and the height of the Mozambican post-independence war. I have chosen this earlier starting-point in order to enable discussion of historical texts that document the initial colonial reification of the specific brand of imperial sexual politics, intrinsically bound up with post-Berlin Conference Portuguese border anxiety, that this study holds as the precedent for the frameworks of gender and sexuality successively imposed on twentieth-century Mozambique and reflected in its national literary texts. Taking as its unifying theme the notion of borders and boundaries, this extended historical background thereby intends to shed light on the ways in which gender and sexual constructs were first established as, and how they have consistently remained, the contested sites upon which Mozambican territorial, political and affective boundaries have been discursively negotiated.

The ways that two authors, José Craveirinha and Paulina Chiziane, have worked within and beyond these constructs and boundaries is the subject of Chapter 2, which begins the study's literary analyses with a conventional Western feminist and poststructuralist starting point represented by the theories of Judith Butler and R. W. Connell. This framework serves to situate the study within an understanding of gender that acknowledges the fundamental instability of gendered categories while at the same time opening that potentially Western-centric framework up to interrogation. From here, the chapter examines the role of masculinities in shaping the aesthetics of José Craveirinha's first published collection, *Xigubo* (1964), placing particular emphasis on the recurring motif of the colonized male subject's 'return' to an imagined state of heroic African authenticity assumed to have been lost or erased by the dominant culture. The first chapter's second section explores these same themes in Paulina Chiziane's novel *O Sétimo Juramento* (2000), which is seen as satirically undermining the male 'hero' trope reflected in Craveirinha's work, exposing its oppressive implications by means of a strategic deployment of parody, excess and realism.

This tactical use of oppressively racialized and gendered tropes as the means to a subversive end is further explored in Chapter 3, which examines the ways that Noémia de Sousa's pre-independence poetry and Ungulani Ba Ka Khosa's post-independence short stories and novels handle the ideals of femininity imposed by the late colonial regime, the anticolonial movement and, in the case of Khosa, by the post-independence Frelimo government. The chapter makes use of the theories of 'disidentification' originally developed by Chicana feminists Chela Sandoval, Norma Alarcón and Gloria Anzaldúa, and queer Latino theorist José Esteban Muñoz, to propose that despite the apparent dissimilarities between de Sousa and Khosa's respective bodies of work, we can identify a clear common thread between the two, tied to the disavowal or deferral of gendered boundaries of identity. While this reading of de Sousa hinges on her subtle linguistic play of metaphysical subjectivities, Khosa by contrast roots the impact of his work firmly in gendered reproductive corporealities, which become a symbolic site for critique of Frelimo's post-independence espousal of reproductive futurist ideals. This use of corporealities is understood using theories of the damaged, pained or grotesque body as expounded by Elaine Scarry, Mary Russo and Laura Mulvey, with Carolyn Nordstrom's ethnography of the Mozambican post-independence conflict and queer theorist Lee Edelman's notion of reproductive futurism providing further theoretical angles.

Chapter 4 carries forward this critique of reproductive futurism as part of its exploration of work by Lília Momplé and Suleiman Cassamo, using a framework informed by Achille Mbembe's theory of necropolitics, a postcolonialist reworking of Michel Foucault's biopolitics. This final chapter looks beyond gender constructs to examine the notion of corporeality more broadly, focusing specifically on the role of death in Portuguese imperial thought and in Frelimo discourse as a gateway to understanding Momplé's and Cassamo's presentations of suicide, hunger, and haunting in their short stories and novels. These deeply affective and complex themes are explored in terms of their capacity both to represent the gendered subject's negotiation of agency from within a position of subjugation, and at the same time to question the West's historical and contemporary constructions of Africa as embodying meaninglessness and death.

The conclusion to this study aims to bring each chapter's analysis forward to the present day, with reference to the 2015 abandonment of the 1886 Portuguese Penal Code in Mozambique. Among the changes made to the country's legal framework was the scrapping of a law prohibiting 'unnatural vices', which the Western media embraced as an officially codified decriminalization of homosexuality. Mozambicans themselves were not so sure. It is at this juncture of imperial imposition, post-independence rhetoric, Western mythification and material reality that the ongoing relevance of the study's prevailing themes of corporeality, agency and subjectivity is brought to the surface.

Boundaries, Borderlands and Bodies: Gender and Sexuality in Mozambique's Long Twentieth Century

> Dos seus milhões de hectares, quantos são ocupados por gentes bravias, que só poderão ser subjugadas em guerras que custariam num dia mais do que as suas terras renderiam num século, ou por criaturas ínfimas que a civilização mal poderá aproveitar para instrumentos rudes de trabalho? Quantos outros são areias estéreis, pântanos que exalam morte, juncais impenetráveis, leitos de oceanos efémeros que o sol depois muda em esbraseadas charnecas, serranias de cabeleira hirsuta em que se dobra o fio dos machados, chão pobre, chão de refugo, chão maldito, que só merece ser explorado quando não houver mais terra inculta no mundo?

> [Of its millions of hectares, how many are occupied by defiant peoples, who can only be subjugated via wars that cost more in a single day than their lands could yield in a century, or by worthless creatures that civilization could barely make use of, even as the crudest tools of labour? How many others are infertile wastelands, swamps exhaling death, impenetrable marshlands, ephemeral saltwater beds that the sun dries into charred scrub, rocky outcroppings covered in hirsuit growths that can bend the blade of an axe, poor earth, pitiful earth, that would only be worth exploring were there no more hidden land in the world?]
> — ANTÓNIO ENNES'S report to the Portuguese government on Mozambique (1893: 12)

2015 marked 600 years since the Portuguese invasion of Ceuta, hailed not only as Portugal's first act of imperialism on mainland African shores but also as the first step in European maritime expansion as a whole (Blackmore 2009: xii–xiv). In addition, it marked forty years since the official end of Portugal's handover of power to Samora Machel's Frelimo government on

25 June 1975,[1] more than a year after the fall of the New State regime and nine months after the Lusaka Accord put an end to Portugal's long and bitter war with the Mozambican independence movement (Newitt 1995: 540–1). These two moments bookend a span of time in which the complex trajectory of Portugal's imperial endeavour came to establish itself in a position of violent symbiosis with identities both Portuguese and African, ensuring that imperial relations would continue to make their presence felt in relation to those identities long after empire's official end. Gender and sexual identities, despite frequently occupying a latent subtextual position in official documentation, are no exception. Deconstructing the texts that document the duration and aftermath of Portugal's imperial presence in Mozambique, in a way that acknowledges the importance of silence, ellipsis and coded language, can thus reveal the insistent influence that gender and sexuality exerted on Portugal's interpellation of Africa into a discourse of empire, while in turn being shaped by it.

Understanding this symbiotic relationship, produced and reified over more than half a millennium, is an essential step in the process of identifying and analysing gendered and sexual modalities in the cultural output of Mozambique, casting new light on patterns and motifs that might otherwise go unnoticed. Similarly, recognizing the ways in which this dynamic connection between imperialism, gender and sexuality came to bear on Mozambican lives both during and after the era of empire provides vital insight into the reflection of those patterns and motifs in the work of Mozambican writers, and thus in turn helps to parse the strategies writers might use to subvert them.

1   Both 'FRELIMO' and 'Frelimo' are used to refer to the Frente de Libertação de Moçambique. Academic convention is that the capitalized FRELIMO was used up until the party's Third Congress in 1977, when it became the 'Partido Frelimo' (Owen 2007a: 222n; Dinerman 2006: 298n). The party itself used the term 'Partido FRELIMO' at least as late as 1980, however (e.g. '3ª Conferência da OMM: Integrar a Mulher na Tarefa Principal' 1980: 38–42). For the sake of consistency, I will use 'Frelimo' throughout to refer to both the independence movement and the political party.

New Imperialism, New Anxieties

Gendered meanings and ideologies have played a subtextual role in the Portuguese writing of Africa since the very earliest days of expansionist encounter.[2] It was in the final decades of the nineteenth century, however, that these discontinuous thoughts were actively welded into the official apparatuses of Portuguese colonial sovereignty, becoming discursively intertwined with the long-disputed borderlines that locked Mozambique in place 'like a piece of a jigsaw puzzle' (Newitt 1995: 355) in 1891. This tentative agreement of borders was finalized in the wake of decades of conflict between Portugal and Britain over southern and central Africa, a conflict that intensified following the Berlin Conference in 1884–5, Portugal's subsequent claiming of the territories between Angola and Mozambique with the production of the 'Mapa Cor-de-Rosa' [Pink Map], and the British Ultimatum, the name given to the 1890 Cecil Rhodes-led British response to this latter Portuguese project.[3] During these decades, the contested reaches and frontiers of Portugal's African empire were defined by their fluidity, uncertainty and instability, and while the 1891 agreement brought multilateral recognition of Portugal's territorial claims, it did little to curtail the political manoeuvring or internal uprisings that threatened them (Newitt 1995: 341–5). The profound anxiety of borders and boundaries that dominated Portuguese imperial discourse on Africa during this period became, inevitably, a cornerstone of the state-building processes that followed it, with the reification of gender and sexual constructs emerging as one such process.

2   cf. Blackmore (2002, 2009). While gender is not the central analytical lens for either work, both texts explore the interpellation of African and Portuguese bodies into narratives of empire in a way that clearly indicates the gendered meanings underlying early expansionist texts. Also important to note here is the growing body of work examining the gendered and sexual implications of Luís de Camões's seminal epic of Portuguese expansionism, *Os Lusíadas* (e.g. Klobucka 2002).

3   For more detailed analysis of the lasting effect of the British Ultimatum on contemporary Mozambican identity and Mozambican–Portuguese relations, see Rothwell (2001).

An influential 1893 treatise commissioned by the Portuguese government to provide direction on how best to exploit Mozambique's economic potential, written by Mozambican High Commissioner-to-be António Ennes and quoted as the epigraph to this chapter, provides an unintentional narrative on this process, exposing the anxieties at its heart. What characterizes the presentation of gender and sexuality in Ennes's text is a deep sense of racialized unease, centred around the perceived refusal of the African or non-white body to conform to the naturalized rules and categories central to Portuguese state discourse. This non-conformity enacts a troubling of the boundaries between and around those categories, destabilizing not only the text's delineations of racial, ethnic and sexual differences themselves, but also its distinctions between land and inhabitants, colonizer and colonized. Perhaps unsurprisingly given the text's ostensibly economic drive, these blurred distinctions and uncertain causalities coalesce primarily around issues of fertility and economic yield. The perceived inability or unwillingness of Mozambique's native inhabitants to adequately adhere to normative gender roles, and particularly the failure of African men to 'properly' perform masculinity, is implicitly correlated with the land's incompatibility with agricultural production. In turn, the apparent hostility of the Mozambican terrain is seen to disrupt the ability of European men and women to successfully reproduce, troubling the flow of power between colonizer and colonized.

The connection between gender performance and agricultural production first becomes evident in Ennes's descriptions of the southern African Vatua people, a Tsonga subgroup, whom he first affirms should be regarded as the 'inimigo irreconciliável [da civilização], porque esterilisa o chão que pisa' [irreconcilable enemy [of civilization], because they sterilize the very ground that they tread] (1893: 23). This 'sterilizing' effect is framed as resulting from the Vatua's bellicose nature: they are 'opressores sensuais' [lustful oppressors] (23), with a tendency to violently appropriate the lands, resources, and women of other groups (23–4). In short, the Vatua men are here characterized as displaying traits of excessive and aberrant masculinity. Men from other groups, in contrast, are defined by their deficient masculinity, manifest in their 'gosto [...] pelo adorno' [taste for adornment] (25) and displays of 'infantil vaidade' [infantile vanity] (24).

These traits, Ennes admits, can be exploited to colonial advantage; none-theless, such preoccupations impede effective cultivation of land. Present here is an implied relationship between the supposedly faulty masculinity of African men and an inability to produce yield from land – or, perhaps more aptly, to inseminate it. This characterization of the Vatua is further-more significant in its foreshadowing of the 1895 indigenous uprising in Gaza, spearheaded by notoriously tyrannical Vatua chief Ngungunhane. The uprising and its subsequent defeat represented both the climax and downfall of Ngungunhane's long-standing role as the principal antagonist of Portuguese territorial security in the south of Mozambique.[4]

The correlation between erroneous performance of masculinity and poor agricultural potency is reinforced by Ennes's prolonged indictment of the alcohol abuse he claims is rampant among Mozambique's native inhabitants (1893: 43–50). Alcoholism, which Ennes observes to be par-ticularly common among migrant workers who can neither 'juntar o preço de uma mulher' [get together the price of a wife] nor find other means of satisfying 'essa ambição de sensualidade' [these sensual desires] (46), robs Mozambicans of 'a razão e a virilidade' [reason and virility], and drives them to 'desvergonhamentos sensuais' [shameful displays of sensuality] (49). This distortion of proper masculinity, itself implicitly resulting from an inadequacy of the same, goes hand-in-hand with improper agricultural practices, leading men to abandon the cultivation of cash crops in favour of distillable sugar cane or pineapple (46).

Ennes's portrayal of African men thus maps the gendered body onto the Mozambican terrain, illustrating the ways in which the perceived failure of said men to conform to naturalized European gender roles was inter-twined with Portuguese imperial anxieties over the potential fragility of their colonial presence. Alongside construing the African male body as

---

4   Ngungunhane would, however, stage a symbolic (and, in terms of his mortal remains, literal) return to Mozambique as an icon of the post-independence nationalist move-ment. Ungulani Ba Ka Khosa's contemporary retelling of the Gaza Uprising, *Ualalapi*, is explored in Chapter 3; Portuguese cavalry officer Joaquim Augusto Mousinho d'Albuquerque's 1896 account of the campaign against Ngungunhane is briefly exam-ined in Chapter 4.

improperly masculine and at the same time insufficiently prolific, Ennes introduces another figure of flawed masculinity into his text: that of the subcontinental Asian man.⁵ While the ostensibly faulty masculinity of African men is implicated with low agricultural yield and drunken promiscuity, however, in Asian men it is entangled with an excess of agricultural productivity and economic efficiency.

The influx of Asian men into Mozambique is framed by Ennes as a plague of intruders, 'densos e vorazes como os gafanhotos' [dense and voracious as locusts], that is 'incessantemente renovada' [relentlessly renewed] (1893: 51). The company of these invaders 'não é de certo agradável à vista nem ao olfato' [is disagreeable to both eyes and nose] (51) due in part to their refusal to wear trousers, a point frequently reiterated by the author. Yet they have 'muitas utilidades e pouquíssimas necessidades' [many skills and very few needs] (55), and 'não há ramo que eles não cultivem' [there is no branch they will not cultivate] (53), meaning that they can emigrate 'só com a roupa que mal lhe cobre o corpo' [with only the clothes that barely cover their backs] (55), and still rapidly accumulate wealth. Additionally, Asian men have specifically persuasive powers over Africans, a notion that Ennes couches in the language of seduction, describing the 'indígenas que o Asiático seduz, exibindo-lhes às portas das cubatas os panos vistosos e as missangas multicolores, e movendo-lhes com a sedução a colherem cocos ou a cultivarem amendoim [...]' [natives that the Asian seduces, flaunting his eye-catching cloths and colourful beads at the doors of their huts, and inciting them by means of this seduction to gather coconuts or cultivate peanuts] (56).

Ennes's choice of words here reveals a further way in which gendered meanings came to be discursively enmeshed with the late Portuguese Empire's anxiety toward its presence in Mozambique, centred this time on the permeability of the colonial territory's borders and the imperial state's vulnerability to displacement. Asian immigration is framed as an

5   While Ennes generally uses the ambiguously generic term 'asiáticos' to refer to the men in question, it is clear from his treatment of the word as interchangeable with the India-specific 'baneane' and the pejorative 'monhé', and his references to Indian currency (rupees) that he is referring specifically to men of subcontinental origin.

imminent threat to Portuguese sovereignty precisely because Asian men can inseminate and produce yield from land *too* efficiently. Within the specific context of late nineteenth-century Mozambican colonial discourse, then, Asian men perform the compulsory reproductivity of masculinity too well: not only are they able to penetrate Mozambique's borders in innumerable droves, but they are also able to more fruitfully penetrate the land itself. Indeed, Ennes's use of sexualized language to describe Asian soliciting of African labour implies Asian masculine superiority even in the arena of sexual dominance. The author's attempts to denigrate Asian masculinity through repeated displays of contempt toward their manner of dress and willingness to subsist in demeaning circumstances serve only to underscore the perceived threat that the Asian presence poses.

The text's anxious interweaving of thoughts on African and Asian masculinities with economic and agricultural concerns is brought into particular relief by Ennes's presentation of white men, white women and black women later in his treatise. It is here that the emasculating effect on white men of the Mozambican landscape and its inhabitants is made explicit, reifying the author's hitherto latent gendered unease. The black woman, until now almost entirely absent from Ennes's text, is furthermore introduced here, highlighting late nineteenth-century Portuguese constructs of black femininity.

The deleterious effects of Mozambique on white Portuguese male settlers are condensed by Ennes into two interrelated concerns: the inability to reproduce, and *cafrealização* (1893: 192–6).[6] The first, the author explains, is a direct result of Mozambique's hostile climate, which impedes white men's 'propagação da sua raça' [propagation of their race] (194) by destroying white women's reproductive capacity, 'fazendo-a sofrer especialmente nos órgãos e perturbando-lhe as funções a essa missão destinados' [causing them to suffer particularly in the organs, and impeding the functions, that are dedicated to that mission] (194). Children that are moved to Mozambique by their parents 'quase não parecem brancas, tão macilentas são' [almost

6   *Cafrealização* loosely translates into English as 'going native'; the racial perjorative 'cafre' in Portuguese imperial discourse is roughly equivalent to 'kaffir' in the British correlate.

do not seem white, they are so lean] (194), and more often than not end up 'minadas por consumpções, devoradas por febres' [hollowed out by consumption, devoured by fever] (194).

Thus deprived of the reproductive proof of hegemonic masculinity, Portuguese men are driven to a state of *cafrealização*, defined by Ennes as 'uma espécie de reversão do homem civilizado ao estado selvagem' [a sort of regression of the civilized man to a state of savagery] (1893: 193). The catalyst for this process of 'going native' is the black woman, whom the author describes as 'a hedionda negra, – porque não há negra que não seja hedionda!' [the hideous black woman – because there is no black woman that is not hideous!] (193). Yet in much the same way that Ennes's disgust toward Asian and African masculinities barely conceals a latent sense of fear and menace, his description of African women as 'hideous' directly precedes the affirmation of their power to 'conquista[r] [...] os altivos conquistadores do Continente Negro' [conquer the proud conquerors of the Black Continent] (193): in short, to usurp the masculine sovereignty of Portuguese men, and to thus subvert the naturalized colonial power structures of both gender and race.

This brief passage neatly illustrates the intense unease within late nineteenth-century Portuguese colonial discourses toward the sexual triangulation of black women, white men and white women in the Mozambican context. White men are presented as literally emasculated by Mozambique, denied the racial propagation that would consolidate their position at the apex of racial and gendered hierarchies; white women are similarly stripped of their childbearing destiny. Black women, meanwhile, become implicated in the downfall of both, not only supplanting white women as sexual object choice for white men and thereby polluting white racial purity through miscegenation, but also threatening the very masculinity of white men. The result is a discursive breakdown of racial and gendered boundaries, embodied by the Portuguese émigré children that 'quase não parecem brancas' [almost do not seem white] (Ennes 1893: 194) and by the white settler men reduced to an 'estado selvagem' [state of savagery] (193): a blurring of the distinctions between colonizer and colonized.

The treatise is, of course, only a single example taken from the proliferation of official and unofficial Portuguese colonial documents that emerged after the events of 1884–5. Yet it serves as an emblematic case study of the ways in which gender, sexuality and race became embroiled with imperial economic and border anxieties during this turning point in Lusophone African colonial histories, and of how this series of discursive interconnections was brought to bear on political and legislative thought. Furthermore, the text illustrates the fragility and precariousness of the race and gender categories upholding colonial hierarchies, intimating the means by which future generations would begin to deconstruct them. Indeed, Ungulani Ba Ka Khosa's first novel *Ualalapi* is set during Ennes's era and exploits the anxieties typified by his treatise in service of its subversive drive, as Chapter 3 will demonstrate.

The influence that Ennes's text exerted on Mozambican colonial legislature, from its time of publication until many decades after his death, further contributes to its position as an essential point of analysis in Mozambican gendered and racial history. The 350 pages of legal proposals, amendments and spending projections that follow his treatise became the official blueprint for the extensive administrative reform of the colony that dominated the last five years of the 1890s, and whose social policies would remain at least symbolically in place far beyond the midpoint of the twentieth century. Nowhere is this longevity more evident than in the arena of racial classification and indigenous labour policy, outlined in the thirty-first chapter of the 1893 text (495–513)[7] and officially brought into force in late 1899. The passing of the *Regulamento do Trabalho dos Indígenas* (1899), which obliged all able-bodied black men and boys between the ages of fourteen and sixty to engage in government-approved work and to pay a head tax, and allowed for forced labour to be used as judicial punishment in place of prison sentences for indigenous subjects, was a watershed moment in shaping Portuguese colonial ideology, fixing the racial categories of 'indígena' and 'não-indígena' as its official foundation and making clear that fiscal, civil and legal rights and obligations would be divided along racial lines (Newitt 1995: 383).

7   See Chapter 4 of the current study for further analysis of Ennes's labour proposals.

In addition, the 1899 decree provides an important elliptical statement on gender by excluding women from its regulatory remit. If the decree used racial difference to officially cast black men as discursively, legally and institutionally inferior, and in doing so succeeded in naturalizing the racist paradigms on which Portuguese imperialism had relied since its very beginnings, then it used gender difference to write black women out of discursive, legal and institutional existence altogether. While the vast racial divides of Portuguese colonial society were rendered explicit, ensuring that individual experiences of colonialism would be heavily contingent on skin colour and ethnic heritage, its equally pervasive paradigms of gender difference remained concealed: a succinct reminder that colonial subject positionality could depend as much on silence and blank space as on discourse and legislation.

The exclusion of women from labour legislation enacted by the 1899 decree was not permanent, and amendments made to the *Regulamento* following the fall of the Portuguese Monarchy and inauguration of the First Republic in 1910 do offer limited acknowledgement of women's participation in the indigenous workforce. Within these contexts, however, women are mentioned only to emphasize their ostensibly essential biological difference from men, or as an indirect means of reiterating the inferiority of black masculinity, corroborating Kathleen Sheldon's assertion that precolonial Mozambican paradigms of gender difference were markedly deepened by Portuguese legislative intervention (2002: 46–7). The preamble to the 1914 *Regulamento*, for example, echoes Ennes's 1893 assertion that black men are unable and unwilling to take proper advantage of the land, now depicted as abundantly fertile; the black man lives, according to the text, 'do que a terra fertilíssima lhe fornece espontâneamente como retribuição dum trabalho ligeiro que, em regra, ele não executa, porque obriga as suas mulheres a fazê-lo [...]' [on what the lush earth freely provides him with, in exchange for light work that, as a rule, he does not carry out, because he makes his wives do it] (1914: 948). The *Regulamento* itself dictates that women should not be required to complete 'serviços que só por homens possam ser executados' [services that can only be carried out by men] (963), or to work in the last thirty days before and the first thirty days after childbirth (970); neither should they be required or allowed to

sell sex while working in otherwise legitimate food and drink establish-
ments (974). Evident here is the implication that women have meaning
only in relation to men, either as wives, mothers, or sexual commodities.

Family Ties

This late nineteenth- and early twentieth-century discursive erasure of
women beyond their reproductive and sexual capacities sets a clear and
direct precedent for the gender ideology that emerged in force after the
fall of the Portuguese First Republic in May 1926 and the installation
of three subsequent regimes: the Military Dictatorship (1926–8), the
National Dictatorship (1928–33), and, finally, the New State dictatorship
under António de Oliveira Salazar. The latter regime would remain in
power until the bloodless coup of 25 April 1974, with Marcelo Caetano
taking over as leader after Salazar's death in 1969. In the 1930 Colonial Act,
and the 1933 Portuguese Constitution that would serve as the founding
document for the New State, race and gender difference are reinscribed
into legislature; at the same time, they become enmeshed in a discourse
of Portuguese nationalism that carries within it the latent reflection of
nineteenth-century unease.

The preamble of the Colonial Act describes the reinforcement of
imperial sovereignty as an urgently needed means of protecting Portugal's
dominion from external pressures, recalling the post-1884 border anxieties
underpinning Ennes's 1893 text. While Ennes's text couches these anxieties
in economic terms, however, in the Colonial Act they are tied to more affective issues of national identity and unity. Portugal's essential selfhood, itself
cast in gendered terms as the 'Mãe-Pátria' [literally, Mother-Fatherland], is
what is now threatened by the failure of indigenous subjects to conform to
European norms and bow to Portuguese interests. And what is needed to
ensure its safety, the Act makes clear, is a deep reinscription and enforcement of the rules, categories and differences governing racial hierarchy.
These measures alone will safeguard, as the Act puts it, the 'expansão da

nossa raça' [expansion of our race] (1930: 1309). The need for an ongoing reiteration of hierarchical racial categories thus becomes interwoven with an implicit reassertion of compulsory heterosexuality and binary gender, tied up in the reproductive imperatives of racial preservation and expansion.

If the Colonial Act sought to reinscribe racial hierarchies in the terms of national unity, itself implicitly tied to compulsory sexual reproduction, the 1933 Constitution brought that obligatory conformity with patriarchal – and Roman Catholic – rules of gendered behaviour to the fore, as has been well-documented by Ana Paula Ferreira (1996) and Hilary Owen (2007a: 17–18). Citing 'as diferenças resultantes da sua natureza' [women's natural differences] and '[o] bem da família' [the good of the family] (228), the Constitution excluded women from national citizenship in an addendum to the very article that affirmed the equality of all citizens before the law. Meanwhile, it interpellated the family firmly into New State ideology 'como fonte de conservação e desenvolvimento da raça, como base primária da educação, da disciplina e harmonia social, e como fundamento de toda a ordem política' [as source of the conservation and development of the race, as primary basis of education, discipline, and social harmony, and as foundation of political order] (229), and made the defence of the family, including the avoidance of 'a corrupção dos costumes' [the corruption of customs] (229) and the protection of motherhood, an explicit priority of the state.

This strict binding of women to the maternal, domestic sphere once again excluded them from meaning except in terms of their reproductive potential; in addition, as Ferreira affirms, the construction of the family home as the foundation of state authority forced upon women the burden of responsibility for 'the entire Portuguese nation-family; and also for the behaviour, if not the very thoughts and desires, deemed appropriate for its members' (1996: 135)· In tandem with the Colonial Act, then, the 1933 Constitution naturalized the normative body as white and male, while simultaneously instrumentalizing female and black bodies in service of maintaining that normativity as a central linchpin of, in Owen's terms, a 'single, imagined unity of empire' (2007a: 18). It was during these early days of dictatorship that two of the present study's writers were born: Noémia de Sousa, in 1926, and Lília Momplé in 1935. Craveirinha, the oldest of our writers, was four years old when the Military Dictatorship came into power.

A Lusotropical Climate

Just as the Colonial Act and the 1933 Constitution were finalized, and in the case of the latter voted in by national plebiscite, the Brazilian sociologist Gilberto Freyre was developing a theory that would in later years play a pivotal role in the New State's justification of Portugal's ongoing occupation of its African territories. Known ultimately as Lusotropicalism, the underpinnings of the theory first emerged in Freyre's 1933 *Casa Grande e Senzala* [*The Masters and the Slaves*] (19th edn 1978; trans. Putnam, 1946), an exploration of the relationship between masters and slaves in Brazilian plantation culture in which the author attempts to identify the sociohistorical factors behind what he perceived as the 'success' of Portuguese colonization of tropical countries, or as he put it the 'singular predisposição do português para a colonização híbrida e escravocrata dos trópicos' (1978: 5) [singular predisposition of the Portuguese to the hybrid, slave-exploiting colonization of the tropics] (1946: 4). For Freyre, this success hinged largely on Portuguese men's sexual contact with American and African indigenous women, a phenomenon itself attributed to early racial mixing between the Portuguese and North Africans (5–6).

Freyre's visions of Portuguese colonial sexuality are both Edenic and orgiastic. The Portuguese man is seen 'misturando-se gostosamente com mulheres de cor logo ao primeiro contato' (1978: 9) [sensually mingling with women of colour from the first moment of contact],[8] first entranced by 'a figura da moura-encantada, tipo delicioso de mulher morena e de olhos pretos, envolta em misticismo sexual' (9) [the idealized figure of the

---

8   This line of translation of Freyre's text is my own (all others are taken from Putnam's 1946 edition).

'enchanted Moorish woman', a charming type, brown-skinned, black eyed, enveloped in sexual mysticism] (12), and then in Brazil by 'as índias nuas e de cabelos soltos' (9) [the naked Indian women with their loose-flowing hair] (12). Repeated emphasis is placed on Portuguese men's hypervirility and capacity for proliferate reproduction: they are shown 'dominando espaços enormes e onde quer que pousassem, [...] emprenhando mulheres e fazendo filhos' (1978: 8) [dominating enormous spaces and, wherever they might settle, [...] taking wives and begetting offspring] (1946: 10); 'multiplicando-se em filhos mestiços' (9) [procreat[ing] mestizo sons] (11), and creating, 'pelo intercurso com mulher índia ou negra', a 'vigorosa e dúctil população mestiça' (13) [through intercourse with the Indian or the Negro woman [...] a vigorous and ductile mestizo population] (18). The contrast between Freyre's representations of Portuguese men and black or indigenous women and those of Ennes is stark. Portuguese men are not the victims of a hostile terrain, but rather are uniquely adapted to dominating it; black women do not emasculate them, but rather are the erotically irresistible, subordinate objects and vessels of their sexual prowess and hyperfertility. In the words of Luís Madureira, the indigenous women of Freyre's fantastical narrative 'are a "speculum" of the colonizer's desire [...] figured as disembodied vaginas, and mean only insofar as they are penetrated and inseminated' (1994: 163).

As Cláudia Castelo affirms, Freyre's theories were initially ill-received by New State ideologues (1998: 48). Given the divergence of his ideas from the narrative upheld by Ennes of Portuguese settlers as corporeally pure, long-suffering and heroic quasi-martyrs, this rejection is perhaps unsurprising. It was some years later, as moves toward political autonomy and decolonization began to sweep through colonial Africa and Asia, and Portugal found itself once again facing renewed international and internal pressures on its fragile overseas borders in the shape of United Nations policies and civil unrest, that Salazar's regime revisited Freyre's theories as part of its attempt to present a new public image for the Portuguese Empire. The 1950s saw the 1933 Constitution amended, with the term 'colónia' [colony] replaced with 'província ultramarina' [overseas province] (Newitt 1995: 473), and the 1926 Indigenous Statute, which had laid out the racial hierarchy consolidated in the 1930 Colonial Act, revised to emphasize the supposed means by which (male) black Africans might attain *assimilado* or assimilated citizen status (1954: 21–4). During these years, Freyre's theories came to represent, as Madureira puts it, 'a ready-made ideological justification as well as a pseudo-scientific legitimation [...] for [the New State's] revamped colonial policy' (2006: 139).

Following Freyre's return from a New State-funded 'research trip' to the Portuguese colonies from 1951 to 1952, his theories, now under the name of Lusotropicalism, were incorporated into Portuguese imperial discourse as evidence of the regime's *a priori* racial democracy (Madureira 2006: 142). By 1962, following the official revocation of the Indigenous Statute the year before, Freyre's version of events had become so discursively naturalized that it had almost completely supplanted prior narratives, at least for the benefit of international audiences (Madureira 2006: 140). Madureira cites an interview given by Salazar in May 1962 to the US magazine *Life*, which was republished in the *Boletim Geral do Ultramar* and is replete with instances of this mythic doublethink:

> Nós temos sido muito criticados pela nossa persistente adesão ao ideal da sociedade multirracial a desenvolver-se nos trópicos, como se tal ideal se opusesse à natureza humana, à ordem moral universal ou aos interesses dos povos, quando é o contrário que se verifica. Sem discutir o problema, direi que nós, Portugueses, não sabemos estar no Mundo de outra maneira, até porque foi num tipo social de multirracialidade que, há oito séculos, nos formámos como nação, no termo de diversas invasões, oriundas do Oriente, do Norte e do Sul, isto é, da própria África. Daí nos ficou talvez um pendor natural – que citamos tanto mais à vontade quanto é certo tem sido reconhecido por notáveis sociólogos estrangeiros – para os contactos com outros povos, contactos de que sempre estiveram ausentes quaisquer conceitos de superioridade ou discriminação racial. (6)

> [We have been heavily criticized for our persistent adhesion to the ideal of a multiracial society developing in the tropics, as if such an ideal were contrary to human nature, to the universal moral order or to the interest of the people, when the opposite is shown to be the case. Without wanting to labour the point, I will say that we, the Portuguese, do not know any other way of being in the world, especially since it was a kind of social multiraciality that formed us as a nation eight centuries ago, during a period of multiple invasions from the East, North and South, that is to say, from Africa itself. As a result, we have been left with a natural inclination – which we can claim even more freely now that it has been acknowledged by notable foreign

sociologists – for encounters with other peoples, encounters that have always been
devoid of any notion of superiority or racial discrimination.]

This discursive about-face by the Portuguese state speaks clearly to the
changeability of national myth-making at the intersection of race, gender
and sexuality. At the same time, however, it also exemplifies the means by
which racial, gendered and sexual meanings are upheld and consolidated
beneath the aesthetic layers of the myth itself. While Salazar's statements
above employ Lusotropicalist conclusions to indicate Portugal's ostensible commitment to racial egalitarianism, his words carry within them an
insinuation of Portuguese masculine superiority and virile dominance,
couched in coded terms as 'multiracial' endeavour, that points to an ideological continuity reaching back to the nineteenth century. This veiled
assertion of Portuguese male supremacy in turn casts black masculinity as
inferior and impotent, while black women are defined as hypersexual and
perpetually sexually available.

For the New State, Lusotropicalism thus provided access to the
European post-World War II discursive zeitgeist of democracy and racial
egalitarianism, while at the same time resolving Portugal's colonial border
anxieties by exploiting gendered and sexual meanings to uphold the same
racial hierarchies on which the empire's territorial frontiers had always
relied. Speaking only two months after the interview cited above, Salazar
revealed just how little had actually changed since the nineteenth century
for Portugal's African anxieties:

[O]s grandes problemas africanos não eram, até há pouco, e na verdade continuam
a não ser, os políticos – mas sim a luta contra a doença em climas propícios às mais
variadas endemias; o esforço para manter produtivas as terras arrancadas à selva, que
as forças da natureza a todas as horas para a selva empurram de novo; a abertura das
vias de comunicação como condição indispensável à transformação da economia
africana; a manutenção da ordem para impedir as cruéis lutas de destruição intertribal
[...], etc., etc ... ('Entrevista' 1962: 7)

[The great problems of Africa were never, until very recently, and in reality continue
to not be, political – but rather comprise the fight against sickness in climates favour-
able to the widest range of endemic diseases; the effort to keep productive lands that
were wrangled from the jungle, that the forces of nature are constantly dragging

back into the jungle; the opening up of lines of communication as an indispensable necessity for the transformation of the African economy; the maintenance of order to impede the cruel battles of intertribal destruction [...], etc., etc. ...]

The emphasis here on disease, hostile terrain and innate indigenous 'cruelty' brings Ennes's earlier words into clear focus. During this heyday of Lusotropicalism, the three youngest of the present study's writers – Paulina Chiziane, Ungulani Ba Ka Khosa, and Suleiman Cassamo – were born, in 1955, 1957 and 1962, respectively; between 1948 and 1951, meanwhile, Noémia de Sousa produced her entire published poetic corpus.

Mothers of the Revolution

As the New State resisted the rising tide of international decolonization with linguistic makeovers and PR offensives, the first movements toward an organized anticolonial pushback were germinating just outside Mozambique's borders. As Malyn Newitt makes clear, a viable anticolonial nationalist movement was slow to develop in Mozambique; the population's exceptionally low literacy and education rates went hand-in-hand with the New State's censorship policies and ban on trade unions to insulate the country from events in the wider continent and to nip in the bud any stirrings of dissent (1995: 520). For these reasons, it was among those who travelled beyond the borders of Mozambique – migrant labourers working in the mines of the Rand and the Copper Belt, and the relatively privileged *assimilado* class studying in Portugal, the US or South Africa – that Mozambican nationalist organizations emerged, ultimately coming together in 1962 under the leadership of Eduardo Mondlane to form Frelimo in Julius Nyerere's newly independent Tanzania (Newitt 1995: 521–2).

Mondlane was the product of a traditional Tsonga family, a Protestant schooling courtesy of the Swiss Mission, and a foreign higher education, having attended mission schools in both southern Mozambique and South

18

CHAPTER I

Africa, and having spent a brief interim period at the Universidade de Lisboa
before completing his BA, MA and PhD in the US at Oberlin College and
Northwestern University (T. Silva 1998: 189–99). On 25 September 1964,
with little to no negotiation or build-up due to the refusal of either side to
acknowledge the other's legitimacy, war officially broke out between Frelimo
and the Portuguese government (Newitt 1995: 517). José Craveirinha's first
collection of poetry, *Xigubo*, was published in Lisbon that same year. The
war was to last a decade.

The clandestine propaganda materials distributed by Frelimo in
the early years of the organization's existence, often produced outside of
Mozambique and written in English and French as well as Portuguese,
effectively illustrate the ways in which anticolonial constructs of gender
and sexuality came to bear on the nationalist ideology that would dominate
Mozambican politics and cultural production for many years to come.[9] In
so doing, these materials reveal a latent discursive and affective continuity
between the Portuguese colonial regime and the Frelimo-led nation-building process that would follow independence in 1975, a continuity that has
remained officially unspoken while simultaneously becoming a mainstay
of the Mozambican post-independence literature typified particularly by
the works of Chiziane, Khosa and Cassamo.

An edition of *Mozambican Revolution*, the English-language version
of official Frelimo newsletter *A Voz da Revolução*, distributed two months
before the outbreak of war in 1964 provides early indications that beneath
the radically distinct rhetoric of the anticolonial movement lay a very
familiar gendered framework. An article condemning the Organização
Provincial de Voluntários e Defesa Civil, a paramilitary organization for
colonial loyalists living in Mozambique, ends with a warning: 'We are more
than 7 million people while they are only 100,000, and when 7 million
people are united by one aim, and that aim is freedom, nothing can stop

9   The present study uses the Portuguese versions of these preindependence clandestine
    publications wherever possible. However, judging by their limited availability in the
    archives of Maputo relative to English versions, it appears that the latter texts often
    outlived their Portuguese counterparts; in cases where no Portuguese version could
    be found, the English version will thus be used.

them' ('Organized Civil Oppression' 1964: 5). The article is immediately followed by a piece on a visit to communist China by Selina Simango,[10] and describes how she 'learned many things about the role of women in the revolution; how they must be organized in order to be able to give a direct contribution to the struggle for the complete independence of their country' ('Sister Selina Simango in China' 1964: 6). The article then comments that 'Portuguese colonialists indiscriminately oppress men, women and children. We know of many cases where women, by their courage and determination have been able to save their husbands and children from the hands of the Portuguese fascist police. We have among us in exile women who have followed their men to participate in the struggle' (6).

The juxtaposition of these two brief articles serves to highlight the significant gendered implications underpinning Frelimo's early visions of independence. The former piece's statement that the independence movement unites all Mozambicans under the aim of 'freedom' immediately raises questions of representation and voice – who is claiming that unity? And to whom will this freedom belong? – that the second article effectively answers. This professed unity is led by men; women are present as followers and supporters of their men, and protectors of their children. The statement that 'Portuguese colonialists indiscriminately oppress men, women and children' furthermore points toward a flattening of the gendered specificities of colonized life, itself indicating that freedom is defined along the lines of male experience. Women may be helping to lay the foundations of liberation struggle, but its design will be a male endeavour.

This levelling of gendered experiences of colonialism becomes a key feature of Frelimo's gender discourse as the colonial war stretches on and independence approaches. In many cases the textual means by which this effect is reached can be understood as exemplifying what Sara Ahmed has termed 'non-performativity', wherein a speech act is committed in order to forestall its material realization (Ahmed 2015).[11] An illustrative example

---

10   Selina Simango was the wife of Frelimo founding member Uria Simango. Both were ultimately executed in secret by Frelimo on charges of treason (Igreja 2008: 545–6).

11   Sara Ahmed's 2015 talk, 'Brick Walls: Racism and Other Hard Histories', is unfortunately not available to read (though there are video recordings online as of January

can be found in a 1966 special edition of *A Voz da Revolução*, produced to inform readers of the outcome of an extraordinary session of Frelimo's Comité Central, in which the official disassociation of the short-lived Liga Feminina Moçambicana (LIFEMO) from Frelimo is announced:

> O CC [Comité Central] constata que sob o regime colonial, a mulher moçambicana está submetida à mesma opressão que o resto da população. Mas, além disso, ela está também submetida à discriminação económica e social (em relação aos homens) forçando-a, por exemplo, à imoralidade da prostituição.
>
> Esta situação, e o carácter radical da reivindicação da independência nacional, faz com que a mulher tenha, perante o colonialismo português, uma posição idêntica à de toda a população moçambicana, isto é, na essência e na prática, a posição fundamental das mulheres identifica-se com a do resto da população. ('LIFEMO' 1966, n. p.)[12]
>
> [The Central Committee recognizes that under the colonial regime, the Mozambican woman is subject to the same oppression as the rest of the population. But, in addition to that, she is also subject to economic and social discrimination (in relation to men), forcing her, for example, into the immorality of prostitution.
>
> This situation, and the radical nature of the revindication of national independence, means that women have, in the face of Portuguese colonialism, a position identical to that of all of the Mozambican population; that is to say, in essence and in practice, women's fundamental position can be identified with that of the rest of the population.]

2017); however, an earlier and less specific explanation of 'non-performativity' is included in her 2004 article 'Declarations of Whiteness: The Non-Performativity of Anti-Racism'.

12   Interestingly, the existence of LIFEMO appears to have been somewhat suppressed in official Frelimo history. Particularly compelling examples can be found in Benigna Zimba's *A Mulher Moçambicana na Luta de Libertação Nacional* (2013), wherein the 1966 article cited above is reproduced in full but with all references to LIFEMO replaced with ellipses (27–8), and in the Frelimo-published *Datas e Documentos da História da Frelimo* (Muiuane 2006), which lists the outcome of the 1966 extraordinary session simply as '[a]firmação do princípio da emancipação da mulher como parte integrante da linha política da Frelimo' [the affirmation of the principle of the emancipation of women as an integral aspect of Frelimo's party line] (79).

In this passage, the specificities of women's experiences of Portuguese colonialism are acknowledged, only to be immediately elided into those of men. The boundaries of gender difference are thus reinscribed under the guise of speaking to women's specific needs, while the needs themselves are explicitly erased. A similar pattern is evident in articles dealing with instances of gendered violence; the acts are exposed, often in great detail, but in the very same moment are anchored back in the realm of male experience and suffering. The same publication's 1967 endorsement of the testimony of Father Mateus Guenjere, a Mozambican priest, to the United Nations reflects this discursive process:

> [F]rom the outset you must know that the Mozambican African has no property rights whatsoever. His farms, his fruit trees, huts, wives and children, all belong to the Portuguese government.
> [...]
> I have already told you that the African Mozambican has been deprived of his wife. The Portuguese are an immoral and adulterous people. Where there are Portuguese men there one must expect an abundance of mulattoes. Women and young girls are violated by the Portuguese as if they were bitches set on by a pack of dogs.
> [...]
> This year the doors and windows of an African [...] were broken down by the Portuguese settlers who wanted to get his wife.
> [...]
> The head of the family which lived a few kms. from my mission was savagely beaten up by two white Portuguese settlers because he was refusing to let them sleep with his 9 year old daughter. ('A Mozambican Priest' 1967: 11)

The sexual atrocities of Portuguese settlers are here framed primarily as either the precursor to violence against Mozambican men, or as a violent misuse of their 'property', in addition to evidence of the perversity of Portuguese men. The implication of this presentation of gendered violence is that violence against women is relevant to the liberation struggle only insofar as it threatens men or masculinity. Women and girls are thus used in symbolic terms to prove the validity of anticolonial struggle, while at the same time being divested of a subjective role within it; the consolidation of black masculinity in the face of colonial emasculation, meanwhile, remains the foremost priority.

Following Mondlane's assassination by parcel bomb in February 1969 and a subsequent protracted power struggle, in May 1970 Samora Machel assumed leadership of Frelimo (Newitt 1995: 526–7). Machel's installation as leader signalled a distinct shift to the revolutionary left for Frelimo, culminating in its official espousal of Marxist-Leninist doctrine in 1977[13] and displays of support for the Soviet Union during the Cold War. His leadership also brought with it a strong rhetorical reassertion of the role of women within the anticolonial movement. At the first conference of the Frelimo-run Organização da Mulher Moçambicana [Mozambican Women's Organization] (OMM) in 1973, with Machel in active attendance, the group declared their vision for an independent Mozambique as one that 'recusa qualquer forma de opressão e exploração, de um indivíduo ou grupo ou clase sobre outro, e que visa o estabelecimento de relações humanas sãs e harmoniosas' [refuses any form of oppression or exploitation, by any individual or group or class against another, and that looks toward the establishment of healthy and harmonious human relations] ('Primeira Conferência' 1973: 5). Machel's speech to the conference appears to echo that sentiment, lauding the event as 'um momento histórico, glorioso, na vida da nossa Organização' [a historic and glorious moment in the life of our Organization] (1974: 7) and asserting that women's emancipation 'é uma necessidade fundamental da Revolução, uma garantia da sua continuidade, uma condição do seu triunfo' [is a fundamental necessity of the Revolution, a guarantee of its continuity, a condition of its triumph] (13), the title given to the speech when it was published and distributed in 1974 as a key Frelimo text.

While the optimistic certainty of this rhetoric is undeniably compelling, a deeper analysis of Machel's choice of words here reveals the profound fissures still evident in Frelimo's commitment to women's liberation. Indeed, when viewed in its original context as part of Machel's definitive 1973 speech, the very wording of the oft-repeated maxim quoted above – most significantly, its reference to 'continuidade' – itself exposes the stumbling-block at the heart of Mozambican revolutionary gender discourse: the

13   Frelimo declared itself officially Marxist-Leninist at its third party congress in 1977 (Newitt 1995: 542).

'continuador', a term coined by Machel to refer to Mozambique's children. The figure of the 'continuador' underpins the entirety of the speech, a pervasiveness made explicit in Machel's description of the principal tasks he envisages for women in the revolution:

> Formar a nova geração, criar nas crianças a mentalidade nova que lhes permitirá serem autênticos continuadores da revolução. Ensinar os alunos, para que, assumindo a nossa linha, dominem a ciência e se tornem agentes transformadores da sociedade. Transformar as esposas dos militantes em militantes ativas elas próprias, em autênticas mães da revolução. (1974: 9)

> [To bring up the new generation, to create in children the new mentality that will allow them to become authentic *continuadores* of the revolution. To teach our students so that, when they assume our roles, they dominate the sciences and become transformative members of society. To transform the wives of militants into active militants themselves, into authentic mothers of the revolution.]

Even the latter of these tasks, while apparently offering women a subjective role on the frontlines of the revolution, is ultimately tied back to motherhood as the *sine qua non* of female obligation. The implication of Machel's ostensibly pro-woman stance thus becomes clear: that women are necessary foot-soldiers of the revolution because, and insofar as, they produce and raise children, themselves the embodied proof of the enforcement of compulsory reproductive heterosexuality.

Contagious Colonialism

Following the 25 April 1974 coup in Portugal and the subsequent formal end of the colonial war with the signing of the Lusaka Accord in September of the same year, this demarcation of ideal womanhood was written into official Frelimo policy. A February 1975 policy document made available in popular pro-Frelimo weekly magazine *Tempo* defines the emancipation of the Mozambican woman as her taking responsibility for her roles as 'cidadã, filha, esposa e mãe' [citizen, daughter, wife and mother] ('Organização da Mulher Moçambicana' 1975: 34). Under Frelimo, she would be '[r]esponsável, enquanto a companheira do homem; responsável enquanto educadora da nova geração' [responsible in her role as man's companion, responsible in her role as educator of the new generation] (34). Sexism, meanwhile, is elided into the twin enemies of precolonial traditionalism and (neo-)imperialism, absolving pro-Frelimo men of responsibility for women's emancipation and forestalling any critique of gendered meaning as a discrete axis of oppression.

While the Mozambican anticolonial struggle and subsequent achievement of independence indicated sweeping emancipatory changes for the country's women, then, it is clear that this new era carried with it a burden of age-old prescriptions and restrictions. Not only were women expected to marry and bear multiple children, fulfilling the obligations of a strictly delineated and deeply conservative gender binary; they were also required to bear full responsibility for the eternalization of socialist (and specifically, from 1977, Marxist-Leninist) ideology and the future unity of the Mozambican nation through ideological regulation of the domestic sphere. As Owen demonstrates, drawing on Catherine V. Scott's 1994 work on comparable processes in revolutionary Angola, this reaffirmed association between femininity and the family home served to perpetuate a gendered division of space, rooted in patriarchal traditionalism, in which the domestic sphere was cast as private and tacitly exempt from revolutionary critique (2007a: 34). Women were thus uncritically anchored to a traditionalist and patriarchal domestic role even as they were discursively welcomed into the public sphere, a paradox captured by the iconic imagery of Figure 2. Meanwhile, as Arnfred explains in great detail, various precolonial practices that women themselves often experienced ambivalently, but ultimately as advantageous, such as *lobolo* (bride-price) and polygyny in the south of the country and matriliny and sexual initiation rituals in the north, were banned in the name of 'progress' and female emancipation (2011: 27–31, 40–6, 71–90, 102–3), leaving membership of a nuclear family as the sole officially sanctioned female destiny.

Figure 2: June 1972 front cover of *Mozambique Revolution*, the French-language edition of Frelimo newsletter *A Voz da Revolução*. Author unknown; held by the Arquivo Histórico de Moçambique, Maputo.

This focus on a morally regulated and reproductive nuclear family unit as the cornerstone of post-independence Mozambican nation-building had equally restrictive and prohibitive implications for men and masculinity, as Rothwell notes (2004: 134). Despite Frelimo's dubbing of the ideal revolutionary man as the 'Homem Novo' [New Man], it is clear that there was very little that was actually 'new' about this man. Rather, the attributes valued in Portuguese men by late New State ideology and thereby held as constituting an ideal masculinity in the eyes of the colonial regime – virility, strength, reproductive heterosexual monogamy – were simply transposed by Frelimo onto the equally conservative masculine ideals arising from the southern Mozambican syncretism of traditional Tsonga patriliny with the Protestant puritanism of the Swiss Mission (Arnfred 2011: 57–60). The result was a doctrine of masculinity that sanctioned male engagement with certain elements of (Tsonga) precolonial tradition, namely patriliny and control over female sexuality, while officially condemning others seen as incompatible with Frelimo's selective progressivism, such as the afore-mentioned *lobolo* and polygyny (Arnfred 2011: 46–7, 57–60). It was this prescriptive understanding of masculinity that became fixed, in formal Frelimo ideology at least, as indicative of ideal Mozambican manhood as a whole (Rothwell 2004: 134).[14]

This process speaks, evidently, to the tacit Tsonga ethnocentrism running through Frelimo's ideological production, an undercurrent officially denied by the party but clearly indicated by the makeup of its leadership (Owen 2007a: 33–4). It also suggests that while men's sexuality may have been cast in an overall more subjective light than that of women by Frelimo, it remained equally circumscribed in terms of its position within the matrix of compulsory heterosexuality: a point illustrated by the ongoing silence toward homosexuality perpetuated by each successive Frelimo government, and the parallel preservation of an 1886 colonial law interpretable as prohibiting homosexual practice until 2015.[15]

---

14   As Rothwell shows here, practices deviating from this official ideal did inevitably persist, albeit in an 'under-the-radar' fashion.

15   See the present study's Conclusion for further information on the 2015 penal reform.

Against this restrictive backdrop of biological determinism and gender essentialism, upheld by the lack of a viable theory of gender hierarchy in Frelimo's classical socialist worldview and underpinned by the party's moral and religious inheritances (Owen 2007a: 33), the attempts of women both in and outside Mozambique to acquire limited agency or autonomy by working within oppressive political systems were either ignored or actively denigrated by pro-Frelimo media. The second wave of Western feminist struggle, running more or less contemporaneously with the fight for Mozambican independence, was dismissed as collaborating with capitalism, by turns demonizing men and somehow playing into their hands, and encouraging women to buy into an illusion of individualist emancipation in which the liberated women 'é a que bebe, é a que fuma, é a que usa calças e mini saias, a que se dedica à promiscuidade sexual, a que recusa ter filhos' [is one that drinks, is one that smokes, is one that wears trousers and miniskirts, one that dedicates herself to sexual promiscuity, one that refuses to have children] (Machel 1974: 26).

This identification of women engaged in gender struggle with hypersexuality and promiscuity illustrates the sexual conservatism that characterized Mozambique's post-independence nation-building project. It also suggests a fear of female corporeality and sexuality, epitomizing the affective continuity between post-independence Frelimo policy and the various permutations of colonial rule that had preceded it, beneath the on-paper emancipatory gestures typified by Frelimo's granting of leadership roles within the OMM to some women – who were, it is almost needless to say, almost invariably southern and Protestant-educated (Arnfred 2011: 27) – and its early support of women-run projects such as the Zonas Verdes [Green Zones], a collective of Maputo agricultural cooperatives (Arnfred 2011: 36–8). The emasculation of black men at the heart of colonial discourse, itself a symptom of ingrained gendered and racialized border anxieties, had worked both to reinforce the importance of gender hierarchy as a site of national consolidation and social empowerment and to erode the boundaries of black masculinity. Within this context, the disciplining of black femininity becomes a means of reaffirming black masculine hegemony at the level of affect that the political power granted by independence had failed to reach, a revindication itself affectively correlated with the fortification of nationhood and national boundaries. Nowhere is the deployment of this power mechanism more evident than in Frelimo's post-independence agitprop on the subject of prostitution, which became a mainstay of the party's rhetoric following their assumption of power over state media after the 25 April revolution.[16]

A lead article by prolific Mozambican journalist Albino Magaia, entitled 'Prostituição: Tráfico Sexual Mata a Fome' and run by *Tempo* in October 1974, neatly encapsulates the nature of this burgeoning political obsession. Its opening paragraph describes an imagined encounter with a 'rapariga negra que de noite usa uma mini-saia ultra curta cuja cor condiz com as botas altas; peruca de um milhar de escudos, toda loira [...]; cara pintada com exagero e unhas prateadas; [...] [que] não sabe ler nem escrever mas diz no seu inglês limitado "I love you"' [black girl who at night wears a tiny miniskirt which matches her high-heeled boots; a thousand-*escudo* blonde wig [...]; a heavily made-up face and polished nails; [...] who cannot read or write but can say, in her broken English, 'I love you'] (19). The author imagines that this woman has fled rural famine, engaging in sex work out of desperation, but her motives are presented as of secondary importance to her exaggeratedly Western-coded clothing, wig, and makeup and her 'Mediterranean' dancing style.

This fantasized scenario is followed immediately by the claim, asserted frequently in state-endorsed media of the era, that '[n]ão existia prostitu-ição em África antes da vinda dos europeus' [prostitution did not exist in Africa prior to the arrival of Europeans] (20). This unfalsifiable assertion makes explicit the association between sex work and imperialism, while its juxtaposition with the article's opening description implicitly casts women sex workers themselves as colonial collaborators and traitors to their race. Mozambican men, conspicuously absent from the long list of foreign nationals with whom the imagined sex worker negotiates trans-actions, are thus absolved of responsibility for the thriving sex industry, becoming instead the usurped victims of neo-imperial acts of emasculation.

---

16   Mozambican filmmaker Licínio Azevedo's 2012 feature film *Virgem Margarida* offers a recent (and controversial) critique of Frelimo's anti-prostitution policies.

Diverging sharply from the sympathetic, if heavily paternalistic and fetishizing initial tone of the article, Magaia uses this claim to segue into a lengthy affirmation of the Frelimo line on prostitution. Sex workers are not only the vectors of disease, but are themselves 'uma das doenças crónicas do colonialismo' [one of the chronic illnesses of colonialism], 'um cancro' [a cancer] (1974: 20).[17] They represent an excessive attachment to the 'vida fácil' [easy life], a mentality that is 'ultra-burguesa de um modo quase doentio' [ultra-bourgeois to a point of near-insanity] (24). The anxious casting of black men as the emasculated and usurped victims of this female sexual engagement with neo-imperial foreign intruders weighs heavy in the author's emphasis on the 'violento racismo em relação aos negros' [violent racism toward black men] that he claims is commonplace among black women sex workers (23). Yet despite its outlandish claims as to the commonality of this vilified practice among Lourenço Marques's black female population, any real analysis of why poor black women in particular might enter into such work in the first place is manifestly absent. Within this juxtaposition of visceral disgust and analytical silence lies the implication that women and women's bodies are natural vectors of corporeal and ideological corruption, and natural mediators for neo-imperial endeavour, bringing into focus the symbiotic male unease and misogyny on the flipside of Machel's imagining of women as the bearers of Mozambican culture. This mapping of the prostitute body onto post-independence male corporeal and territorial boundary anxieties is made yet more explicit in an early 1975 policy document, which asserts that '[a]través da prostituição o inimigo pode infiltrar-se' [it is through prostitution that the enemy can infiltrate] ('Problemas Sociais' 1975: 37–8).

As the need to consolidate national unity and stability grew in urgency following the finalization of the decolonization process in June 1975, the anxious sentiments of these early anti-prostitution campaigns intensified into outright eliminationism. An August 1975 report entitled 'Para Onde Foram as Prostitutas?' [Where Have the Prostitutes Gone?] enthusiastically

---

17   For more detailed analysis of Frelimo's pathologization of sex work and other perceived acts of dissent, see my article 'Discipline, Disease, Dissent: The Pathologized Body in Mozambican Post-independence Discourse' (2016).

recounts a vigilante raid carried out on a cluster of *lupanares*, a term that refers to a small dwelling known to operate as a makeshift brothel, describing it as an act of 'fúria popular' [popular rage] during which 'as massas assaltassem os lupanares destruindo as camas e demais haveres das prostitutas' [the masses attacked the *lupanares*, destroying the prostitutes' beds and other belongings] (27) and leaving '[a]s portas arrombadas, as janelas arrancadas, os muros demolidos' [the doors forced open, the windows torn out, the walls crumbling] (27). The women occupying the area are reported to have fled in terror, setting up alternative workplaces alone in individual apartments or turning to streetwalking. There is no mention of the exponentially increased danger for these women resulting from being forced to work alone, nor is there any concern for their wellbeing; a description of the now-derelict former *lupanares* ends simply 'E ainda bem' [Just as well] (28). The desire toward eradication implicit in this silence is reinforced by the article's telling choice of phrasing as it reminds its readers that there is still work to be done if Mozambique is to 'liquida[r] a prostituição e com ela as prostitutas' [eliminate prostitution, and with it prostitutes] (29).

This preliminary discursive shift toward eliminationism anticipates the renewed anti-sex work rhetoric displayed during the implementation of Frelimo's 1983 'Operação Produção' [Operation Production]. This national framework was implemented during the increasingly unstable social climate of early 1980s Mozambique, which saw earlier efforts by the Rhodesian and then South African white minority governments to destabilize Frelimo escalate into a violent and sustained threat to the integrity of the country. Operação Produção aimed to create a sense of national unity and loyalty in the face of these threats, while removing dissident elements from society at large, by rounding up citizens considered socially unproductive and forcibly deporting them to 're-education camps' – penal labour colonies – located mostly in the isolated rural northern province of Niassa.[18] As part of the process, Mozambicans were encouraged to prove their loyalty to Frelimo by reporting the unproductive, antisocial or 'parasitic' behaviour of friends or

---

18   For a retrospective literary critique of this system of 're-education camps', see the 2013 novel from Ungulani Ba Ka Khosa, *Entre as Memórias Silenciadas* (Maputo: Alcance Editores, 2013).

family members to authorities (Castanheira 1983: 20–2).[19] Of the women deported to these camps during the campaign, a significant number were either sex workers or suspected sex workers (Sheldon 2003: 370).

A speech given by Machel in Gaza, historic southern Mozambican kingdom of chief Ngungunhane, in the lead-up to the launch of the operation provides a clear example of the way that the violent eradication of prostitutes came to be framed as an essential part of national consolidation. Following a brief and decisive justification of the use of violence in the righteous exercise of state power, Machel describes Ngungunane's torturous methods of execution for suspected prostitutes, which consisted of live impalement on sharpened sticks driven into the ground (1983b: 20). He immediately slides out from under this graphically violent image by noting that Frelimo is not in favour of the death penalty for prostitutes – but then reiterates that sex workers have long been considered impure and touching them taboo, and finally asks, '[t]erá valor o nosso povo quando misturado com [...] prostitutas?' [can our society have any value when mixed with [...] prostitutes?] (20). This shrewd rhetorical paralipsis seems particularly conspicuous in the light of Frelimo's deification of Ngungunhane; indeed, less than a year later the very same magazine in which this speech was published would dedicate a cover and feature article to the nineteenth-century chief, hailing him as a 'Herói da Luta Anticolonial' [Hero of the Anticolonial Struggle] ('Ngungunhane' 1983: 27–35).

The coincidence of this intensified judicial and rhetorical targeting of prostitution during Operação Produção with the increased aggression of anti-Frelimo factions underscores the prominence of gendered meaning in Frelimo's vision of Mozambican nationhood. If sexual transactions between black Mozambican women and foreign men represented a threat to nascent black masculine hegemony, and if that hegemony was itself affectively embroiled with the consolidation of nationhood, then Frelimo's violently eliminationist anti-sex work efforts worked to symbolically reinforce

---

19   As Castanheira's dispatch shows, even strongly pro-Frelimo *Tempo* could not fail to
      acknowledge that such action on the part of ordinary Mozambicans was more com-
      monly used as a way to punish enemies or get rid of inconvenient wives or mistresses.

national boundaries by reasserting national male sovereignty over the nationalized female body. Meanwhile, the black prostitute body, as the embodied site of foreign penetration both literal and figurative, becomes a disciplining mechanism for all black Mozambican women: a reminder of the dire individual and collective consequences of stepping outside the bounds of approved female conduct.

Killing Utopia

The years following the implementation of the Operação Produção campaign were dominated by the increasingly dramatic and brutal war between Frelimo and Renamo, the name ultimately adopted by what was initially a loose conglomeration of factions and individuals with the singular commonality of opposition to Frelimo.[20] The details of Renamo's initial formation are subject to a high degree of conjecture that varies from source to source, but the broad consensus is as follows: known first as the Mozambican National Resistance (MNR), the organization was founded by white minority Rhodesia's Central Intelligence Organization under Ken Flower (Dinerman 2006: 2; Newitt 2002: 209) in collaboration with former PIDE agent Orlando Cristina (Newitt 1995: 563–4), with its first members recruited in 1976 (Chan and Venâncio 1998: 3).

While disruptive attacks on localized civilian targets began later that year, it was following the death of its first leader André Matsangaissa in 1978 (Newitt 2002: 211), the assumption of leadership by Afonso Dhlakama in 1979, and the independence of Zimbabwe in 1980 (Dinerman 2006: 2–3) that the tactics that would define Renamo's reputation were deployed on a wider scale (Chan and Venâncio 1998: 4). It was at this point that the organization was taken over by the apartheid

20   As with the name 'Frelimo/FRELIMO', the rendering of 'Renamo/RENAMO' (Resistência Nacional Moçambicana [Mozambican National Resistance]) varies across sources; I have standardized the term to 'Renamo' throughout.

South African government (Dinerman 2006: 2), which had the motivation and wherewithal to properly train and arm Renamo's soldiers (Chan and Venâncio 1998: 4). Thus began the terror campaign that led US policy analyst Bill Frelick to dub Renamo the 'Khmer Rouge of Africa' (1989). For Frelick, '[t]he magnitude of RENAMO's record of gratuitous violence and disregard for human life – of murder and mutilation, rape and pillage – makes them stand in a class of their own' (1989: 4). Momplé, Chiziane, Khosa and Cassamo all produced their first publications during these gruelling years.

The sociopolitical circumstances that facilitated the rise of Renamo, and the specific methods used by the organization during the conflict, will be explored in greater detail in Chapters 3 and 4; for the purposes of this contextual chapter, Frelick's expanded summary provides a brief insight into the group's approach to warfare:

> RENAMO has demonstrated utter disregard for the dignity and integrity of the human person. The civilians in its areas are treated – no, mistreated – as chattel. Women and girls in areas of RENAMO control are forced to submit to rape on a frequent and sustained basis. Those who resist are severely beaten, and, in some cases, executed. Refugees consistently testify about being pressed into forced labor. [...] Whether defended or not, civilians are subjected to indiscriminate attack including automatic weapons fire, but also axings, knifings, bayoneting, burning to death, smothering, and forced drownings. Some refugees have reported retribution attacks – mutilation and killing – on young children whose parents fled RENAMO attacks. (1989: 3–4)

As Alice Dinerman notes, this sustained use of arbitrary and devastating violence worked to paralyze the Mozambican population, hand-in-hand with the systematic destruction of essential community centres such as schools, clinics, health posts, and local shops, the creation of man-made famine and energy poverty through disruption of transport systems, and the deliberate hindering of relief efforts (2006: 54).

The ways in which the violence of Mozambique's post-independence conflict manifested speaks clearly to the discursive productions of gendered meanings examined so far in this chapter. The use of sexual violence against women, a practice employed by both sides but utilized in the most systemic manner by Renamo, as a means of exerting domination over local populations is perhaps the most widely documented example. As Carolyn Nordstrom affirms, the rape of women and girls was a central weapon in Renamo's arsenal; featured within their creation of a 'spectacle of violence', it was intended to 'undermine personal integrity and family relations in their most profound sense' (1997: 127). Rape was most notably committed in public, often in view of the victim's family, who were commonly forced to watch. It was also a significant part of the culture in what Robert Gersony's 1988 report to the US Department of State refers to as 'control areas': villages that had fallen entirely under the control of Renamo combatants (18). Rape was used as a disciplining mechanism in these zones, a means of consolidating power and reinforcing hierarchies, as Sheldon confirms (2002: 198).

This use of sexual violence as a prominent means of destroying affective and social integrity on a collective level can be understood in relation to the gender constructs discussed thus far as a grotesque and literal violation of the gendered territorial boundaries upheld by Frelimo. That Renamo sought to destroy Mozambican nationhood in and through the bodies of women, and to assert their own territorial supremacy via the excessive and violent reinscription of their masculinity, thus becomes the horrifying logical conclusion of Frelimo's gendered understanding of nationhood. If, for Frelimo, women were the bearers of culture, the vessels for the utopian next generation of socialist *continuadores*, then rape became for Renamo a violent means of forestalling that culture, that utopia. Women themselves, meanwhile, were left utterly divested of the right to corporeal or affective boundaries, reduced in discursive and often literal terms to embodied sites of contested male prerogatives.

As this analysis of textual and historical moments has sought to demonstrate, gender and sexuality have figured in the last century of Mozambican discourse as inextricably intertwined with cartographic, territorial and political borders, frequently operating as the latent vehicle for the assertion and contestation of border control, and for the expression, resolution and quelling of territorial anxiety. These underlying meanings and purposes have changed little throughout Mozambique's long twentieth century, despite otherwise radical changes to discourse and policy regarding both gender itself and the axes of race, ethnicity and class with which it intersects. It is this very intransigence, however, that imbues the gendered and sexual body with subversive potential, as the following literary analyses seek to elucidate, beginning with two figureheads from chronologically opposite ends of the Mozambican literary canon: José Craveirinha and Paulina Chiziane.

CHAPTER 2

Unma(s)king Hegemony: Negotiating Masculinities in José Craveirinha and Paulina Chiziane[1]

> Tomorrow there will be no master left, because everybody will be the master of himself. This is the lesson of poetry and it is essential for the success of the Revolution.
> — 'The Role of Poetry in the Mozambican Revolution' (1969: 32)

The task of foregrounding the historically marginalized experiences of women has remained axiomatic to feminist gender scholarship since its earliest inception. In a world in which the putatively universal subject of philosophical and political enquiry is still assumed as male, and in which attempts to alter this status quo are diminished in academia as specialist or niche efforts, the privileging of women's histories has rightly been recognized by scholars of gender as a foundational priority. The late 1980s rise of theoretical schemata based on the contingency of gendered categories served to spark an increased engagement of feminist theory with the study of men as gendered subjects themselves, but the development of masculinity studies has nonetheless remained a slow process; as Scott Coltrane affirms, 'research on men is as old as scholarship itself, but a focus on masculinity, or men as explicitly gendered individuals, is relatively recent' (1994: 41). The study of gender in African contexts, itself a nascent field, has presented in a similar pattern, with gender becoming a 'major research focus' while the default universality of the male subject precluded gendered analysis

---

1   This chapter is an expanded version of an article originally published as 'Diminished Returns: Mozambican Masculinities in José Craveirinha's *Xigubo* and Paulina Chiziane's *O Sétimo Juramento*' in *Forum for Modern Language Studies* 52/1 (2016), 81–99, and is used here by permission of Oxford University Press.

of masculinity right up until the early twenty-first century (Lindsay and Miescher 2003: 2).

Mozambique is no exception to this tendency in African studies, and what little scholarship has emerged on men and masculinities in the country is limited almost exclusively to primary qualitative anthropological and socio-logical research.[2] While such research is undeniably pioneering, a clear space remains for the critical discussion of Mozambican masculinities as constructed in cultural texts. This chapter seeks to make use of that space to recentre black masculinities in works by two writers credited with making very different, and yet equally gendered, contributions to the development of the Mozambican lit-erary canon. Poet José Craveirinha comes imbued with the patriarchal authority granted by his symbolic role as the founding father of Mozambican literature (Owen 2007a: 46), with a career spanning four tumultuous decades of the country's recent history. Paulina Chiziane, meanwhile, became the nation's first woman novelist with the 1990 publication of *Balada de Amor ao Vento*, and has henceforth been hailed as the foremost literary and journalistic voice of Mozambican womanhood (Chabal 1996: 91–3). With these gendered interpel-lations firmly in mind, this chapter will take as its primary focus a comparative analysis of the works by each writer in which masculinity features most promi-nently: Craveirinha's first published volume, *Xigubo* (1964; 2nd edn 1980, repr. 2008),[3] and *O Sétimo Juramento* (2000; 3rd edn 2008), Chiziane's third novel and her first to focus on a male protagonist. First, however, it is necessary to

---

2   See, for example, Aboim (2008). Notable exceptions to this generalization can be found in Rothwell (2004) and Sabine (2004).

3   It should be noted here that the 2008 edition of *Xigubo* used for reference in this study follows the format of the 1980 second edition, which places the poems in a different order from that of the original 1964 version (entitled *Chigubo*); the original opens with 'Manifesto', with 'Xigubo' much later in the text, for example. The original edition also contains some minor typographical differences to later editions, for example in line breaks (comparing the 1964 and 1980 versions of 'Manifesto' provides evidence of these small discrepancies). However, the order and renderings used in the 1980 edition appear to have been maintained for all subsequent reprints and editions, in both Portugal and Mozambique, which presumably indicates Craveirinha's prefer-ence. On the meaning of the title: as specified in the glossary to the 2008 edition, the Ronga word *xigubo* refers to a southern Mozambican warriors' dance performed to call or prepare for a defensive or offensive act of war (3).

provide a brief theoretical background to the study of masculinities and the ways in which the Mozambican case both reflects and challenges mainstream Western academic consensus on the same.

Hegemonic, Subordinated, Other

Perhaps the best known, and certainly the most widely utilized contemporary theory of masculinity can be found in R. W. Connell's 1987 text *Gender and Power*. With this theory, Connell sought to maintain the basic feminist premise of acknowledging culturally instituted male domination over women while problematizing what she perceived as the simplistic tendency among feminist thinkers to posit masculinity as a homogeneous monolith. With the aim of articulating a more nuanced and pluralistic understanding of power relations both between and among genders, Connell developed a theoretical framework based around 'hegemonic' and 'subordinated' masculinities. Hegemonic masculinity is here understood as 'constructed in relation to various subordinated masculinities as well as in relation to women' (183) and is necessarily heterosexual and usually white: a cultural ideal of manhood grounded in collective fantasy that 'need not correspond at all closely to the actual personalities of the majority of men' (184) but that nonetheless works to sustain male domination. The maintenance of the hegemonic-subordinated binary implies 'a large measure of consent' (185), with the majority of men on both sides in tacit collaboration to preserve hegemonic supremacy with the latent aim of reaping the benefits of women's subjugation.

While Connell's framework remains the *sine qua non* of masculinity studies, the years since the publication of *Gender and Power* have seen a proliferation of theoretical texts that challenge the uncritical use of her schema on the grounds of its simplistic attitude toward race, ethnicity and sexual orientation, and its overlooking of the negotiation of masculinities in (post)colonial contexts. Harry Brod (1994) evaluates Connell's work against the cultural denigration of Jewish men in the twentieth-century United States, and notes the flaws inherent in using an overly simplistic gendered framework to analyse the complexities of racially subordinated masculinities. Such an approach, Brod asserts, runs the risk of playing down the complicity of racialized men with patriarchal gender systems, thereby regressively absolving such men of responsibility for the oppression of women (86–7). He concludes that nonhegemonic masculinities must therefore always be critically located at the intersection of at least two axes of power: 'the male–female axis of men's power over women within the marginalized grouping, and the male–male axis of nonhegemonic men's relative lack of power vis-à-vis hegemonic men' (89). Michael Kimmel's chapter in the same volume explores the complexities of constructing gay masculinity as subordinate, noting that the fearful silence of gay men in the face of the hierarchical gender system is itself complicit in the perpetuation of that system: '[o]ur fears are the sources of our silences, and men's silence is what keeps the system running' (1994: 131). In terms of upholding male domination, then, the absence of speech acts becomes as important as the acts themselves. These critical evaluations by both Kimmel and Brod, published shortly after the advent of Connell's theory, bring forward the importance of maintaining a sense of cultural specificity in relation to her overarching framework.

Drawing Connell's work into dialogue with postcolonial and poststructuralist theories of gender, Elahe Haschemi Yekani's more recent text (2011) emphasizes the complicating impact that the processes of colonialism, resistance and decolonization have on sociocultural negotiations of masculinity, shoring up the limited value of the hegemonic-subordinated binary for gendered analysis of postcolonial contexts. Lending particular weight to narratives of masculine 'crisis' in terms of their capacity to privilege the hegemonic perspective while at the same time betraying the fragility of hegemonic masculinity as a whole, she notes that the inherent ambiguity of masculinity in postcolonial texts demands a more nuanced approach that acknowledges 'narrative patterns of "*in-between-ness*" and *hybridity* as well as *guilt* relating to the after-effects of colonialism' (36).[4]

---

4   Unless otherwise stated, all italics in this study are present in original texts.

Lisa A. Lindsay and Stephen Miescher echo Yekani's concerns toward Connell's framework in terms of the specific complexities of postcolonial Africa, affirming that productive analysis of the ever-changing axes of power that shape the negotiation of gender, race and class identities in African contexts necessitates a fundamentally dialectic relationship between theory and subject matter (2003: 6). Their work underscores the need to exercise caution when applying Connell's model to these contexts, making clear that the repeated and often violent attempts by colonial regimes to acculturate indigenous African subjects to European value systems created a landscape of competing ideologies wherein 'it was *not* always obvious which notions of masculinity were dominant, or hegemonic, since understandings of gender depend on the specific context and on actors' different subject positions' (2003: 6). Sofia Aboim's qualitative sociological study of masculinities in contemporary urban Maputo confirms the centrality of this uncertainty in the Mozambican case, noting that the men she interviewed could be characterized as '"apanhados entre mundos": o dos "velhos tempos" (os *old days*), das tradições pré-coloniais [...]; as heranças do colonialismo português [...]; [e] o mundo "moderno" da sociedade pós-colonial' ['caught between worlds': those of the 'old days' of precolonial traditions [...]; the legacy of Portuguese colonialism [...]; [and] the 'modern' world of post-colonial society] (2008: 276).

This need to acknowledge the intrinsic diversity and changeability of masculinities in African contexts is facilitated by the approach of Belinda Bozzoli (1983), who problematizes the uncritical application of Western social theory to African settings in an essay predating Connell's work by several years. Bozzoli's critique is not primarily concerned with gender theory, making use instead of examples from the apartheid South African resistance movement's utilization of Marxist social theory. Nonetheless, her proposal that the term 'patriarchy' should be used in a plural sense to refer to specific power structures within a given era or society, with colonial and post-independence systems imagined as 'a "patchwork-quilt" – a system in which forms of patriarchy are sustained, modified and even entrenched in a variety of ways depending on the internal character of the system in the first instance' (1983: 149), offers a valuable strategy for reworking Western-centric theories of masculinity to productively fit the Mozambican context.

Robert Morrell, who like Bozzoli takes South Africa as his primary case study, further advocates this notion of a 'patchwork of patriarchies', with 'patriarchy' pluralized in line with 'masculinities' and 'femininities', and confirms that the coexistence of distinct patriarchies is necessarily inherent to colonial and postcolonial states (1998: 613–14). In the same vein, he warns in a later text against the temptation to assume that the dichotomous gendered and racial value systems of colonial states could be superimposed onto colonized societies in any neat or absolute way, noting that while 'colonialism may have destroyed the material base of the African economies, [it] did not destroy the history which was woven into a myriad of gender rituals which served to legitimate the sexual division of labour and male power' (2001: 13). To buy into such simplification, Morrell affirms, is therefore to wrongly deduce that colonialism was successful in dissolving preexisting social hierarchies and values, implicitly crediting the imperialist notion of precolonial Africa as a primordial *tabula rasa* (1998: 612).

Morrell's critique furthermore functions as a warning against extrapolating theories arising from the study of black Western masculinities to black masculinities in Africa. Increased academic interest in black masculinity in the United States and Britain closely followed the emergence of masculinity studies as a whole,[5] and while the resulting research enriches the fields of study of both masculinity and race, its focus on societies in which black men occupy an indisputably subordinate societal position as numeric and power minorities severely limits its use as an approach to African contexts. The situation of men in postcolonial sub-Saharan Africa is far more complex: while black men today represent numerical and power majorities across the region, that status cannot erase the lasting legacies of colonialism, state racism and anticolonial struggle that continue to loom large in the collective living memories of many African nations. The ethnic and class tensions, political heterogeneity and pervasive Western economic pressures specific to Africa, alongside the disproportionate prevalence of whites in the upper echelons of many African societies, further complicate issues relating to masculinity in a way that Western-centred scholarship

5   See, for example, Mac an Ghaill (1994); Segal (1990); Westwood (1990).

cannot account for. Moreover, as Morrell demonstrates, such scholarship is of little to no use for understanding the influence of indigenous social institutions upon quotidian life in postcolonial Africa; nor can it be used to analyse the role of those institutions in forging a sense of national unity during independence struggles and subsequent nation-building projects (1998: 611).

This tight knot of influences, struggles and tensions lies at the heart of gendered power negotiations in Mozambican national and literary discourses, and brings the methodological and theoretical difficulties of approaching the country's literary portrayals of masculinity into stark relief. Understanding the representation and utilization of masculinity within this context evidently demands a critical and interrogative approach to Western-centred gender theory. The problematization of established gender theories brought about by the complicating effects of colonial imposition and postcolonial nation-building is not, however, the only barrier to producing an effective understanding of Mozambican masculinities; a further stumbling-block can be found in the failure of many of the foundational texts of anti- and postcolonial theory to consider the ramifications of gender for their understandings of colonial power mechanisms. Frantz Fanon's seminal work *Black Skin, White Masks* (1967; trans. Markmann 1986) provides a classic example of this elision of gendered oppression. Fanon's work, of course, does not reflect the diversity of postcolonial theory as a whole. Nonetheless, its status within postcolonial studies as a 'classic' text or cornerstone of the field means that its interarticulation of postcoloniality and masculinity offers a useful lens through which to productively examine other anti- and postcolonial materials.

Emasculating Blackness

As Gwen Bergner notes, it is somewhat ironic that Fanon's scathing study of the role of colonial infantilization in instilling 'inferiority complexes' among colonized people, in which he 'transpos[es] Freud's question of the

other from gender to race', passes over the unique colonial infantilization
of black women (1995: 76–8). Indeed, despite the pivotal role of the text
in foregrounding racial difference within psychoanalysis, Fanon's consistent use of man as default universal subject erases gender as an axis of
oppression almost entirely, excluding black women from the reclamation
of agency at the centre of his vision of racial empowerment (Bergner 1995:
76–7). His use of castration as an analogical metaphor for the experience
of colonization (Fanon 1986: 112) provides a succinct example of this uni-
versalization of male experience and consequent suppression of women's
voices. In addition, within that metaphor lies the significant implication
that the empowerment of colonized men is essentially reliant upon the
revindication of black male virility, itself tacitly predicated on the sexual
submission of women.

Further proof of the legitimacy of this interpretation can be found in
Fanon's discussion of colonized women in the chapter 'The Woman of Color
and the White Man' (1986: 41–62). Bergner notes that in this chapter, as in
the text as a whole, 'women are considered as subjects almost exclusively in
terms of their sexual relationships with men; feminine desire is thus defined
as an overly literal and limited (hetero)sexuality' (1995: 77). That said, this
passive reduction of women to sexual object status takes something of a
background role to Fanon's active denigration of black women in terms of
betraying the misogyny within his framework. The black woman subject
of the chapter, a Martinican woman named Mayotte Capécia whose autobiography expresses a desire to marry a white man in order to bolster her
social standing, is described numerous times along with other black women
as a 'girl'; the autobiography is said to have been written out of 'a motivation whose elements are difficult to detect' (42), carrying the 'imbecilities'
(53n) and 'infantile fantasies' (44) of a 'mudslinging storyteller' (53n) that
reflect 'the most ridiculous ideas proliferated at random' (42). She is, in
summary, the ultimate traitor to her race. Black men who harbour sexual
or romantic feelings toward white women are characterized, by contrast, as
'anxious [men] who cannot escape [their] bodies', and who are 'enslaved by
[their] inferiority' (60). While the sexual object choices of black men are
here framed as naturalized social phenomena, the inevitable consequence
of centuries of emasculation at the hands of white colonizers, black female

sexuality is cast as quite outside of this oppressive framework, representing instead an informed, individual network of cynical and voluntary choices (Bergner 1995: 83).

Fanon's excoriating denunciations of Capécia's narratives of her experiences as a black woman under colonial rule do not serve only to deny her subjective and individual lived reality. They also frame the control of black women's sexual and romantic choices, and the ringfencing of sexual access to the black female body, as a necessary step in the journey toward black empowerment, here implicitly held as a purely male preserve. For Fanon, the reclamation of black subjectivity in the face of colonial disempowerment thus becomes contingent on the consolidation of black male hegemony, itself reliant on the enforcement of a rigidly demarcated gender binary. While *Black Skin, White Masks* is a text ostensibly concerned with the psychology of colonized black subjects, then, it is also, crucially, a treatise on black masculinity: a culturally significant crystallization of the relationship between masculinity and anticoloniality that is captured poetically in Craveirinha's work.

Penetrating the Past: José Craveirinha's *Xigubo* (1964)

The academic sidelining of the significant gendered dimensions of such foundational anticolonial texts as *Black Skin, White Masks*, along with the inadequacy of established frameworks with which to understand these intersectional complexities, perhaps goes some way to explaining the critical silence around the gendered and sexual aspects of Craveirinha's poetry. Despite the relatively high degree of academic engagement with Craveirinha, including Ana Mafalda Leite's dedicated monograph (1991) – a rare phenomenon indeed in Mozambican literary criticism – gender and sexuality have so far not featured in a single piece of accessible published scholarship on his work. Nonetheless, as the first half of this chapter seeks to demonstrate using the complexities raised in the above theoretical review,

gendered meanings are in fact fundamental to his early poetic output, and
deserve detailed consideration.

Craveirinha's perceived location within a tradition of negritude is a
common touchstone for analysis of his poetry, particularly in terms of his
construction of a poetry of 'moçambicanidade' or essential Mozambicanness (Chabal 1996: 40–2). Despite Craveirinha's self-professed ignorance
of the 'Négritude' movement itself (Chabal 1994: 97) – that is to say, the
'specific literary movement born in Paris in the [nineteen-]thirties' (Chabal
1996: 8n) – it is certainly true that many of his best-known early poems
reflect the stylistics of 'negritude', where negritude is defined, per Patrick
Chabal, as 'the attempt to recover, redeem and proclaim African indigenous culture as the basis for African literature' (1996: 41). Russell G.
Hamilton describes Craveirinha's early work as 'convey[ing] an African
regionalist fervor' that speaks to a discourse of black affirmation (1975: 202);
similarly, Chabal sees some of these first published poems as 'stand[ing]
the values of the European coloniser on their head as a way of redeeming
that which is Africa' (1996: 42), concluding that 'by writing about some
of the strongest African traditions the poet asserts the value of that very
culture' (43). Leite, meanwhile, finds the stylistics of negritude embedded in Craveirinha's attempt to 'instituir um novo conceito de *beleza*,
vinculado à noção de raça, enquanto civilização e cultura, normalmente,
no contexto colonial, anulado pela invisibilidade ou fortemente alienado'
[establish a new concept of beauty, linked to the notion of race, and to a
civilization and culture normally rendered invisible or heavily marginalized in the colonial context] (1991: 43). Craveirinha's early espousal of a
poetic approach resonant with the aesthetics of negritude is thus critically
identified as a means of revindicating black Mozambican subjectivity in
the face of institutionalized racial and cultural oppression, while asserting
the author's strategic antiassimilationism through the claiming of solidarity
with black subaltern identity despite his biracial heritage and recourse to
the educational and class privilege therein.

What these established analyses overlook, however, is that the racial
solidarity Craveirinha affirms in his early poems has a strongly gendered
identification at its core, tied to the reclamation of a black Mozambican
masculinity that is often, too, implied to be specifically southern by means of

the author's use of Ronga, a precolonial language of southern Mozambique. Representing far more than mere poetic devices, masculinity and male subjectivity are the foundations upon which his delineation of Mozambican identity rests. An idealized vision of black masculinity is established as a leitmotif in *Xigubo* with the eponymous opening poem, which begins:

> Minha Mãe África
> meu irmão Zambeze
> Culucumba! Culucumba! (2008: 17)

> [My Mother Africa
> my brother Zambeze
> *Culucumba*! *Culucumba*!][6]

Establishing an immediate filial connection between poet and land, this first stanza implicitly figures Africa as woman, mother, and passive object of address, while the poet is cast in the role of active male subject. This paradigm is further reflected in the fourth and fifth stanzas:

> E negro Maiela
> músculos tensos na azagaia rubra
> salta o fogo da fogueira amarela
> e dança as danças do tempo da guerra
> das velhas tribos da margem do rio.

> E a noite desflorada
> abre o sexo ao orgasmo do tambor
> e a planície arde todas as luas cheias
> no feitiço viril da insuperstição das catanas (18)

> [And the black man Maiela
> muscles tense on the red spear
> leaps over the flames of the yellow fire
> and dances the dances of wartime
> of the old tribes from the riverbank.

6   *Culucumba* is a Ronga word meaning God or godlike spirit.

And the deflowered night
opens her sex to the orgasm of the drum
and the plains burn every full moon
under the masculine magic of knives beyond superstition]

Craveirinha here juxtaposes two images, both palpably corporeal: the first a textual close-up of a black male character's musculature, in visible tension around his phallic spear, and the second an erotic evocation of the night as a passively open and penetrated vagina. This latter image functions as a means of consolidating the phallic masculinity of the male subject through the oppositional constitution of a sexually available and passive female object, itself an abstract extension of the opening stanza's feminization of the African landscape. The sexual penetration of an objectified, symbolic feminine enacted in these lines is framed as a climactic moment, prefacing the scene of indigenous unification and uprising that ends the poem:

E as vozes rasgam o silêncio da terra
enquanto os pés batem
enquanto os tambores batem
e enquanto a planície vibra os ecos milenários
aqui outra vez os homens desta terra
dançam as danças do tempo da guerra
das velhas tribos juntas na margem do rio. (18)

[And voices shred the silence of the land
as feet stamp
as drums beat
and as the plains vibrate with thousand-year echoes
here once again the men of this land
dance the dances of wartime
of the old tribes together on the riverbank.]

While the desire reflected in 'Xigubo' to return to a lost Africa of maternal origins has hitherto been identified as a means of voicing universal black solidarity and collectivity (Laranjeira 1995: 414–26; Leite 2001: 31–3), what becomes clear with a gendered reading of the piece is that this African 'origin' is essentially sexed: it is both embodied by, and in turn serves to symbolize, the feminine. The imagined 'return' of the male subject to this mythopoetic feminine 'origin' is presented as an act of racial and cultural empowerment, in Leite's words 'um acto de legitimação e de conquista de poder simbólico' [an act of legitimation and a symbolic act of conquest] (1991: 38), but it is couched in a specific semiotics of *sexual* conquest that casts that empowerment as a male preserve predicated on women's sexual subjugation. The revindication of black Mozambican identity is thus framed as a consolidation of masculinity necessarily enacted in and through the female body.

Craveirinha's espousal of an anticolonial racial empowerment consolidated through the reinforcement of black male subjectivity is once again reflected in the final stanza of 'África', a poem that confronts the erasure of precolonial Mozambican cultures and the internalized racial degradation that ensued:

> E ao som másculo dos tantãs tribais o eros
> do meu grito fecunda o humus dos navios negreiros ...
> E ergo no equinócio da minha Terra
> o moçambicano rubi do nosso mais belo canto xi-ronga
> e na insólita brancura dos rins da plena Madrugada
> a necessária carícia dos meus dedos selvagens
> é a tácita harmonia de azagaias no cio das raças
> belas como altivos falos da ouro
> erectos no ventre nervoso da noite africana. (2008: 23)

> [And to the masculine sound of tribal drums the eros
> of my cry seeds the soil of slave-ships ...
> And thus in the equinox of my Land
> the Mozambican glows with our most beautiful Ronga song
> and in the sudden whiteness of the loins of the broad Dawn
> the longed-for caress of my savage fingers
> is the silent harmony of spears in the races on heat
> beautiful like proud phalluses of gold
> erect in the nervous womb of the African night.]

Reducing the feminized night to an open womb, Craveirinha here reinscribes the paradigm of sexual penetration employed in 'Xigubo' and intensifies its evocation of corporeality by introducing an implicit element of violence into the text's active male–passive female binary, thereby

reinforcing its gendered power matrix. At the same time, the pluralization of the explicitly phallicized 'spears' frames the sexual penetration of
Craveirinha's imagined 'Mãe África' [Mother Africa] as a collective event, a
means of consolidating male unity and solidarity by means of shared sexual
conquest. Intrinsic to the poet's offer of a path to anticolonial resistance
through reconnection with a mythopoetic African authenticity is the tacit
assumption of male dominance leading the way.

'Manifesto', the poem that most clearly illustrates Craveirinha's sub-
scription to the aesthetics of negritude, uses the black male body as a touchstone for this essentially masculine imagining of anticolonial resistance.
A celebratory reclamation of the narrator's black southern Mozambican
maternal heritage, characterized by its abundant use of Ronga, and by its
incantatory repetition of first-person pronouns and possessive adjectives,
the poem posits virility at the centre of black masculine physicality:

> Oh! Meus belos dentes brancos de marfim espoliado
> puros brilhando na minha negra reencarnada face altiva
> e no ventre maternal dos campos da nossa indisfrutada colheita
> de milho
> o cálido encantamento da minha pele tropical.
>
> Ah! E meu
> corpo flexível como o relâmpago fatal da flecha de caça
> e meus ombros lisos de negro da Guiné
> e meus músculos tensos e brunidos ao sol das colheitas e da carga
> e na capulana austral de um céu intangível
> os búzios de gente soprando os velhos sons cabalísticos de África. (2008: 39)

> [Oh! And my beautiful white teeth of polished ivory
> pure and shining in my face reborn majestic black
> and in the maternal womb of the fields of our uneaten crop
> of maize
> the burning wild enchantment of my tropical skin.
>
> Ah! And my
> body lithe as the lethal lightning strike of the hunting arrow
> my smooth black Guinean shoulders
> my muscles tense and bronzed from bearing burdens of harvests in the sun

and the southern *capulana*[7] of an untouchable sky
resounds with the mysterious ancient sounds of Africa.]

Defined by its subjective sexual agency and physical potency, the black male body as metonym of essential masculine selfhood is once again defined in opposition to the abstract, passive and maternal femininity symbolized by the 'capulana austral de um céu intangível' [southern *capulana* of an untouchable sky]. The image of the body as a 'flecha de caça' [hunting arrow], echoed later in the piece by the line 'eu azagaia banto' [I, Bantu spear], invokes the possibility of military struggle against the oppressor, but its juxtaposition with the 'ventre maternal dos campos' [maternal womb of the fields] recalls the violently phallic imagery of previous poems. In doing so, the image serves only to recentre the matrix of male dominance and female passivity in the anticolonial struggle, the latter rendered figuratively telluric through its transposition onto the Mozambican terrain.

The poem's sixth stanza reinforces this symbolic interchangeability of woman and land, this time through the use of a sexualized image of northern Mozambican Makonde women:

Ah, Mãe África no meu rosto escuro de diamante
de belas e largas narinas másculas
frementes haurindo o odor florestal
e as tatuadas bailarinas macondes
nuas
na bárbara maravilha eurítmica
das sensuais ancas puras
e no bater uníssono dos mil pés descalços. (2008: 39)

[Ah, Mother Africa in my brilliant dark face
with its beautiful wide masculine nostrils
twitching as they savour the forest's scent
and in the naked
tattooed Makonde dancers

7   The *capulana* is a staple item of Mozambican women's dress, consisting of a printed length of cloth commonly worn as an ankle-length wrap skirt but also used in various other ways (e.g. as a headscarf, shawl, swaddling cloth, etc.).

in the barbarous eurythmic wonder
of pure and sensual hips
and in the unified beating of one thousand bare feet.]

Having recalled the implicit filial relationship between land and narrator established in 'Xigubo' and 'África' with the invocation of the Mãe
África trope, these lines furthermore serve to condense Craveirinha's
drive toward a romanticized black solidarity into the bodies of 'tatu-
adas bailarinas macondes | nuas' [naked | tattooed Makonde dancers],
who are here cast in the role of embodied gatekeepers and guards of the
authentic Mozambicanness previously presented as the catalyst for black
male liberation. Restricted to the status of sexual or maternal object, the
abstract feminine becomes no more than a symbolic counterweight with
which the narrator can elevate his essentially masculinist understanding of
Mozambican subjectivity. The climactic achievement of pan-Mozambican
black male solidarity following this objectification of femininity, expressed
through the narrator's espousal of the diverse subject positions of 'chefe zulo'
[Zulu chief], 'negro suaíli' [black Swahili], 'caçador de leopardos traiçoei-
ros' [hunter of treacherous leopards] and 'xiguilo no batuque' [*xiguilo* in
the *batuque*][8] (2008: 40) further affirms that Craveirinha's understanding
of anticolonial subjectivity hinges on the perpetuation of women's object
status.

Consolidating Maleness: Revirilizing Blackness

The three poems discussed thus far, in addition to offering clear evidence
of Craveirinha's early engagement with a stylistics of negritude, present
an imagining of anticolonial masculinity that speaks to its inherent complexity, exemplified by the latent tension reflected in the poems between
Craveirinha's biraciality, his identification with a black pan-Mozambican

8   *Xiguilo* denotes a war dance; a *batuque* is a series of dances set to drum beat.

and pan-African masculine solidarity, and his reinforcement of a specifically southern Mozambican idealization of masculinity. A brief return to
Black Skin, White Masks is here useful as a means of situating the poetic
work studied so far in relation to the broader cultural intersection of anticoloniality and masculinity.

The interconnection between Craveirinha's poetic construction of
anticolonial masculinity and the psychoanalytical version expounded by
Fanon is perhaps best understood in terms of their shared position within
a collective narrative of crisis and resolution, identified by Yekani as an
intrinsic attribute of literary portrayals of masculinity (2011: 36). While
Yekani uses the concept of 'crisis narratives' primarily to describe the textual
representation of colonial men's self-perceived loss of sexual potency, in
gendered terms the works of both Fanon and Craveirinha can nonetheless
be located on a similar schema. We have seen how Fanon's imagining of
the racial objectification central to the colonizing regimes of Africa and
the black Caribbean is described in terms of emasculation and specifically
castration. For Fanon, this use of emasculation as a means of exerting power
over colonized peoples is particular to the oppression of black men; con-
trasting their situation with that of Jewish men, he notes that in 'the case
of the Jew, one thinks of money and its cognates. In that of the Negro,
one thinks of sex. [...] No anti-Semite, for example, would ever conceive
of the idea of castrating the Jew. He is killed or sterilized. But the Negro is
castrated. The penis, the symbol of manhood, is annihilated, which is to say
that it is denied' (1986: 160–2). The author's specific imbrication here of
colonization with the denial of sexual capacity and potency clearly speaks
to a sense of masculine crisis, an affective 'complex' to which he affirms
there is 'only one solution': to 'assert [him]self as a BLACK MAN' (115).
Yet Fanon's writing on women tacitly divulges an alternative or complemen-
tary strategy to this singular tactic, in the shape of affectively reclaiming
privileged sexual control over and access to the bodies of black women.

Craveirinha's early poetry implicitly casts the experience of colonization as one of emasculation, thereby drawing itself into line with the crisis
narrative reflected in *Black Skin, White Masks*. Both writers, moreover,
figure sexual control over women as the resolution to their masculine
crises. The nuances of these respective crisis narratives, however, and the

subtle distinctions in the ways in which women are situated within them, bring their differences into the foreground. While Fanon conceives of black masculine crisis as predicated on the colonized man's lack of sexual subjectivity, perceived in terms of his restricted sexual access to women both white and black, and thus imagines this privilege of access as the linchpin of racial autonomy, Craveirinha's crisis narrative is predicated primarily on a sense of affective alienation from an 'authentic' Africanness, which itself is figured as feminine. For Fanon, then, sexual access to women is a signifier of male power; for Craveirinha, women are the corporeal gateways to it. In Craveirinha's work, sexual penetration of the Mãe África figure as the embodiment of a nostalgic, imagined authentic past furthermore becomes a symbolically collective event: a means of consolidating male unity in the face of colonial oppression.

Craveirinha's engagement with this specific semiotics of emasculation and resolution provides a firm reminder of the legacy of Portuguese colonialism in Mozambican literary culture, specifically the sexual and gendered elements that made the latter years of New State imperialism unique. As Chapter 1 of this study illustrated, in the euphemistic rhetoric that defined the period, heavily indebted to Lusotropicalist pioneer Gilberto Freyre, the putatively innate virility of the Portuguese man made him the natural vector for a romanticized 'racial democracy' achieved through the 'whitening' effect of miscegenation imposed on local populations (Owen 2007a: 18–19). This framing of Portuguese masculinity relied upon the wholesale denial of native women's sexual agency and power to consent (Madureira 1994: 163), which, as Mark Sabine notes, in turn demanded 'the concomitant and brutal imposition on black men of the label of inadequate or aberrant masculinity' (2004: 25).

The deification of the black male subject in Craveirinha's work represents a clear attempt to shake off this imposed masculinity, challenging the myth of the white man's greater grasp on 'civilization' by providing a counternarrative centred on the black male hero. The antepenultimate stanza of 'África', preceding the heroic scenes cited above with a detailed list of white male atrocities, exemplifies this pattern:

E aprendo que os homens que inventaram
a confortável cadeira eléctrica
a técnica de Buchenwald e as bombas V2
acenderam fogos de artifício nas pupilas
de ex-meninos vivos de Varsóvia
criaram Al Capone, Hollywood, Harlem
a seita Ku-Klux-Klan, Cato Manor e Sharpeville
e emprenharam o pássaro que fez o choco
sobre os ninhos mornos de Hiroshima e Nagasaki [...] (2008: 21)

[And I learn that the men who invented
the comfortable electric chair
the machinery of Buchenwald and the V2 bomb
sparked fireworks in the eyes
of the once-living children of Warsaw
created Al Capone, Hollywood, Harlem
the Ku-Klux-Klan, Cato Manor and Sharpeville
and impregnated the bird that laid its eggs
into the warm nests of Hiroshima and Nagasaki [...]]

Black Mozambican men, meanwhile, are cast as the counterheroes to these
industrialized atrocities, the discoverers of a lost, authentically African mas-
culinity symbolized by their 'azagaias no cio das raças | belas como altivos
falos de ouro' [spears in the races on heat | beautiful like proud phalluses of
gold] (2008: 23). Yet while Craveirinha's words appear to push back against
Lusotropicalist mythologies of the superiority of white masculinity, the
means of his resistance are ultimately predicated on the equally pernicious
Portuguese colonial notion of black femininity. If Lusotropicalist ideology
held black women as merely the means by which the Portuguese mission
of miscegenation was enacted, giving them meaning, in Madureira's terms,
'only insofar as they [were] penetrated and inseminated' (1994: 163), in the
poems discussed here they are likewise divested of agency, reduced at best
to the status of obligatory reproductive bearers of a telluric and ahistorical
'subjectivity', and at worst to disembodied sexual or reproductive organs,
illustrated by the 'ventre nervoso' [nervous womb] (Craveirinha 2008: 23)
of 'África', the 'ventre maternal' [maternal womb] (38) of 'Manifesto', and
the open 'sexo' [sex] (18) of 'Xigubo'.

Cracks and Fissures

Craveirinha's perpetuation of colonial ideology in his early attempts to revindicate black Mozambican subjectivity can be fruitfully analysed by engaging his work with the broad theoretical framework of compulsory heterosexuality, in this case understood as the basis on which racially delineated imperialist gender and sexual dynamics are constituted and upheld. While the critical concept of compulsory heterosexuality, originally popularized within radical feminist discourse in Adrienne Rich's 1980 essay 'Compulsory Heterosexuality and Lesbian Existence' (1993: 203–24) and later extensively developed by poststructuralist queer theorists Eve Kosofsky Sedgwick (1985) and Judith Butler (2007, 2011), has long been rightly perceived as resoundingly Western-centric, its adaptation to certain specificities of Portuguese imperialism can shed potential new light on the resilience of colonial gender ideology within anticolonial sentiment. As explained in the Introduction to this study, for Butler the maintenance of 'a stable and oppositional heterosexuality' (2007: 31) symbiotically requires and produces a rigid gender binary, which becomes a disciplining mechanism for circumscribing gendered and sexual conduct in order to 'consolidate and naturalize the convergent power regimes of masculine and heterosexist oppression' (2007: 46). The achievement of discursive intelligibility, understood as the societal recognition and validation of one's identity and autonomous selfhood, within this system of compulsory heterosexuality depends upon the subject's ability to 'institute and maintain relations of coherence and continuity among sex, gender, sexual practice, and desire' (2007: 23). To fail to maintain this cohesion is to be relegated to the peripheral zone of the abject, against which the discursively intelligible shape their identities (Butler 2011: xiii).

Viewed through this conceptual lens, the racially motivated emasculation imposed by the Portuguese colonial regime on African societies can be interpreted as a means of perpetually destabilizing the cohesion of the black male subject's body, desire and sexual practice, rendering him abject and subhuman and divesting him of agency and subjectivity, as a way of bolstering white male dominance. In this way, black masculinity is pushed

out of the realm of the colonial self in order to assuage the profound gendered anxieties identified in Chapter 1 as intrinsic to Portuguese imperial
thought. Within this dynamic, the reconsolidation of masculine identity
becomes axiomatic to the reclamation of anticolonial male subjectivity
– and if masculinity as a naturalized discursive construct represents the
apex of a hierarchical gender binary enforced through compulsory heterosexual practice, then its consolidation is necessarily contingent upon the
performative enactment of male sexual control over women. To borrow
Andrea Dworkin's terse phrasing on the matter, 'the legitimacy of a man's
civil dominance depends on the authenticity of his masculinity, which is
articulated when he fucks' (2007: 188).

In Craveirinha's case, the reclamation of black masculinity from the
abject realm of the colonial regime is enacted by means of an excessive
reinscription of compulsory heterosexuality that requires black women
to be sexually available and, significantly, maternal. Maternity, within this
framework, represents the crystallization of compulsory heterosexuality, the embodied proof of continuity between anatomical sex, gender
identity and heterosexual practice. Craveirinha's repeated invocation of
the metonymical African or Mozambican 'womb' thus becomes a reiterative act of consolidation of black masculine identity, which is nonetheless
dependent on an imperial imagining of authentic African-ness as passive,
telluric and female, and on the framing of reconnection with that authenticity as an exclusively male prerogative. Meanwhile, his casting of female
objectification and penetration as a group act, aside from confirming black
masculinity as a collective identification in the face of political and ethnic
heterogeneity, serves to reinforce male hegemony by allowing individual
men to symbolically share in sexual dominance. Sedgwick, writing on literary representations of male homosocial relations, proposes that 'sharing
sexual territory with other men' offers a way for men to strengthen their
collective and individual identities by 'participating in a supraindividual
power over women' (1985: 36–7). In the context of Craveirinha's early work,
the collective penetration of a feminized 'Africa', expressed through the
recurrent image of a singular female figure or body part set against a male
group, thus confirms both shared African origin and shared domination
of women, consolidating individual and collective black masculinities.

It is the reiterative nature of this oppressive gendered paradigm, however, that makes its subversion possible. For Butler, gender is fundamentally fragile, consisting of nothing more than the 'sedimented effect of a reiterative or ritual practice' (2011: xix) that is 'never fully what it is at any given juncture in time' (2007: 22). The performance of a gender that appears substantial thus requires the subject to repeatedly disavow that which is 'masculine' or 'feminine' in a 'tacit collective agreement to perform, produce and sustain polar genders' (2007: 190). It is in the spaces between these repeated acts – the fissures left behind by a performance of gender that can never be fully materialized – that potentialities for destabilizing the hierarchical gender binary manifest (2011: xix). Working from this basis, if Craveirinha's work demonstrates the necessity for a confirmation of masculine identity through a ritual reinscription of the gender hierarchy that tacitly perpetuates colonial gender ideology, then it must also hold within it multiple concealed possibilities for deconstructing that exclusionary identity. In Chiziane's *O Sétimo Juramento*, through the strategic interarticulation of hyperbolic excess, parody, and realism, these fissures, spaces and possibilities in Craveirinha's poetry are thrown wide open.

Sexualizing Satire: Paulina Chiziane's *O Sétimo Juramento* (2000)

O Sétimo Juramento, Chiziane's third novel, was received upon publication in 2000 (3rd edn 2008) as something of a departure from her previous work. While her previous two novels, 1990's *Balada de Amor ao Vento* and 1993's *Ventos do Apocalipse*, had foregrounded women protagonists, *O Sétimo Juramento* narrates the story of a man, with less of the intense lyricism that had come to be associated with her storytelling (Mata 2001: 188). The novel tells the story of David, an ethnically Tsonga Maputo factory owner and former Frelimo independence fighter. On hearing of the probability of strike action by workers at his factory in response to failed wage payments, the result of gross incompetence, embezzlement and corruption on his part, David chooses to pin his misconduct on his wife Vera, and beats her (Chiziane 2000: 38–40). Fleeing the house, he finds sanctuary in a bar, and encounters his old friend Lourenço, who encourages David to turn to the supernatural order of precolonial southern Mozambique to resolve his difficulties (45). David dismisses his advice as nonsense and heads instead for his favourite brothel, wherein he purchases the services of Mimi, a young girl orphaned during the post-independence conflict, and rapes her (52).

Days later, David's factory workers revolt, and he learns that his fellow company board members have betrayed him by giving the workers access to evidence proving his criminal activities (Chiziane 2000: 66–71). In furious desperation, he allows Lourenço to guide him through a series of increasingly fantastical and exaggerated supernatural encounters and rituals that culminate in a journey to Lourenço's parents' mansion, located near the isolated southern town of Massinga. David learns that Lourenço's father is the legendary *feiticeiro* Makhulu Mamba, 'um personagem das lendas de terror do universo mítico dos tsongas' [a character from the horror stories of the Tsongas' mythological universe] (139). It is here that David makes the Faustian 'seventh oath' of the novel's title, swearing absolute loyalty to Makhulu Mamba in exchange for supernatural abilities (168). He arrives home to find that his factory, including the paperwork incriminating him, has been destroyed in a fire, and that the company's commercial director has suffered severe burns and is in a coma – just in time to prevent him from making David's fraud public (175).

Emboldened by this stroke of fortune, David realizes that in order to maintain his power, he must make a sacrifice to Makhulu Mamba: a virgin 'escolhida entre as mais queridas' [chosen from among your most beloved] (176). David sends Vera and their son Clemente to Swaziland, and, in their absence, drugs and rapes his young daughter Suzy (181–2). Thereafter, his luck seems boundless: the commercial director, who had been steadily recovering, dies suddenly (209); his secretary and lover Cláudia, and young sex worker Mimi, both pregnant by him, are killed in a freak car crash (241–2). However, unbeknownst to David, Vera and Clemente have also sought supernatural help, and have become aware of the danger David poses. Clemente receives training as a *curandeiro*, a traditional healer, and returns to confront David. Face to face with his son's superior powers, David ultimately dies, deranged by terror (265).

The initial chapters of the novel display various characteristics of the standard contemporary narrative of an inner 'crisis of masculinity', identified by Yekani as so common among male narratives that 'it is in question whether there has ever been a "stable" male identity which was not constructed as being in crisis' (2011: 18). David feels emasculated by Vera, perceiving her as financially exploiting him, and extrapolates his feelings to the behaviour of all women:

> As mulheres delicadas, bonitas, sensíveis, são aranhas. Oferecem-te o sorriso de gata e prendem-te na sua teia. Escravizam-te. Como bruxas da meia-noite, sugam-te o sangue, o suor e obrigam-te a cometer loucuras por amor a elas. (Chiziane 2000: 39)

> [These delicate, pretty, sensitive women are spiders. [...] They flash you their cat-like smile and ensnare you in their web. They enslave you. Like witches at midnight, they drink your blood, your sweat, and drive you to madness with your love for them.]

His persecution complex extends even to the factory workers he has failed to pay, whose revolt provokes a deep sense of anguish in him and causes him to weep uncontrollably (40). In one particular comment, so typical of mainstream discourses on male 'crises' as to render it wryly comical, he blames Vera's supposed exploitation of him on feminists, who are 'por todo o lado, reclamando direitos sobre coisas que nunca construíram' [all over the place, demanding rights over things they had no part in creating] (38).

Excessive(ly) Sex(ed)

With the actions David takes to resolve this perceived crisis, however, Chiziane's tale takes a darkly satirical turn away from the relative ordinariness of its premise, to a point where the text can be read as a somewhat irreverent echo of the eroticized fantasies reflected in Craveirinha's poetic rendering of anticolonial ideology. Evidence of this turn to the parodical can be found in Chiziane's use of lurid sexual images, which increase in both frequency and obscenity as David becomes more and more entangled in the world of sorcery. David's participation in the macabre ceremony that cements his initiation into the supernatural world provides an especially compelling example of this use of sexuality. Arriving at the event, David is presented with '[s]eis raparigas vestidas de igual, seis pessoas verdadeiras, de carne e osso, todas sorrindo para ele' [six girls, all dressed identically, six real-life people, flesh and blood, all smiling at him] (Chiziane 2000: 92). Gazing on this vision of '[v]irginidade pura. Beleza. Sensualidade' [pure virginity. Beauty. Sensuality], his mind fills with memories of 'as orgias antigas: amor a quatro, troca de casais, bebedeira, soruma e tabaco, aventuras perigosas' [the orgies of days gone by: group sex, wife-swapping, drinking, marijuana and tobacco, dangerous adventures] (92–3). Imagining himself as the proprietor of a vast harem, he feels elevated, liberated, 'como se uma vassoura mágica tivesse varrido todos os seus problemas' [as if a magic broom had swept away all of his problems] (95). As the ceremony progresses, he watches one of these women collapse in visible pain while dancing, as if stabbed with an invisible dagger, but minutes later she appears to have recovered, and approaches David, beckoning to him in seductive tones (100–1). David is perturbed, recalling myths in which 'um só corpo pode ser possuído por [...] uma virgem e uma prostituta' [a single body can be possessed by both virgin and prostitute] (102), and in which possessed women rape, strangle and drink the blood of their male victims (103).

Coupled with David's affective responses and viewed within the context of his ongoing quest for lost power, the resonance of these images with the sexual symbology discussed in Craveirinha's work is clear. The six subservient virgins, whose presence evokes a feeling of calm and confidence in David, recall Craveirinha's 'tatuadas bailarinas macondes | nuas' [naked | tattooed Makonde dancers] with the 'sensuais ancas puras' [pure and sensual hips] (2008: 39) that soothe and empower the narrator of 'Manifesto', consolidating his masculinity through an exoticized performance of femininity. Likewise, the scene in which one of the six appears to be stabbed with an invisible dagger reflects Craveirinha's figurative descriptions of weaponized sexual penetration. Chiziane's specific framings of these tropes, however, demonstrate a careful use of abjection and excess, consistent with Butler's proposed tactics for the subversion of hierarchical gender constructs, which allows her to satirically deconstruct the racialized masculinism underlying anticolonial aesthetics like that of Craveirinha. The strategies Butler identifies, namely 'hyperbole, dissonance, internal confusion, and proliferation' (2007: 43), allow the subject that espouses them to destabilize gender categories by rendering their place within the gender binary uncertain or unintelligible, thereby foregrounding the abject realm. Given that the repudiation of the abject is the means by which subjects are originally constituted, in a disavowal that must be repeatedly enacted, the deliberate exhibition of abject elements threatens to destabilize or disrupt the subject's base assumptions (Butler 2011: xiii). While Butler sees her proposed tactics most clearly embodied by drag performance, in which subjects enact an excessive version of a gender discontinuous with their bodily makers and thus through 'hyperbolic conformity to the command [...] reveal the hyperbolic status of the norm itself' (2007: 181), the ambiguous and diffuse potentialities suggested by her strategies can be identified in a hypothetical multitude of gender identities and expressions, including the hyperbolic performance of one's assigned gender.

A closer reading of Chiziane's afflicted dancing woman uncovers the subversive effect of this excessive conformity to the gender suggested by one's anatomical markers. The dancer's initial demeanour is virginal and submissive, and she serves David as if she were part of his fantasized harem, but following her violent 'penetration' she transforms into an excessively sexual 'sedutora' [seductress] (Chiziane 2000: 101). With this rapid about-face, she comes to embody both the passive femininity and compulsory heterosexuality underpinning Craveirinha's work, but in a performance so hyperbolic and mercurial that it ultimately exceeds itself. Her performance of a constructed femininity is so outlandish, so grotesque, that it threatens to expose the artifice of femininity itself, troubling the naturalized understanding of femininity on which male hegemony relies. The anxiety that David experiences as he watches the woman, channelled into the profound fear that she might sexually violate him, makes clear the disturbing impact of her performance; he feels that she could literally transgress his physical boundary between 'inner' and 'outer', 'self' and 'not-self', destroying the illusions of corporeal impermeability and safety from the abject sphere implied by his maleness. Later in the ceremony, in a visceral display of sexual excess and violence, he has sex with the dancing woman in a ritual bath of blood, taken from a black female goat that has been stabbed in the neck with a spear (108). As the blood washes over the pair, the woman is returned to a submissive state, while visions of penetrative weapons – 'balas, punhais, baionetas' [bullets, daggers, bayonets] – race through David's mind (108). He feels his masculine power has been restored, that he will after all achieve '[o] poder, a riqueza e a longa vida' [power, wealth and longevity] (109). The sequence, with its obscenely graphic images of violent sexuality and penetration, thus comes to offer a hyperbolic rewriting of the drive toward male sexual domination latent in anticolonial narratives like those employed by Craveirinha, satirizing the reinscriptions of compulsory het-erosexuality central to the negritude aesthetic while exposing the anxiety underpinning them.

This hyperbolic overstatement of negritude's masculinist underpin-nings, centred on the excessively sexed body, is furthered by a subsequent scenario in which David engages in a series of tests to prove his loyalty to Makhulu Mamba. Prior to beginning his quest, David, along with other men seeking alliance with the sorcerer, is ordered to remove his clothes and replace them with a loincloth (Chiziane 2000: 161). David feels 'um guer-reiro antigo' [an ancient warrior] being reborn within him (162). As the hunt progresses, David passes through an increasingly primordial landscape, filled with '[a]nimais extintos [...]. Dinossáurios. Insectos do tamanhos de pássaros. Sáurios voadores. Plantas carnívoras' [extinct animals [...]. Dinosaurs. Insects the size of birds. Flying reptiles. Carnivorous plants] (163). Finally, he is required to hunt and kill a lion; he succeeds, stabbing it in the mouth (164). He is pronounced a hero, and is carried 'para a palhota pelas mãos dos fiéis, tal como acontece aos heróis' [back to the hut by the hands of the faithful, as is befitting of a hero] (165), envisioning himself as a Bantu king (167).

As Hilary Owen affirms, here David 'anxiously reinforces his new sense of ancestral masculinity by performing an exaggerated version of Bantu male identity' (2007a: 197). His sudden bloodlust and adoption of the stereotypical loincloth and phallic spear, alongside the delusions of grandeur that accompany his hero's return, act as performative elements of this hyperbolic masculinity. In an oppositional reiteration of the virgin-seductress's dance, David's self-consciously gendered performance embodies a romanticized idealization of Bantu – specifically Tsonga – masculinity so obsessively that it becomes cartoonish, absurd. Taking the mythopoetic role of masculine hero that dominates anticolonial literature such as that of Craveirinha, and having an otherwise seemingly three-dimensional character perform it to caricatured excess, Chiziane here reveals the absolute fictitiousness of the role itself, exposing the hero, the pinnacle of idealized masculinity, as nothing more than a mirage. In so doing, she troubles the notion of idealized masculinity in its entirety, shifting and rocking its place at the apex of the gender hierarchy. The latent misogyny of the masculinist hero motif of anticolonial artistic expression is thereby brought to the fore, while more local discourses of southern Mozambican manhood are revealed as absurd fantasies.

Chiziane's casting of David, a former Frelimo fighter, in this role of cartoonishly overstated precolonial warrior serves a further key purpose: to draw out the hypocrisy of Frelimo's simultaneous repudiation of precolonial practices, and deification of specific precolonial southern male 'heroes' such as Gazan chief Ngungunhane, itself indicative of the ongoing latent presence of a nostalgic masculinism reminiscent of Craveirinha's negritude aesthetic in the ostensibly forward-looking and sexually egalitarian Frelimo imaginary. As Arnfred makes clear, Frelimo's abolitionist stance toward traditional practices often divested women of certain positions of power and prestige granted to them by precolonial belief systems (2011: 102–3); the party's ethnocentric heroization of precolonial southern figureheads, meanwhile, served as tacit endorsement of some of the most aggressively patriarchal facets of those same systems. A clear example is Samora Machel's elliptical support for Ngungunhane's anti-prostitution measures, detailed in Chapter 1 of this study. David's rapid abandonment of any remaining pretence to the progressivist 'New Man' role implied by his past, in order to embrace the trappings of an absurdly exaggerated, sexually promiscuous pseudo-nativism, encapsulates this hypocritical and patriarchally driven ideological cherrypicking on the part of Frelimo in comically satirical fashion, calling into question whether the 'New Man' was ever anything more than a rhetorical device.

Daughters of the Revolution

While the initiation ceremony and hunt sequence emphasize the vital role of hyperbole and excess in Chiziane's scathing critique of the Tsonga masculine ideals embedded in Mozambican anticolonial rhetoric, realism also has a firm place in her arsenal, acting as a means of shedding light on the material lives and bodies in which that rhetoric is 'staked' (Owen 2007a: 171). Her unflinching portrayal of the rape of child prostitute Mimi, who is repeatedly described in terms of her childlike appearance and first encountered as David attempts to resolve his affective emasculation, is a clear case in point. As David waits in the brothel, we see 'behind the scenes' as brothel madam Lúcia attempts to soothe the sobbing young girl with promises of bread, a bed and pretty clothes (Chiziane 2000: 51). In a moment of dark irony, she turns on the radio and is reminded that '[n]o campo, as mulheres tocam tambores e simulam uma festa para abafar os gritos dos parturientes, para que as crianças não percebam o sofrimento da mulher na hora de parto' [in the countryside, women play drums and act out a party to drown out the sounds of labouring women, to keep children ignorant of how women suffer during childbirth] (51); then, presenting the pacified girl to David, she wishes him '[b]om apetite' [*bon appetite*] (51).

After a fleeting moment of deliberation over whether or not he should have sex with Mimi, whom he places at an age similar to that of his young daughter, David concludes that even if he desists she will be raped by someone else that day all the same. Having given her whiskey 'tal como o bom médico anestesia o seu doente preparando-o para uma operação dolorosa' [just like any good doctor anaesthetizes his patient before a painful operation] (Chiziane 2000: 52), he aggressively strips and rapes her. Upon waking beside Mimi following the attack, David experiences a wave of rejuvenation, feeling that he has awoken within himself 'o gigante adormecido e está pronto para conquistar o mundo' [a sleeping giant, and is ready to conquer the world], and muses on the refreshing properties of the child prostitute's body, deciding to 'fazer dela uma dama' [make a lady of her] by negotiating her purchase from Lúcia (63). During his next visit to Mimi, he feels 'uma vontade louca de despedaça-la' [a wild urge to tear her apart], and attacks her; she is, after all, 'simples puta' [just a whore] (120). Immediately after this incident, David learns that Mimi is pregnant (120–1).

Chiziane's message here seems resoundingly clear: that the gender binary upon which the rhetoric of post-independence Mozambican nationhood is implicitly predicated is enforced in and through the bodies of women, and that the romanticized imagining of Mozambican women as the vessels for the genesis of the independent nation often conceals a quotidian reality of exploitation and violence. The author's figuring of David, a Mozambican 'hero', as resolving his crisis of masculinity through the rape of war orphan Mimi acts as an extreme reflection of paradigmatic sexual politics in a society that is ostensibly postcolonial but in which women remain, for Chiziane, manifestly colonized. If, as Isabel Fêo Rodrigues and Kathleen Sheldon propose, the maintenance of masculine power in post-independence Lusophone Africa 'rests on specific forms of silence aimed at maintaining social control' (2010: 79), Chiziane's representation of the relationship between David and Mimi shatters that silence, bringing the reality of the Mozambican nationalist 'hero' narrative into sharp focus.

Chiziane reiterates this desire to reveal the violent truth behind anti-colonial hero narratives with David's incestuous rape of his daughter Suzy as a 'sacrifice' in exchange for further powers from Makhulu Mamba. When viewed as a successive event to the rape of Mimi, this scene charts the logical progression of a masculine hegemony predicated on female passivity; while David relied on Mimi's desperation for her compliance, he renders Suzy's body literally passive by drugging her (Chiziane 2000: 181–2). His literal violation of Suzy's physical boundaries through rape denies her coherent selfhood and autonomy, confirming in Dworkin's terms that as a girl she is 'intended to have a lesser privacy, a lesser integrity of the body, a lesser sense of self, since her body can be physically occupied and in the occupation taken over' (2007: 155). In the specific context of early southern Mozambican cultural nationalism, the rape furthermore acts as a grotesque inversion of the Mãe África trope frequently employed by Craveirinha. While Craveirinha's male heroes successfully pursue power and fortitude through a fetishized and sexualized mother-son relationship, poetically figured as the romanticized penetration of a passive and telluric Mãe África, David's quest reaches its climax with the forceable penetration of his young daughter's inert body, romanticized for him as 'voa[ndo] com ela por paraísos sem fim' [soaring with her through an infinite paradise] (182). This disturbing image of father-daughter rape, a literal inversion of the protected mother-son adoration of Craveirinha's poetry, takes the sexual subjugation of women implicit in the eroticized nationalist Mãe África motif to its excessive extreme.

Chiziane's invocation of incest renders the attack all the more grotesque when we consider Butler's theory of the internalization of the incest taboo as the primary moment that constitutes gender identity (2007: 184). By breaking the incest taboo, David asserts the regulatory power that he considers part of his hegemonic position, but in doing so he threatens that very position by failing to disavow the abject realm. The author's violent use of this taboo thus serves to turn the poetic trope of Mãe África inside out, rendering it abject and unthinkable, while David's role in the process of abjection troubles the seemingly hermetic contours of his masculinity, destabilizing gendered boundaries in a way that sets the scene for the novel's subversive denouement.

Uprooting Mythology

The climactic ending of *O Sétimo Juramento* serves to consolidate the troubling of masculine hegemony that Chiziane lays out throughout the novel, exemplified most significantly by David's death, the physical manifestation of his terminal loss of internal coherence and selfhood. Her presentation of the protagonist's demise, 'de medo, num estado de absoluta loucura' [from fear, in a state of absolute madness] (2000: 265), underlines the ultimate fragility of the masculinity he has constructed for himself; his

repeated repudiation of femininity, enacted through the degradation of
women and girls including his own daughter, in pursuit of a masculinity
untouched by any element of the feminine, has ultimately destroyed him.
Chiziane thus reveals this notion of absolute or 'pure' masculinity to be a
mere fantasy, demonstrating in line with Lynne Segal that such masculinity 'depends upon the perpetual renunciation of "femininity"', and that
'while the "feminine" may be dispatched in the insouciant bravado of
masculine endeavour, it will always return to haunt the conquering hero'
(1990: 114). David's dissolution into terror confirms that his attempts to
consolidate his masculinity by repeatedly inscribing male domination on
the bodies of the women around him have served only to underscore his
subconscious fear of femininity's encroachment. And, in the end, it is the
feminine – embodied by Vera and by Clemente, who consistently fails to
disavow femininity sufficiently to 'correctly' perform masculinity – that
obliterates him entirely.

Emerging here too, meanwhile, is Clemente's 'deficient' performance
of masculinity as an alternative gendered potentiality: a possible blueprint
for future generations of young men that diverges from the hypermas-
culinity David aspires to embody. Latent doubts are cast on Clemente's
masculinity from the early chapters of the novel, as Vera recalls that during
his baptism the candle went out not once – a bad omen – but three times,
foreshadowing an inundation of tragedy at the point of puberty (60). Even
his name – an attribute given great importance in the novel via the author's
repetition of the Ronga aphorism 'a vito i mpondo' [a name is worth a
pound] (59) – comes from the name of a goddess, Clementia. His persistent nightmares and histrionic outbursts, which often feature his father in
the role of antagonist and are dismissed by a frustrated Vera as 'medo de
crescer, medo de ser homem' [fear of growing up, fear of becoming a man]
(56) and by David as neurotic (177), further stress the character's perceived
lack of masculine stoicity. Yet as the novel progresses, these fits of emotion
and fear are revealed to be the premonitions of a Cassandra-esque prophet.
It is, then, in Clemente's very failure to adequately perform masculinity
that his power manifests, allowing him to physically overcome his father's
oppressive exercise of maleness while symbolically undermining the hierarchical significance of maleness itself.

By framing David's death as the ultimate consequence of his attempt to achieve an unshakeable hegemonic masculinity, Chiziane thus exposes the fragility of both southern Mozambican masculine ideals and masculine hegemony as a whole. Her parodic portrayal of David's transition from former Frelimo fighter to a cartoonish incarnation of the negritude 'hero' works to reappropriate the 'return to origins' narrative underpinning poetic imaginaries such as that of Craveirinha, removing it from its masculinist foundations and recasting it as a means of threatening male dominance in the putatively egalitarian society of post-independence Mozambique. It furthermore serves to reveal the misplaced nostalgia toward a romanticized 'authentic' masculinity lying just beneath the progressivist veneer of Frelimo's imagined 'New Man'. While the character of David, as Owen demonstrates, does indeed chart 'the continuity of patriarchal and patrilinear structures through Christian colonialism, [anticolonial] Marxist-Leninism, resurrected Bantu tradition, and neoliberal capitalism' (2007a: 195), then, his ironic demise disrupts that continuity by displacing the naturalized fundamentality of masculine domination. If Craveirinha's engagement with the negritude style represents the assertion of a counternarrative to the oppressive Lusotropicalist mythology of white male heroism that nonetheless perpetuates colonial narratives of black femininity, then Chiziane's novel acts as a wholesale rejection of the shared foundation of each: a means of returning to mythic origins, only to uproot them.

Conclusion: No More Heroes

This comparative analysis of constructs of black Mozambican masculinity in Craveirinha's 1964 collection *Xigubo* and Chiziane's 2000 novel *O Sétimo Juramento* has demonstrated that while Craveirinha's engagement with the aesthetics of negritude might seek to resolve the disempowerment and objectification of colonized subjects, the imagined subjectivity that he creates is ultimately an exclusively male prerogative, contingent on the reinscription of a rigid gender binary that serves only to reinforce the object status of black women repeatedly reiterated during the colonial era. The mythopoetic black male 'hero' of his work therefore becomes the subject of a counternarrative to colonial emasculation that ironically relies upon the perpetuation of colonial gender ideology, centred around a strictly enforced compulsory heterosexuality, for its realization. His recurrent use of the sexual penetration of a passive female body with a symbolic phallus or weapon as a climactic motif exposes this foregrounding of male sexual dominance over women as central to his imagined reclamation of black Mozambican subjectivity.

Chiziane's novel, by contrast, protests this ostensibly resistant early anticolonial counternarrative through a strategic deployment of outlandish excess and unsettling realism, constructing a satirical alternative narrative that foregrounds the female subjugation underpinning both colonial and anticolonial endeavour. Her uncompromising depictions of sexual exploitation and violence uncover the grim reality behind the Mozambican cultural nationalist use of romanticized gendered tropes and Frelimo's hypocritical tacit perpetuation of the same, while her parallel use of cartoonish hyperbole underscores their ultimate falsity. The bodies of both the black male 'hero' and the violated black woman are thus reappropriated, becoming the contested sites of this literary protest.

While this chapter has illustrated the means by which counter- and alternative narratives of masculinity might be constructed for subversive intent, Chapter 3 will explore the notion of identification with narratives of femininity. The works of Noémia de Sousa and Ungulani Ba Ka Khosa, roughly contemporaneous with those of Craveirinha and Chiziane respectively, also foreground the gendered and sexed body as literary devices. For de Sousa and Khosa, however, the displaced or damaged body itself becomes the means of rejecting gendered impositions, and indeed utopian political narratives more broadly, in a process of 'disidentification'. Gendered subversion thus becomes not only an end in itself, but also a strategy for resistance of wider disciplinary mechanisms, as Chapter 3 will make clear.

Strategies of Disidentification: Rewriting Femininity in Noémia de Sousa and Ungulani Ba Ka Khosa

With each new manifestation of imperial venture that constituted the half-millennia of Portuguese presence in sub-Saharan Africa, one construct saw itself consistently reiterated at the levels of both discourse and practice: that of the black body as at once repellant and beguiling, inferior and threatening. From the early narratives of expansionism that transformed the profound fear of the unknown into the ideological framework of imperialism, thereby framing the black body as both *tabula rasa* for Western cultural and spiritual inscription and as a savage menace to the social order, to the justifications of slavery that emerged in the seventeenth and eighteenth centuries to rationalize the brutal instrumentalization of Africans in service of European desires;[1] and from the anxious conceptions of racial hygiene that became officially intertwined with colonial border uncertainties in the late nineteenth century, typified by António Ennes's 1893 treatise, to the romanticized Lusotropicalist doublethink of 'racial democracy' at the heart of Salazar's racist dictatorship, fear and loathing of black corporeality provided the consistent axis on which Portuguese imperial thought and action turned. Within this ambivalent and prohibitive framework, black Mozambican women were discursively cast as both racially despised and sexually fetishized. At the level of policy, meanwhile, living under a regime that precluded both women and the vast majority of black men from citizenship, black women were doubly excluded from participation in public life.

As the first two chapters of this study sought to demonstrate, anticolonial movements both in and outside Mozambique brought with them a

---

1   These manifestations of imperialism are examined in greater detail in Chapter 4, 'States of Exception'.

strong reclamation of black somatic autonomy, expressed in part through the literary revalorization of the black body. This move toward literary revindication played a key role in shaping Mozambique's anticolonial cultural output, with Craveirinha's work the most often-cited example. The official rhetoric of the revolutionary independence movement echoed this literary trend in political terms, and the words of Samora Machel in particular appeared to carve out a space for gendered as well as racial emancipation for the exploited black Mozambican body, promising a leading role in the new nation for women as the 'autênticas mães da revolução' [authentic mothers of the revolution] (1974: 9). These putatively liberating 'new' blueprints for gender relations, however, turned out all too often to echo colonial paradigms, and while women gained the on-paper equality denied to them by the colonial regime, their specific emancipatory needs went unacknowledged, decried as a bourgeois distraction from Frelimo's Marxist-Leninist socioeconomic goals. Meanwhile, the colonial imagining of the black female body as the fundamentally sexually available catalyst for the spreading of whiteness via miscegenation was altered only along racial lines; the apex of women's usefulness now lay in the expansion of the Mozambican nation-state, reflected, of course, by Machel's words, above. Black women remained deprived of agency in all but the most abstract sense, with black femininity still devalued, fetishized or erased altogether.

This chapter aims to deconstruct the ways in which works by Noémia de Sousa and Ungulani Ba Ka Khosa – two very different writers, a generation apart – can be read as dismantling the constructs of femininity upheld by each iteration of Mozambican state authority. While Chapter 2 sought to analyse Craveirinha's poetic identification with a specific trope of masculinity and Chiziane's subversion of that trope, this chapter will examine de Sousa's and Khosa's shared *dis*identification with imposed femininities, both as an aim unto itself and as a strategy for calling into question the validity of imperial Portuguese and post-independence Mozambican political narratives more broadly. Their works will be compared in terms of the distinct ways in which they reject colonial, anticolonial and post-independence gender ideologies, effectively deferring gendered identities in their work. The chapter will show how, through this disavowal of gendered identities, de Sousa's work can be read as both using and displacing the sexed female body as the means to enact a subtle yet steadfast rejection of the boundless and contradictory imperatives inscribed on black Mozambican women. Khosa's work, often read as utterly distinct from that of de Sousa in terms of both aesthetics and objective, will meanwhile be recast as thematically indebted to it despite their stylistic dissimilarity. Through the strategic use of motifs of embodied grotesquery and abjection, Khosa will be shown to radically refuse post-independence circumscriptions of the black female body, while furthermore making use of the body as an instrument of resistance to post-independence narratives of national unity as a whole.

Weaving Between and Among

Queer theorist José Esteban Muñoz's concept of 'disidentification' represents a synthesis of ideas that emerged primarily from the writings of women and queer people of colour in the United States during the latter decades of the twentieth century. 'Third World' feminist theory is cited as a specific influence on his attempt 'to chart the ways in which identity is enacted by minority subjects who must work with/resist the conditions of (im)possibility that dominant culture generates' (Muñoz 1999: 6), making a particular contribution to the concept of 'identity-in-difference' (6), an umbrella term denoting forms of subaltern identity based on the rejection of dominant modes of identification. Referred to as 'differential consciousness' by Chela Sandoval in her influential 1991 paper 'U.S. Third World Feminism' (2–3), this mode of, effectively, identifying in opposition to identity is proposed as the primary means by which oppressed subjects might empower themselves. For Sandoval, the differential mode of consciousness allows the oppressed subject to 'learn to identify, develop, and control the means of ideology, that is, marshal the knowledge necessary to "break with ideology" while also speaking in and from within ideology' (1991: 2). This act of 'weaving "between and among" oppositional ideologies' (Sandoval 1991: 14), utilizing dominant modes of expression while enacting gestures of resistance to that very domination, creates a space 'within which subjugated citizens can either occupy or throw off subjectivities in a process that at once both enacts and yet decolonizes their various relations to their real conditions of existence' (11).

Reconciling Sandoval's theory with the work of Chicana feminists Gloria Anzaldúa and Cherríe Moraga and that of black feminists Audre Lorde and bell hooks, Norma Alarcón identifies this kinetic mode of consciousness as representing 'a process of "determinate negation", a nay-saying of the variety of the "not yet", that's not it' (1996: 129). This repeated process of rejection of identity, the position of 'not yet/that's not it', can be seen as the foundation of both Anzaldúa's and Lorde's work, as well as that of other prominent feminists of colour. In her groundbreaking text *Borderlands/La Frontera* (1987; 4th edn 2012), Anzaldúa terms this position the 'conciencia de la mestiza': a hybrid consciousness that demands 'divergent thinking, [...] a tolerance for contradictions, a tolerance for ambiguity' (101) and that allows the mestiza subject to '[reinterpret] history and, using new symbols, [to shape] new myths' (104). Lorde writes of the necessity for North American women of colour to channel the anger turned against them, 'to learn to orchestrate those furies so that they do not tear us apart[;] to move through them and use them for strength and force and insight within our daily lives' (1984: 129). bell hooks, meanwhile, affirms that women of colour 'need to know that they can reject the powerful's definition of their reality – that they can do so even if they are poor, exploited, or trapped in oppressive circumstances' (1984: 90).

This complex process of rejecting dominant modes of identification while utilizing dominant modes of expression to enact resistance is the cornerstone of what Muñoz terms 'disidentification'. While the above-named writers describe this process of disidentification along the broad lines of gender, race and sexual orientation, Jack Halberstam's groundbreaking work on female masculinity uses the term to explore the specific disconnect between gender identity and performed gender negotiated by female drag kings (1998: 248).[2] Referring to a particular category of female

2   While Halberstam published this volume under his previous, female-identified name Judith Halberstam, he has stated in more recent interviews and blog posts that he

drag performance characterized by the performer's ability to 'pass' as male, Halberstam emphasizes that these performers do not seek assimilation with maleness; rather, they enact 'an active disidentification with dominant forms of masculinity, which are subsequently recycled into alternative masculinities' (1998: 248). Though the performer is utilizing the modes of expression and aesthetics associated with dominant maleness, and, indeed, may 'pass' as male, the very act of stage-performing a gender distinct from her embodied gender identity enacts a sliding of the signifier that serves to produce a new, alternative variant of masculinity. Halberstam thus offers a succinct example of a concrete way in which a subject can, in Sandoval's terms, '"break with ideology" while also speaking in and from within ideology' (1991: 2). For Muñoz, such acts of disidentification achieve 'a third term that resists the binary of identification and counteridentification', via 'a reformatting of self within the social' (1999: 97).

It is this concept of an identity of slippage, the disavowal of a fixed subject position in favour of one that shifts, slides and refuses explicit definition, that this chapter seeks to utilize in its analyses of de Sousa's and Khosa's work. While the theoretical models described above are based on the perceptions and lived experiences of minority subjects in North America, using them in a careful and critical manner that weaves 'high' theory models together with the memoir and creative prose that inspired them produces an innovative lens through which to examine anti- and postcolonial Mozambican texts: one that acknowledges the centrality of subject position and standpoint without fixing the subject within them.

'mostly [goes] by "Jack" nowadays' (Halberstam 2012), and that 'people are calling me "he" nowadays. I'm going with that' (Sexsmith 2012).

Out from Under: Noémia de Sousa's *Sangue Negro* (1948–51)

Despite having been dubbed, in affectionate and somewhat grandiose terms, 'A Mãe dos Poetas Moçambicanos' [The Mother of Mozambican Poets] (Saúte 2011: 125), de Sousa has garnered little meaningful critical attention for her work. She is often cited in overviews of Mozambican literature, but rarely appraised; what little criticism does exist of her work is all too often either dismissive or actively disparaging. Embedded within such critiques, furthermore, is the consistent gendered image of de Sousa as the purveyor of an oral rather than written poetics, a categorization that limits her role to one of nostalgic storytelling rather than active cultural production. As Hilary Owen notes, the casting of women writers as such 'allows men to step forth as nationhood's "natural" narrators while women, bound to the primary nostalgia of the oral sphere, become, once again, the fantasized, ahistorical and excessively embodied "other" through which male projections of national utopia come to be narrated' (2007a: 22). In the preface to de Sousa's fellow Mozambican poet Rui Knopfli's 1969 collection *Mangas Verdes com Sal* [*Green Mangos and Salt*], Portuguese critic Eugénio Lisboa dismisses de Sousa as 'um mito que não vale a pena manter de pé, por mais simpatia que possam merecer as boas intenções dos seus poemas tão pro-lixos como balbuciantes' [a myth that is not worth maintaining, no matter how much sympathy her poems, as prolix as they are stammering, might deserve] (1969: 8). Russell G. Hamilton, in the first book-length English-language overview of Lusophone African literature, expresses similar sentiments – though in less abrupt terms – by implying that de Sousa's prestige owed more to her ability to speak to the emotional zeitgeist of the early Mozambican independence movement than to her poetic talent: 'in the fifties, when most of her poems were written, she seemed to raise her voice at the right time to echo the collective spirit among a handful of *mestiço* and black Mozambicans who were in the process of developing self awareness' (1975: 199). In other words, her poetry was in the right place, at the right time. For Hamilton, the value of de Sousa's work lies in her 'sort of high-pitched emotional tone and full-throated passion', and her cultivation of 'a solidarity of the black man of the world', but he nonetheless concludes that 'it almost seems natural that Noémia de Sousa's own collective voice should wear thin and then finally fade away' (199–202). Patrick Chabal, in his more recent review of Lusophone African writing, mentions her four times in his chapter on Mozambique; in each citation, her name is referenced only in relation to Craveirinha, her contemporary (1996: 26, 32, 40, 95). Her work itself is neither quoted nor analysed.

A notable exception to this 'in name only' attitude toward de Sousa's legacy is Pires Laranjeira, who has considered de Sousa's work, alongside that of more celebrated Mozambican poets, as playing an important role in the construction of a literature of 'moçambicanidade'. In his comprehensively detailed volume on the emergence of the aesthetics of the Francophone Négritude movement in Lusophone African poetry, he presents her work in terms of its use of the characteristics of that movement, emphasizing her identification with a pan-African commonality and solidarity (Laranjeira 1995: 270). He furthermore highlights her work as pioneering in its refusal of colonial gendered and racial exoticism, singling out her poem 'Negra' specifically as 'um dos primeiros marcos da ruptura explícita com a estética e a ética coloniais da poesia antecedente' [one of the first signs of an explicit break with the colonial aesthetics and ethics of earlier poetry] (340). Though Laranjeira's work on de Sousa is undeniably important, his focus on locating it within an existing poetic movement, drawing out its similarities with other work rather than exploring its divergences, precludes any detailed engagement with the gendered aspects of her poetry, even when gender emerges as a key theme (as it does, indeed, in 'Negra').

A further scholar who has engaged at length with de Sousa's work, this time as the object of analysis in its own right, is Owen, who has written comprehensively on de Sousa's poetic negotiation of race, ethnicity, gender and class, and on the way these factors have come into play in the construction of her role as the 'mother' of Mozambican poetry. Owen demonstrates that de Sousa's association with this role as the maternal counterpart of Craveirinha serves to exclude her work from the discourse of nation-building, limiting it instead to a sphere that is 'secondary, presymbolic, inchoate, intuitive' (2007a: 46). Focusing specifically on de Sousa's representation of hybridity, Owen's analysis explores the poet's privileging of women's experiences of 'the race dramas of miscegenation and assimilation' (47), and draws parallels with Anzaldúa's work on *mestizaje*, noting that the works of both women represent 'a feminist reinvestment of the hybridity metaphor as a liberating deconstruction of male historical boundary anxiety' (51). For Owen, de Sousa's work frames Mozambican female subjectivity as in flux, emphasizing 'states of transition and instability, moments of crisis and change' (51).

Building on Owen's foregrounding of de Sousa's ambiguous subject position, this analysis explores three strategies employed by the poet to effect an identity of gendered slippage: the use of ungendered first-person plural pronouns and conjugations; the reversal and blurring of male–female, subject–object positionality; and the adoption of a male poetic voice. Contesting the traditional interpretations of her work as excessively vocal or florid, I aim to demonstrate that the subversive potential of de Sousa's poetry lies not in flamboyant gestures of rebellion and refusal, but instead in the use of constraint and nuance central to her subtle play of subject positions. This reading will furthermore challenge the reduction of de Sousa's poetic work to a timely but technically lacking expression of racial solidarity and anti-assimilationism, showing that her writing can in fact be read as an anticipation of later postmodern literary representations of the Mozambican nation-building project, not least those produced by Khosa.

Refracting Collectivity

Sangue Negro [*Black Blood*] (2001; 2nd edn 2011), the only published collection of de Sousa's poetry, divides her work into six thematic groups. The first of these is entitled 'Nossa Voz' [Our Voice], and comprises six poems written between 1949 and 1950: the eponymous 'Nossa Voz'; 'Nossa Irmã a Lua' [Our Sister the Moon]; 'Súplica' [Plea]; 'Abri a Porta, Companheiros' [Open the Door, Companions]; 'Passe' [Pass]; and 'Justificação' [Justification]. All six have black solidarity as their subject matter, and all six are written in the first person plural ('we'), with masculine (i.e. neutral) agreement, implying that de Sousa is speaking for both black women and black men. It is thus no surprise that these poems have been interpreted as a statement of solidarity and identification with a hypothetical black universality of experience. Laranjeira, highlighting the importance of possessive pronouns in de Sousa's poetry, notes that in 'Nossa Voz' and 'Passe' they 'pontuam um discurso sedento de identidade comum por parte de responsáveis pela enunciação, que se querem afirmar como africanos e moçambicanos *de sangue* e de direito' [indicate an urgent discourse of shared identity on the part of those responsible for their enunciation, who seek to affirm themselves as Africans and Mozambicans *by blood* and by right] (1995: 270).

While it would be difficult to contest Laranjeira's interpretation as one purpose behind such expressions of collectivity, the specificities of de Sousa's use of the first person plural in these two poems bear further analysis. The poem 'Passe' (1950) begins:

A ti, que nos exiges um passe para podermos passear
pelos caminhos hostis da nossa terra,
diremos quem somos, diremos quem somos: (2011: 28)

[To you, who demand from us a pass so that we might pass
along the hostile paths of our land,
we will tell you who we are, we will tell you who we are:]

De Sousa thus creates an immediate division between the plural subject of the poem, within which her persona is included, and the singular addressee, for whom she uses the informal 'tu' [you]. This structure lends weight and power to the subject, challenging the ostensible power of the addressee to refuse the subject entrance or passage. However, it also serves to avoid the question of the subject's gender categorization, adopting instead a sense of multiplicity or neutrality. The piece continues:

[...]
Nós somos os filhos adoptivos e os ilegítimos,
que vossos corações tímidos, desejosos de comprar o céu – ou a vida –,
vieram arrancar aos trilhos ladeados de micaias,
para depois nos lançarem, despidos das peles e das azagaias,
– ah, despojados dos diamantes do solo e do marfim,

despojados da nossa profunda consciência de homens –
nos tantos metros quadros dos bairros de zinco e caniço! (2011: 28)

[We are the adopted and illegitimate children
whom your weak hearts, which seek to buy the heavens – or life itself –,
come to haul from paths flanked by *micaias*,[3]
only to throw us, stripped of our hides and spears,
– ah, dispossessed of the diamonds and ivory of the earth,
dispossessed of our deepest consciousness as men –
into the few metres squared of the slums of zinc and reed!]

De Sousa here identifies the plural subject with a shared past of forced
displacement, locating that past in southern Mozambique with the use of
Ronga-derived word 'micaia'. Her evocation of masculine symbology with
the word 'azagaia' [spear] and her reference to the subject's 'consciência de
homens' draw attention to the subject's ambiguous gender identity without strictly defining it, since 'homens' can be used in both a masculine and
gender-neutral sense. The ongoing inclusion of de Sousa's own persona,
assumed as female, within the speaking subject contributes to this sense
of ambiguity. The following stanza reads:

Nós somos sombras para os vossos olhos, somos fantasmas.
Mas, como estamos vivos, extraordinariamente vivos e despertos!
Com sonhos de melodia no fundo dos olhos abertos,
somos os muchopes de penas saudosas nos chapéus de lixo;
e zampunganas trágicos – xipócués vagos nas noites munhuanenses,
e mamparras coroados de esperança, e magaíças,
e macambúzios com seu shipalapala ecoando chamamentos ...
No cais da cidade, somos os pachiças
e na Vida digna, somos aqueles que encontraram os lugares tomados,
somos os que não têm lugar na Vida, ah na Vida que se abre, luminosa,
com cada dia de pétala! (2011: 28)

[We are shadows before your eyes, we are ghosts
But how alive we are, extraordinarily alive and alert!

3   *Micaia* denotes the *acacia nigrescens*, a tall hardwood tree native to Mozambique.
    'Vera Micaia' was also one of the many pseudonyms de Sousa used to avoid New
    State secret police (PIDE) scrutiny (Owen 2007a: 44).

With melodic dreams in the depths of our open eyes
we are the *muchopes*, with sad feathers in our hats of trash,
and the tragic *zampunganas* – *xipócués* wandering through the Munhuana nights
and the *mamparras*, crowned with hope, and the *magaíças*,
and the *macambúzios* who come with the echoing cries of the *shipalapala* ...
In the city docks, we are the *pachiças*
and in this noble Life, we are those who find their places already taken,
we are those who have no place in Life, oh in this Life that opens out, luminous,
with each petal-like day!]⁴

In contrast to the affirmation of commonality made in the previous stanza, here the multiplicity of the plural subject is emphasized via the listing of specific occupations: *muchope, zampungana, mamparra, magaíça, macambúzio*. De Sousa thereby shifts from a shared, singular identity to a proliferation of identities, without identifying the 'I' implied within the 'we' with any single one. These plural identities are moreover juxtaposed with references to nonidentity or unintelligibility, both in terms of the subjects' erasure in the eyes of the addressee, and in terms of self-conception: they are 'sombras' [shadows] and 'fantasmas' [ghosts], 'xipócués vagos' [wandering phantoms] and 'os que não têm lugar na Vida' [those who have no place in life].

In the stanzas that follow, the poem's subject is once again homogenized, with the emphasis returned to a shared identity:

Somos os despojados, somos os despojados!
Aqueles a quem tudo foi roubado,
Pátria e dignidade, Mãe e riqueza e crenças, e Liberdade! (2011: 29)

[We are the disposessed, we are the disposessed!
Those from whom everything was stolen,
Fatherland and dignity, Mother and wealth and belief, and Freedom!]

4 *Muchope*: Lourenço Marques (Maputo) public worker; *zampungana*: a man who empties neighbourhood latrines at night; *xipócué*: phantom or otherworldly spirit; Munhuana: a poor suburb of Lourenço Marques; *mamparra* and *magaíça*: a migrant worker in South Africa's mines (*mamparra* is also a perjorative meaning stupid, ignorant); *macambúzio*: rural shepherd; *shipalapala* (also spelled *xipalapala*): an antelope horn used to sound a warning or call to action; *pachiça*: a member of the working class.

With this repeated shifting of the meaning attached to the poem's plural subject – from a homogeneous mass to a multiplicity of individual identities and nonidentities, and back again – de Sousa renders the subject in this poem ambiguous, uncertain and indefinable. Meanwhile, her use of the first person plural, within which her own female subjectivity is both implicit and concealed, troubles the subject's assumed masculinity.

A similarly ambiguous subject is presented in the eponymous poem from the same group, 'Nossa Voz' [Our Voice] (1949). The title itself speaks to that ambiguity, attributing a singular noun to a plural possessive pronoun. The juxtaposition of plural subject and singular voice, repeated in an incantatory manner throughout the piece, is upheld by the singular adjectives and verbs that follow it, until it seems that the voice has become a subject itself:

Nossa voz molhada das cacimbadas do sertão
nossa voz ardente como o sol das malangas
nossa voz atabaque chamando
nossa voz lança de Maguiguana
nossa voz, irmão,
nossa voz trespassou a atmosfera conformista da cidade
e revolucionou-a
arrastou-a como um ciclone de conhecimento. (2011: 21)

[Our voice wet with the dew of the wilderness
our voice burning like the sun inside a fresh-cut *malanga*[5]
our voice a drum calling
our voice Maguigana's[6] spear
our voice, brother,
our voice transgressed the conformist atmosphere of the city
and revolutionized it
coursing through it like a cyclone of knowledge.]

5   *Malanga*: a root vegetable, similar in appearance to a yam, with a bright white flesh.
     Thanks to Catarina Fouto for suggesting this translation.
6   Maguiguana (sometimes spelled Magejana) was an indigenous Mozambican warrior,
     the leading general and advisor of late nineteenth-century Gazan chief Ngungunhane
     (Wheeler 1968: 589).

This use of a singular noun and plural pronoun allows de Sousa to once again insert herself into the poem's subject while avoiding the espousal of a fixed identity. In the last lines of the antepenultimate stanza, 'nossa voz milhares, | nossa voz milhões de vozes clamando!' [our voice thousands, | our voice millions of voices hollering!] (21) and again in the final line of the poem, 'nossa voz milhões de vozes clamando, clamando, clamando!' [our voice millions of voices hollering, hollering, hollering!] (21), the 'voice' is pluralized, refracting the collective identity implied by the pairing of plural pronoun and singular noun into a multiplicity of identities. Just as the 'voice' appears to take on a singular subjectivity of its own, it splits and fragments, resisting fixed definition. As in 'Passe', de Sousa's poetic manipulation of subjectivities in this piece creates a space where she can sound her own voice while simultaneously disguising it.

De Sousa's use of the ungendered, ambiguous 'nós' can be read in terms of the 'not yet/that's not it' positionality that Alarcón (1996: 129) identifies as central to the analytical frameworks of North American Chicana and black feminisms. Expounding the theory of 'mestiza consciousness', Anzaldúa, for example, notes that for the mestiza woman,

> [r]igidity means death. [...] *La mestiza* constantly has to shift out of habitual forma-
> tions; from convergent thinking, analytical reasoning that tends to use rationality to
> move toward a single goal (a Western mode), to divergent thinking, characterized by
> movement away from set patterns and goals and toward a more whole perspective,
> one that includes rather than excludes. (2012: 101)

For Anzaldúa, the key to maintaining a coherent selfhood as a woman at the crossroads of multiple cultures and oppressions is, therefore, to develop the above-mentioned 'tolerance for contradictions, a tolerance for ambiguity' (2012: 101). In this way, rather than resisting the ambiguity and contradictory cultural messages brought about by her position as a black, mixed-race woman, with one foot in the middle classes of a society anticipating unforeseeable upheaval, de Sousa can be seen as exploiting the uncertainty brought about by that status to disavow the identities that might be imposed on her by both colonial and anticolonial factions. In addition, employing the vocabulary of racial and class solidarity allows her to realize this disavowal by stealth, outright rejecting the colonial value system while at the same time disidentifying with the similarly restrictive role constructed for her by the masculinist rhetoric of the anticolonial movement. Patricia Hill Collins, quoting Lorde (1984: 114), has commented on the value of this tactic for the subject that experiences oppression along multiple axes, noting that African-American women "'become familiar with the language and manners of the oppressor, even sometimes adopting them for some illusion of protection" while hiding a self-defined standpoint from the prying eyes of dominant groups' (Collins 1991: 91). In this way, de Sousa creates a space for her own self-definition, taking her, in Anzaldúa's terms, 'from being the sacrificial goat to becoming the officiating priestess at the crossroads' (2012: 102).

Shifting Surfaces

De Sousa's enactment of disidentification can further be seen in her blurring and reversal of the male subject–female object positionality that characterizes both colonial exoticism and anticolonial 'emancipation' rhetoric. While the poem 'Poema para um Amor Futuro' [Poem for a Future Love] (1950) is, on the surface, an ode to an imagined male object of the poet's desire, it also effects a degree of gendered slippage that problematizes this simple interpretation. De Sousa's reversal of gendered subject–object positionality becomes apparent in the poem's first sentence:

> Um dia
> – não sei quando nem onde –
> das névoas cinzentas do futuro,
> ele surgirá, envolto em mistério e magia
> – o homem que eu amarei. (2011: 42)

> [One day
> – I do not know when or where –
> from the grey mists of the future,
> he will appear, shrouded in mystery and magic
> – the man that I will love.][7]

---

7   All translations of 'Poema para um Amor Futuro' are by Hilary Owen (2007a: 86–7).

Not only is the object of her piece unambiguously male, he is also wrapped up in the ahistorical romanticism and exoticism – 'mistério e magia' – associated more frequently with colonial depictions of black women. While de Sousa goes on to specify that he will not be 'herói de livro de fantasia, | príncipe russo' [a storybook hero | a Russian prince] or 'actor de cinema' [a film star], her exoticization of this male object creates an immediate sense of irony. The poem continues:

> O homem que eu amarei
> será tal qual eu, no fundo.
> Suas mãos, como as minhas,
> estarão calejadas do dia a dia
> e seus olhos terão reflexos de aço
> como os meus.
> Sua alma será irmã minha
> com a mesma angústia e o mesmo amor,
> com o mesmo frio ódio e a mesma esperança. (2011: 42)

> [The man that I will love
> will be just like me, deep down.
> His hands, like mine,
> will be calloused with his daily work
> and his eyes will have glints of steel
> like mine.
> His soul will be my sister soul
> with the same sorry and the same love,
> with the same cold hatred and the same hope.]

De Sousa's identification of the male object's corporeality with her own establishes her own body as originator, as though she has created the object of her desire in her own image. Rather than acting as the passive surface for the inscription of colonial desires and anticolonial ideology, here the female body becomes the default. This reversal of roles, the demarcation of the male body according to the female, is furthered by de Sousa's characterization of her future love's soul as specifically female, 'irmã minha' [my sister]. The man she describes appears devoid of agency or identity beyond that of de Sousa herself; instead, he represents de Sousa's persona in fantasized male form. This singularity of identity is underscored by de

Sousa's affirmation that she and her love will be 'da mesma seiva generosa' [of the same generous spirit], and that he will be perfect only 'quanto a nossa condição o permitir' [as our circumstance permits], an echo of the singular/plural slippage discussed above with reference to 'Nossa Voz'.

The implication of singularity in these initial stanzas is ruptured in the third, wherein de Sousa describes the hypothetical consummation of the pair's love:

> E meu corpo adubado de ânsias,
> abrir-se-á à charrua do seu desejo,
> à semente do seu amor.
> Serei então irmã gémea da Terra,
> carregando em mim o mistério da vida,
> machamba aberta à chuva benéfica
> e ao sol fecundo do seu amor.
> E quando em mim se fizer o milagre,
> quando do meu grito de morte
> surgir a vitória máxima da vida,
> ah, então eu estarei completa. (2011: 43)

> [And my body steeped in longing,
> will open itself to the ploughshare of his desire,
> and the seed of his love.
> Then I will be the twin sister of the Earth,
> bearing in me the mystery of life,
> the planted ground open to the goodness of the rain
> and the fertile sun of your love,
> And when in me the miracle occurs,
> when from my deathly cry
> there springs the greatest victory of life,
> oh, then and only then will I be complete.]

Here, de Sousa courts the familiar language of telluric femininity that reflects both colonial imaginings of Africa as fertile virgin land and, as Owen has affirmed, the anticolonial symbology of the female body as the vessel for regenerative reproduction (2007a: 59). However, her prior establishment of herself as originating subject subverts the implied female passivity in this stanza, casting her as creator, with the 'vitória máxima da vida' [greatest victory of life] her own accomplishment. This rejection of passivity is confirmed by de Sousa's repeated declaration that the lovers' consummation will be realized only 'depois da paz descer sobre o meu campo da luta, | [...] quando nossa Mãe África nos estender seus pulsos libertos' [after peace has come to my battlefield, | [...] when our Mother Africa reaches out to us her unbound wrists] (2011: 43–4). While the 'luta' in question refers, on one level, to the independence struggle, de Sousa's use of the first person possessive pronoun 'meu' to qualify the metonymical 'campo de luta' [battlefield] implies another, more personal battle for liberation. Until the battle(s) are won, de Sousa asserts, the lovers' shared singularity of identity and objective will remain: 'Antes, seremos companheiros da mesma obra, | operários construindo o nosso mundo' [Before that, we will be comrades in the same struggle, | workers building our world together] (43). As in 'Nossa Voz' and 'Passe', here de Sousa speaks to solidarity while implicitly affirming her own agency. However, while in the former two poems this affirmation is achieved via a manipulation of a plural subjectivity that allows her to evoke a multiplicity of identities without espousing any single one, thus creating a space in which she can define herself, in 'Poema para um Amor Futuro' she enacts a reversal of gendered subject positions that confirms her participation in the independence struggle while realizing her disidentification with the gender roles therein.

This use of familiar language as a cover for the disidentificatory slippage of subject positions is key to the subversive potential of 'Se Me Quiseres Conhecer' [If You Really Would Know Me] (1949). The title invites the reader to 'know' the poem's subject, and, by extension, de Sousa herself. The piece begins:

> Se me quiseres conhecer,
> estuda com os olhos bem de ver
> esse pedaço de pau preto
> que um desconhecido irmão maconde
> de mãos inspiradas
> talhou e trabalhou
> em terras distantes lá do Norte. (2011: 33)

> [If you really would know me,
> look closely with eyes prepared to see
> this piece of dark wood

that an unknown Makonde brother
with inspired hands
carved and fashioned
in distant lands of the North.][8]

De Sousa here instantly breaks with the 'me' of the poem's title and first
line, as the poem's persona is revealed to be a Makonde carving. As Owen
notes, the evocation of this specific type of carving is significant, carrying
with it a tradition of rebellion and defiance against colonial cultural and
religious imposition (2007a: 56). With de Sousa's invitation to 'study', the
carving becomes both the subject and object of the piece, a provocation
of voyeurism. The second stanza reads:

Ah, essa sou eu:
órbitas vazias no desespero de possuir a vida,
boca rasgada em feridas de angústia,
mãos enormes, espalmadas,
erguendo-se em jeito de quem implora e ameaça,
corpo tatuado de feridas visíveis e invisíveis
pelos chicotes da escravatura ...
Torturada e magnífica,
altiva e mística,
África da cabeça aos pés,
– ah, essa sou eu: (2011: 33)

[Oh, she is who I am:
Eye sockets empty in despair at possessing life,
mouth torn open in wounds of anguish,
giant, empty outstretched hands
raised as one who begs and threatens,
body tattooed with visible and unseen wounds
from the whips of slavery ...
Tortured and magnificent,
proud and mystical,
Africa from head to foot,
– Oh, she is who I am:]

8   All translations of 'Se Me Quiseres Conhecer' are by Hilary Owen (2007a: 83).

Having shifted out from under the poem's persona, here de Sousa rein-serts herself. The exclamation of 'essa sou eu' [she is who I am] serves to both identify her (eu [I]) with the carving (essa [she/it]) and to distance herself from it. It also splits the subject and object of the piece, rendering uncertain the identity of both: is she describing 'essa', or 'eu', or both? The provocation of voyeurism initiated in the first stanza is thus partially over-laid onto de Sousa's own body. Meanwhile, the fetishism of the Western gaze is evoked with the exoticizing lines, 'Torturada e magnífica, | altiva e mística, | África da cabeça aos pés' [Tortured and magnificent, | proud and mystical, | Africa from head to foot]. This evocation of the Western gaze continues into the following lines:

> Se quiseres compreender-me
> vem debruçar-te sobre minha alma de África, (2011: 33)

> [If you would really understand me
> come put your ear to my African soul,]

The invitation to the reader to 'debruçar-[se]', which translates literally as 'hunch over', demands that they come closer still, recalling the intrusiveness and voyeurism of colonial ethnography. The Western gaze is thus turned on itself, becoming the partial object of the narrative. The piece ends:

> E nada mais me perguntes,
> se é que me queres conhecer ...
> Que não sou mais que um búzio de carne,
> onde a revolta de África congelou
> seu grito inchado de esperança. (2011: 33)

> [And do not ask me anything more,
> if you really want to know me ...
> For I am no more than a shell of flesh
> in which the rising up of Africa froze
> its cry swelled with hope.]

Subject and object are once again assimilated, rendering both ambiguous. Indeed, the last lines of the piece are ones of radical nonidentity, removing any comforting possibility of coherent identification and leaving only a 'búzio de carne' [shell of flesh].⁹

Through evoking the Western gaze and casting herself, in transient and unstable terms, as both subject and object of 'Se Me Quiseres Conhecer', de Sousa engages in a strategic form of autoethnography. Using the mystifying vocabulary of Western ethnography – the references to 'terras distantes' [distant lands], the 'corpo tatuado' [tattooed body], her 'alma de África' [African soul], the 'batuques frenéticos' [wild *batuques*]¹⁰ and the 'estranha melancolia [...] | duma canção nativa, noite dentro' [strange melancholy [...] | from a native song, deep into the night] – only to reveal an empty shell of flesh, she enacts an ironic performance of exoticizing discourses that ultimately serves to refuse the Western gaze entirely.

Muñoz has noted the subversive potential of autoethnographic performance for colonized subjects, demonstrating that it 'worries easy binarisms such as colonized and colonizer [...] by presenting subaltern speech through the channels and pathways of metropolitan representational systems' (1999: 82). De Sousa's use of autoethnography extends beyond this framework, however, to further challenge the specifically gender-based othering of Mozambican anticolonial rhetoric. Laura Mulvey, writing on artist Cindy Sherman's photographic parodies of the Hollywood film industry's gendered voyeurism, describes how 'Sherman-the-model dresses up into character, while Sherman-the-artist reveals her character's masquerade' via an 'overinsistence on surface' that 'starts to suggest that it might be masking something or other that should be hidden from sight', while 'a hint of another space starts to lurk inside a too plausible façade' (1991: 141). Sherman's photographs, which both feature and are taken by Sherman herself, provoke an uneasy, unstable voyeurism because 'just as she is artist and model, voyeur and looked-at, active and

9 The image of the 'búzio' or cowry shell is one that recurs in later anticolonial texts written prior to independence: for example, in Craveirinha's poem 'Manifesto', discussed in Chapter 2, and in the final lines of Luís Bernardo Honwana's short story 'Dina' (1964; 2nd edn 1980: 53). Whether this recurrence indicates an allegorical or coded reference within anticolonial discourse, or whether Craveirinha and/or Honwana may have been citing de Sousa, would merit future research.

10 A *batuque* is a series of dances set to drum beat.

passive, subject and object, the photographs set up a comparable variety of positions and responses for the viewer' (142). Sherman uses the 'accoutrements of the feminine' (141) to create a surface appearance of conformity with a Hollywood-sanctioned ideal femininity, while simultaneously dissolving any illusion of stable subject positionality for herself or for the viewer.

'Se Me Quiseres Conhecer', in a comparable manner, uses the vocabulary of the exoticizing colonial gaze and that of masculinist anticolonial discourse to create the 'surface' of the Makonde carving, while sliding in and out of the positions of subject and object, rejecting the fixed role of object for either Western fetishism or anticolonial political symbology. The final stanza's revelation that de Sousa's unstable and transient performance as sometime-object was simply a play of surfaces, behind which there is only an empty shell of flesh, finalizes her disidentification with both discourses, rendering her identity radically uncertain. In Muñoz's Althusserian terms, de Sousa has realized the 'formatting of the self within the social' that allows her to '[resist] the interpellating call of ideology that fixe[s] a subject within the state power apparatus' (1999: 97).

Transgressive Abjection

While de Sousa's enactment of disidentification in the poems examined thus far depends on the placing of the identity of her poetic persona in limbo, her adoption of an explicitly male identity can also be understood as part of a disidentificatory strategy. In 'Zampungana' (1949), de Sousa espouses the poem's eponymous persona, a male worker of low social class who empties cesspits during the night. The piece begins:

> Ó noite, ó minha mãe carinhosa
> com tua quente capulana negra!
> Ai embrulha-me bem, noite,
> ai embrulha-me tão bem
> que só tu e mais ninguém
> sejas testemunha da minha humilhação, (65)

[Oh night, oh my tender mother
with your warm black *capulana*![11]
Oh swaddle me well, night,
oh swaddle me so well
that only you and no-one else
can witness my humiliation,]

The vocabulary in this first stanza is typical of the anticolonial imagery discussed with relation to Craveirinha's work in Chapter 2. The night is feminized and maternalized, becoming an anonymous source of protection and comfort in the face of suffering. The following stanza, however, marks a swift departure from this narrative:

E deixa deslizar, sombra ou xipócué,
pelos caminhos perdidos das Munhuanas ...
Que só tu me vejas, só tu me sigas,
passo a passo, cúmplice e material,
enquanto cumprir meu destino irremediável de besta humana.
E eu sombra, e eu fantasma, e eu animal,
de latrina em latrina,
arrepiado até às raízes da alma,
vómitos de náusea recalcados
(e a revolta subindo em maré cheia, subindo)
carregarei à cabeça, enlouquecido,
as latas de excrementos, excrementos, excrementos! (2011: 65)

[And let me slither, shadow or *xipócué*,[12]
through the lost streets of Munhuana ...
May only you see me, may only you follow me,
step by step, complicit and tangible,
while I fulfill my hopeless destiny of human beast.
And I shadow, and I ghost, and I animal,
from latrine to latrine
sickened down to the roots of my soul,
my nauseous heaves held back

---

11   The *capulana* is a staple item of Mozambican women's dress, consisting of a printed length of cloth generally worn as an ankle-length wrap skirt.
12   *Xipócué*: phantom or otherworldly spirit.

(and my disgust rising to high tide, rising),
will carry upon my head, delirious,
the vats of excrement, excrement, excrement!]

The character of the zampungana is undoubtedly male, but his assimilation with the filth of his occupation has diminished his sense of coherent and intelligible selfhood, leaving him to conceive of himself as a non-being, a 'sombra' [shadow], 'xipócué' [phantom], 'fantasma' [ghost], 'animal' or 'besta' [beast]. De Sousa is thus not only 'dragging' in the poem, using a male persona in the first person; she is also taking on a persona whose place within a hierarchical gender binary is fundamentally problematized by his lacking, in Butlerian terms, the fully coherent 'illusion of an abiding gendered self' (2007: 191): in short, by his status as abject.

For Julia Kristeva, whose theorization of abjection is the basis for Butler's specifically gendered elaboration, the abject is that which 'lies outside, beyond the set, and does not seem to agree to the latter's rules of the game' (1982: 2): it upsets the constructs of social order, and yet it is only via the reiterated disavowal of the abject that the subject is able to establish physical boundaries and surface. The abject is continually banished, and yet, 'from its place of banishment, the abject does not cease challenging its master' (2), encroaching constantly on the subject's illusory and contingent boundaries. Expanding on Kristeva's theory, Elizabeth Grosz notes that body fluids and waste 'attest to the permeability of the body, its necessary dependence on an outside, its liability to collapse into this outside [...]. They affront a subject's aspiration toward autonomy and self-identity' (1994: 56). For Andrea Dworkin, it is the perceived dirtiness of the female body specifically that lies at the foundation of the hierarchical gender binary: a woman 'is not just less; she and the sex she incarnates are a species of filth. [...] The dirt in which women are buried alive is not a matter of attitude; it is not in the eye of the beholder' (2006: 215). What is demarcated as abject thus has a heavily gendered component; as Grosz demonstrates, the female body is constructed as a threat to order, coherence and autonomous separateness, 'a formlessness that engulfs all form, a disorder that threatens all order' (1994: 203). The zampungana, mired nightly in bodily filth and unable to resist its encroachment upon his physical and psychic boundaries, sees his sense of coherent individual selfhood gradually eroded. Furthermore, his sense of gendered self, bound up with the social coding of masculinity as that which is *not* abject, is also threatened by this 'horror | do meu próprio asco dia a dia renovado' [horror | of my own disgust renewed each day] (de Sousa 2011: 66). The unstable masculinity embodied by de Sousa's poetic persona is evident in his lack of ability to participate in the compulsory heterosexuality that, for Butler, is essential for the maintenance and reiteration of a hierarchical gender binary: 'E até as mais baixas mulheres me recusam' [And even the lowliest of women refuse me] (66).

This espousal by de Sousa of an essentially abject male persona provides the locus of subversive potential in 'Zampungana'. Both Butler and Halberstam have spoken to the destabilizing influence of female drag performers on hegemonic masculinity, with Halberstam specifically affirming that female drag artists expose the elements within masculinity 'where nonperformativity has ideological implications' (1998: 30). In other words, dragging as male reveals the artificial and constructed nature of the very elements of masculinity perceived as compulsory. In her poetic performance of the role of a specifically abjectified man, de Sousa is able to expand this revelatory power, severing the ties not only between masculinity and maleness, but between abjection and femininity, thus revealing the ultimate artificiality of these naturalized associations. Moreover, the abject masculinity in the poem is constructed against a femininity that speaks from within anticolonial gendered stereotypes of ahistorical maternalism, as seen in the first stanza, while simultaneously refusing them, making the feminine element in the piece the subjective bearer of knowledge, light and transcendent purity. The zampungana is shown speaking with the feminized night in the tone of a prayer to an omniscient being, asking 'her' to assure him that 'há infelicidade maior | e [...] que há degradação pior | do que esta [...] humilhação sem nome' [there is some greater unhappiness | [...] some lower degradation | than this [...] nameless humiliation] (65). The final lines of the poem read:

> também quero sentir cegar-me com seu forte clarão
> essa luz maravilhosa que está nascendo para todos
> essa luz radiosa e libertadora que nem sei donde vem
> nem nunca vi
> mas que adivinho diferente de todas as outras! (66)

[I too want to blind myself in your brightest light
that incredible light emerging for all
that radiant, liberating light that comes from I don't know where
nor have I seen
but that I imagine different from all others!]

This association of the feminine with light, purity and omniscience, held against the poem's backdrop of abject masculinity, effects a break with both colonial and anticolonial gendered binaries, making the feminine element a subjective, liberating guide. De Sousa rejects the fixed mantle of femininity and femaleness by performing a masculine role, but her choice of an utterly abject male persona confirms her disidentification with masculinity's naturalized superiority. Once again, she resists interpellation into any one identity or ideology, deferring instead to Alarcón's position of 'not yet/ that's not it' (1996: 129).

Anzaldúa has affirmed that '[a]ll reaction is limited by, and dependent on, what it is reacting against. [...] At some point, on our way to a new consciousness, we will have to leave the opposite bank, the split between the two mortal combatants somehow healed so that we are on both shores at once and, at once, see through serpent and eagle eyes. [...] The possibilities are numerous once we decide to act and not react.' (2012: 100–1). While the work by Craveirinha discussed in Chapter 2 can be understood as a reaction, a counteridentification with colonial discourse that is nonetheless limited to its underlying binaries and modalities, de Sousa's work represents a profound and heavily performative attempt to work from within those discourses while ultimately rejecting them. Lying beneath the false familiarity that her work constructs is a radical severance between sign and signifier that indicates her desire not to react, but to act.

The lyrical shifts and playful subtleties of de Sousa's poetry are far removed from the narrative techniques that dominate the prose fiction of Ungulani Ba Ka Khosa forty years later. It is thus perhaps no surprise that these two authors' works have hitherto never been comparatively analysed. What I seek to demonstrate in the section that follows, however, is that viewing Khosa's narratives through the lens of critical gender theory reveals a clear thread connecting these two very different writers, tied to the use of the sexed black body – and particularly the anticolonial figuration of the black female body as 'Mãe África' [Mother Africa] – as the means to enacting disidentification. Much as de Sousa takes the Mãe África trope, a talisman of both colonial thought and Mozambican anti-colonial collectivity, and deconstructs it in order to critique hegemonic political narratives while rejecting the selective blindness of any singular ideology, Khosa deconstructs the racially idealized, symbolic and strictly gendered African body, the linchpin of Frelimo discourse despite their supposed post-racialism and gender egalitarianism, to achieve the same ends.

However, while de Sousa foregrounds the Mãe África motif in order to offer a quiet disavowal of certain imposed roles and modalities, making use of subjective ambiguity to slide out from under the trope's corporeal surface, Khosa stakes out that corporeality as catalyst for the rejection of political identification as a whole. While the value of the gendered body in de Sousa's work, then, lies in its ephemerality and capacity for displacement, for Khosa that resistant potential is found in the body's very physicality. His emphasis on corporeal primacy allows him to privilege the events of the post-independence period, while his disavowal of fixed identities forestalls the use of said events as part of a sectarian discourse. His work thus comes to represent a drastic breaking with accepted historical and artistic narratives both official and marginal, signalling the Mozambican post-independence turn toward postmodern expression anticipated by de Sousa's slippage of subject positions.

Backs to the Future: Ungulani Ba Ka Khosa's *Ualalapi* (1987) and *Orgia dos Loucos* (1990)

In the four decades between de Sousa's most prolific years and the publication of Khosa's first novel, *Ualalapi* (1987; 2nd edn 1990), Mozambique experienced changes so dramatic, complex and entangled that succinctly describing them remains fraught. Having led the Mozambican people through a prolonged and gruelling anticolonial struggle, in June 1975 Frelimo took definitive control of the nation. In doing so, the party inherited a country in disarray, facing a populace often unwelcoming of attempts to impose a radically anti-traditionalist model of Soviet socialism unsuited to the specificities of southern Africa, particularly in the traditionally matrilineal north of the country, in addition to increasing external hostility from the white minority governments of Rhodesia and South Africa (Newitt 2002: 207). Meanwhile, Frelimo's Soviet identification and open opposition to the South African apartheid regime thrust Mozambique onto a world stage dominated by Cold War paranoia and *realpolitik* (Newitt 2002: 195).

It was within this climate of uncertainty, distrust and widespread poverty that the MNR, later better known as Renamo, was able to flourish. Born of the post-1975 alliance between white Portuguese former colonialists and the black Portuguese-recruited troops taking shelter across the border in Rhodesia, and overseen by Rhodesian military intelligence and later by apartheid South Africa, Renamo had the singular and uncompromising aim of destroying Frelimo's socialist project. The attacks and raids orchestrated in service of that aim provoked the bloodiest conflict in Mozambican living memory. Spanning the sixteen years between 1976 and the signing of a final peace agreement between Frelimo and Renamo in Rome in 1992, the brutality and destruction that defined the post-independence war defy easy representation. While the intertwined combination of testimony and reportage that made it out of Mozambique during and after the war years provides the onlooker with some sense of the elements that constituted the conflict – the arbitrary use of murder, atrocious torture and mutilation; man-made famine (Frelick 1989: 4); the death or displacement of at least 40% of Mozambique's population; the ubiquity of sexual abuse, including that perpetrated by 'peacekeeping' forces (Sheldon 2002: 197–202); Renamo's forced recruitment of child soldiers (Minter 1989: 5); the targeting of schools, hospitals, clinics, and shops (Gersony 1988: 30) – the magnitude, reach and totality of its violence resist words spoken or written.

Khosa's prose fiction attempts to bridge this void of representation, narrating both individual and collective acts of brutality in order to enshrine their importance in world history as well as in Mozambican cultural memory. His work speaks to an intense overarching disillusionment with the realities of the post-independence nation-building project,

underscoring the demonstrable falsity of the pan-Mozambican collectivity at the centre of Frelimo rhetoric while forcing acknowledgement and
analysis of Renamo atrocities. The emphasis on gendered corporeality that
defines Khosa's work is uniquely equipped to drive these twin projects of
exposition and disidentification, with the bodies of his narratives, in their
damaged, truncated and grotesque states, allowing the author to put words
to an intensity of sensation that resists direct language. What his work provokes is thus a visceral, affective response, which troubles the naturalized
integrity of socially constructed identities and thus symbolically destabilizes the false collectivities dominant on all sides in post-independence
Mozambican rhetoric.

Corporeal Dis-ease

Pivotal to Khosa's use of gendered bodies as the sites of disidentification
are his recurrent portrayals of grotesque corporeality, reflecting the characterization of the grotesque first introduced into contemporary literary
criticism by Mikhail Bakhtin. Explicating the relationship between the
grotesque body and 'low', folkloric and carnivalesque subcultures, Bakhtin
defines the essential principle of grotesque cultural expression as 'degradation, that is, the lowering of all that is high, spiritual, ideal, abstract [...]
to the sphere of earth and body in their indissoluble unity' (1984: 19–20).
In contrast with the bodies of classical canon, the grotesque body 'is not
a closed, completed unit; it is unfinished, outgrows itself, transgresses its
own limits' (26). This essential corporeal openness is illustrated by emphasis
on the body's 'apertures [or] convexities, or on various ramifications and
offshoots: the open mouth, the genital organs, the breasts, the phallus', and
on events including 'copulation, pregnancy, childbirth, the throes of death,
eating, drinking, or defecation' (26). The body is thus cast as unfinished,
unstable, uncontrollable. It has no limits, 'no façade, no impenetrable
surface' (339).

For Bakhtin, birth and death are especially grotesque events, bringing the body's inherent changeability and ephemerality into relief; he cites as an especially grotesque image certain figurines among the Kerch terracotta collection that represent '[laughing,] senile pregnant hags' (1984: 25). In the bodies of these figures, explains Bakhtin, 'there is nothing completed, nothing calm and stable' (25). Rather, their bodies 'combine a senile, decaying and deformed flesh with the flesh of new life, conceived but as yet unformed' (25–6). This intimate link between birth and death is embodied in Bakhtin's text by the recurrent image of the womb as a particularly potent site of grotesquery: the womb, for him, is a 'bodily grave', evoking earth, that which 'devours, swallows up [...] and gives birth at the same time' (21). Bakhtin's imagining of the womb makes clear that at the crux of his theory lies a clear relationship between femininity, death, and the grotesque. Indeed, the three are so closely linked in his work as to be elided, synonymous; femininity is necessarily grotesque and the grotesque is necessarily feminine.

This uncritical alignment of femininity and the grotesque is, evidently, far from unique. As Mary Russo affirms in her own work on the grotesque body, the 'archaic tropes' that '[posit] a natural connection between the female body (itself naturalized) and the "primal" elements' provide a potential starting point for the 'easy and perilous slide [...] to the misogyny which identifies [the] hidden space with the visceral' (1994: 1–2). Yael Shapira likewise demonstrates that the trope of femininity repeatedly referenced in Bakhtin, that of 'a female body dominated by gaping orifices and flux', is a key weapon in 'the historical arsenal of misogyny, a way of grounding women's "aberrance" in their distasteful corporeality' (2010: 53). And, as Bakhtin's work makes clear, the 'gaping orifices' and sense of corporeal flux that provide 'proof' of the female body's essential grotesqueness are nowhere more evident than in the reproductive cycle. Menstruation, (heterosexual) intercourse, childbirth and lactation serve to demonstrate, on this schema, the permeability and openness of women's bodies; their inherent lack of purity, their unpredictability, their unruliness (Grosz 1994: 193–4).

While the use of the grotesque might thus appear antithetical to feminist intent, implicit within Bakhtin's thesis that the grotesque can be deployed for subversive ends in terms of class and subculture is the possibility that the gendered grotesque might have similar potential. Indeed, both Russo and Shapira themselves showcase such subversive outcomes. In Russo's text, Cindy Sherman's photographic piece *Untitled #175*, a graphic representation of the decaying debris of a bulimic woman's binge-purge episode displayed on a large canvas (119cm x 182cm), is shown to present a metacommentary on the naturalized association between the female and the grotesque by forcibly confronting the viewer with an excessive version of its disturbing logical conclusion (1994: 2). Meanwhile, Shapira's analysis of Margaret Atwood's short story 'Hairball', which details a woman's excessive attachment to a dermoid cyst removed from her ovary, shows that Atwood's use of the grotesque reappropriates the 'disorder' of women's bodies as the potential catalyst for 'an exhilarating challenge to oppressive social boundaries' (2010: 53). Central to the successfully subversive outcome of both examples is a strategic use of excess, manifested in making literal and overt what is usually latent or cloaked in metaphor. Both Sherman and Atwood exploit the fear and sense of menace concealed behind the trope of the feminine grotesque, harnessing their ability to unsettle and disrupt.

The affective sense of latent menace that represents both the core of the female/grotesque association and the key to its subversive deployment is a clear example of abject threat, as theorized by Kristeva and outlined above with reference to de Sousa's 'Zampungana'. For Kristeva, the abject manifests as 'a threat that seems to emanate from an exorbitant outside or inside, ejected beyond the scope of the possible, the tolerable, the thinkable' (1982: 1). Cast out from within the boundaries of the self, it becomes the element against which the subject is constituted, its ever-present encroachment an incorrigible threat on coherent subjectivity itself: 'a weight of meaninglessness, about which there is nothing insignificant, which crushes me. On the edge of nonexistence and hallucination, of a reality that, if I acknowledge it, annihilates me' (2). Yet it is this persistent threat to subjectivity and thus to the sociocultural power structures within which subjectivity is negotiated that endows an abject response with the potential to upset social hierarchies. If individual and collective identities and subjectivities can be troubled by the encroachment of abject elements, so too can their naturalized status positions. The corporeal grotesque, by provoking an abject response, provides the means to harness this disruptive power. And if female corporeality is by nature grotesque, then the grotesque female body can be reclaimed from its position as a weapon of gendered subjugation, becoming instead ammunition for the dismantling of hierarchical social relations. To reiterate Grosz's words, the female body under patriarchy has been so defined by its openness that it has come to represent 'a formlessness that engulfs all form, a disorder that threatens all order' (1994: 203). In Khosa's work, it is that threat of formlessness and disorder that comes to play the same role as de Sousa's linguistic elisions and play of subjectivities, providing both a vehicle for expression and a means of social and political disidentification.

The female grotesque comes to occupy a position of particular significance in the context of independence-era Mozambique, as the gendered body was once again discursively transposed onto the anxiously delineated borders of the nascent Mozambican nation-state. One example of the relationship between this interconnection and notions of the grotesque can be found in a series of speeches given by Frelimo leader Samora Machel in the northern regions of Mozambique in 1983, as the party struggled to construct a viable socialist nation-state amid the burgeoning chaos of the post-independence conflict. Typically for the post-independence period, the speeches are dominated by denunciations of perceived threats to the cause from both inside and outside Mozambique's borders; tribalism and imperialism, respectively, are chief among them, characterized as the barriers to Machel's progressivist vision of socialist unity. While these twin enemies are the explicit focus of the speeches, a closer look at Machel's use of language and metaphor reveals an underlying alternative theme: a profound anxiety centred around boundary purity, embodied by the abject menace of the female grotesque.

This sense of concealed threat comes to the fore during the speech given by Machel in Montepuez, Cabo Delgado, the northernmost province of Mozambique and, in Machel's words, the place in which the independence movement learned 'que era preciso matar a tribo para que pudesse nascer a Nação' [that it was necessary to kill the tribe to give birth to the Nation] (1983a, iv: 3). This birthing metaphor, invoking the Mãe África trope, recurs throughout the series of speeches Machel gives in Cabo Delgado: the province is not only the birthplace of the nation, but also the vessel of its gestation, watered and fertilized with 'o sangue vertido pelo povo Moçambicano' [the blood spilled by the Mozambican people] (32). If this feminized region is the mother of the Mozambican nation, however, then her embodied representatives – individual mothers – are responsible for the tribalism among her (their) children. Tribalism is cast as a disease, the 'cancro [...] que corrói a sociedade' [cancer [...] that corrodes society] (39), a threat to the young, those that are 'vulneráveis, [...] permeáveis' [vulnerable, [...] permeable] (21). And, as Machel affirms, this sickness is contagious, and mothers are the vectors, since 'o tribalista não se forma já adulto' [the tribalist is not formed as an adult] (69). In fact, tribalism is passed to the victim at their youngest and most vulnerable: 'chupando o leite viciado com estas ideias' [suckling on the milk poisoned with these ideas] (69). Within a maternal woman's inscrutable body, the contagion is engendered, and she must thus be careful to feed her child not 'leite tribalista' [tribalist milk] (69), but rather 'o leite puro da mulher moçambicana' [the pure milk of the Mozambican woman] (72).

Machel's symbolic framing of breast milk, an essentially maternal body fluid normally associated with the nourishment and sustenance of life, as a source of societal breakdown brings the abject ambivalence toward female corporeality concealed within Mozambican independence discourse into relief. The maternal body is transposed onto the land, engendering life in Machel's vision of the birth of an independent nation, but hidden within its porous borders lurk the seeds of chaos and destruction. The act of breast-feeding, blurring the lines between self and other, subject and object, and inner and outer, shores up the permeability and instability of the female body – in short, its grotesqueness – while breast milk itself secretly pollutes, poisons and contaminates. The ability of female corporeality to trouble subjectivity via its grotesqueness becomes clear, demonstrating that within the objectifying trope of Mãe África lies the key not only to its own sub-version but also to the problematization of the collectivity it stands for: the implicit fear that with Mother Africa's ability to engender life comes the power to destroy it.

A Disorder that Threatens All Order: *Ualalapi*

Khosa's first and best-known novel, 1987's *Ualalapi*, foregrounds the disordering potential of the female grotesque as a pivotal narrative element. Loosely structured as a fragmented series of stories, textual images and diary entries that blur the lines between official history, fiction and myth, *Ualalapi* narrates the final days of Nguni emperor Ngungunhane's reign over the southern Mozambican Gaza Empire before its fall to the Portuguese in December 1895. The novel provides a scathing counternarrative to official discourses both colonial and anticolonial, imbuing the character of Ngungunhane with a profound ambivalence that rejects both his racially charged denigration under colonialism and his uncritical heroization by Frelimo – which reached fever pitch with the return of Ngungunhane's mortal remains from the Azores to Mozambique in 1985[13] – while underscoring the violence and brutal subjugation common to both the Portuguese and Nguni imperial projects.

At the literal and figurative centre of the text is the portentous death of Damboia, Ngungunhane's transgressive and childless aunt, who suffers an agonizingly excessive and prolonged menstruation that ultimately proves fatal (Khosa 1990: 61–72), foreshadowing the apocalyptic final defeat of the Gaza Empire by Portuguese forces. The complex layers of gendered grotesquery and abjection at play in Damboia's narrative, working within a late nineteenth-century contextual landscape of multilateral expansionist anxieties and paranoia allegorical of early Frelimo rule, represent an important precedent for Khosa's later uses of sex and gender as the loci of a disidentificatory discourse.

---

13   For examples of Frelimo's uncritical, and indeed often hypocritical, heroization of Ngungunhane see 'Ngungunhane: Herói da Luta Anticolonial' (1983), and the following articles, all published in Mozambican daily *Notícias* as part of a report on the transfer of Ngungunhane's remains: 'Ngungunyane Regressou à Pátria: Povo Recebeu Herói da Resistência' (1985), Naroromele (1985), A. Lopes (1985), Machel (1985).

True to these contextual environs, the death of Damboia foregrounds borders: the anxiogenic permeability of the body's boundaries, the encroachment of the inner on the outer, the polluting and poisoning effects of the body's effusions and effluvia, and the distortion of the corporeal surface. The opening lines of her narrative make these emphases clear:

> Tirando o dia, a hora, e pequenos pormenores, todos foram unânimes ao afirmar que Damboia, irmã mais nova de Muzila, morreu de uma menstruação de nunca acabar ao ficar três meses com as coxas toldadas de sangue viscoso e cheiroso que saía em jorros contínuos, impedindo-a de se movimentar para além do átrio da sua casa que ficava a uns metros da residência do imperador destas terras de Gaza que, a seu mando, colocou guardas reais em redor da casa de Damboia, impedindo olhares intrusos e queimando plantas aromáticas que não tiravam o odor nauseabundo do sangue que cobriu a aldeia durante aqueles meses fatídicos [...]. (Khosa 1990: 61)

> [Though disagreeing about the day, the time, and other minor details, all were unanimous in declaring that Damboia, the youngest Sister of Muzila, died of a never-ending menstruation which for three months left her thighs in a continual gush of sticky, pungent blood, preventing her from venturing farther than the forecourt of her house, situated but a short distance from the residence of the emperor of these lands of Gaza. Upon his orders, guards were placed round Damboia's house, to inhibit prying eyes and to burn aromatic plants which failed to remove the nauseating odor of the blood that covered the village during those fateful months.] (Brookshaw 2010: 382)[14]

Damboia's body is established as defined by its openness, unpredictability and unruliness, overflowing with a viscous fluid that nauseates with its smell and abundance, emanating via that most concealed and fetishized of bodily openings, the vagina. As cited above, Grosz asserts that body fluids play a crucial role in destabilizing the boundaries of the subject; by providing a perpetual reminder of the body's permeability, they 'affront a subject's aspiration toward autonomy and self-identity [and] attest to a certain irreducible "dirt" or disgust, a horror of the unknown or the unspecifiable that permeates, lurks, lingers, and at times leaks out of the body' (1994: 193–4). Body fluids are thus by nature grotesque, troubling

---

14   Unless otherwise stated, all translations of *Ualalapi* are from David Brookshaw's 2010 translation of the Damboia excerpt. Brookshaw's translations are henceforth indicated by the page numbers in parentheses after the square brackets.

the hermetic constancy on which the illusion of coherent selfhood relies, and reminding the subject of what is hidden, to borrow Bakhtin's terms, in the 'lower bodily stratum' (1984: 20).

Within this framework, menstrual blood is the grotesque body fluid *par excellence*: essentially female and thus always-already grotesque, inconsistently both liquid and solid, it represents an encroachment of the outside on what 'should' be inside, constituted by blood and tissue normally associated with injury and death, and containing within it no potential of new life as the blood of childbirth does and in fact directly negating that potential. It furthermore carries the specific near-universal cultural weight of the menstrual taboo, in which the blood is perceived as uniquely dirty and polluting (Kristeva 1982: 71). The traditional Tsonga belief systems of southern Mozambique are no exception to that taboo, holding menstrual blood and menstruating women as dangerous and pollutive presences that threaten human and animal life (Gengenbach 2003: 199). Paulina Chiziane has confirmed that these beliefs persist in contemporary southern Mozambican culture, stating that they pervade belief systems to the point that the burden of blame for all natural and social catastrophe is tangentially placed on women because 'é o sangue podre das menstruações, dos seus abortos, dos seus nado-mortos que infertiliza a terra, polui os rios, afasta as nuvens e causa epidemias, atrai inimigos e todas as catástrofes' [it is the rancid blood of menstruation, miscarriage and stillbirth that sterilizes the earth, pollutes rivers, scares away clouds and causes epidemics, and attracts enemies and all a manner of catastrophes] (1994: 12). Clear here is the implication that the ingrained cultural fear of menstruation and menstrual blood in the southern Mozambican context goes beyond anxiety over contamination or disease risk and speaks instead to a metaphysical horror, a perceived ever-present threat of chaos and destruction consistent with Kristeva's notion of menstrual blood as representing 'society threatened by its outside, life by death' (1982: 71). Machel's words on breast milk, another essentially female-coded body fluid, implicitly reflect this metaphysical and ultimately intangible fear and loathing.

Menstrual blood is furthermore troubling within patriarchal discourses because it signifies a failure of male virility, as Argentine novelist Luisa Valenzuela suggests in her essay 'Mis brujas favoritas' [My Favourite

Witches] (1982). For Valenzuela, who makes extensive use of the female grotesque in her work (Christoph 1995), the role of menstrual blood as confirming lack of pregnancy demonstrates the failure of individual men to comply with their 'tarea de fecundador' [fertilizing task], becoming a monthly reiteration of the fallibility and contingency of masculine power as a whole (1982: 90). If, as Butler proposes, the hierarchical gender binary is upheld by and in turn serves to uphold an equivalent matrix of compulsory reproductive heterosexuality (2007: 30–1), then menstrual blood provokes a doubly abject response, forcing acknowledgement of both the body's essential instability and the contingency of the natural-ized gender binary.

Damboia's presence in *Ualalapi* is thus potentially threatening on multiple levels. Her body's excessively violent and grotesque expulsion of pollutive menstrual blood troubles illusions of purity and corporeal integ-rity, while also signifying a dramatic negation of both maternal possibil-ity and male virility. The novel's subversive success, however, depends not only on Damboia's presence in itself, but also on the ways in which Khosa harnesses her destabilizing potential by exploiting the abject response her grotesque body engenders, a subtle manipulation that becomes clear as the narrative progresses.

As Damboia bleeds uncontrollably, disorder begins to creep into her village, accelerating as time passes: first, shells from the 'profundezas abissais do mar distante' (64) [fathomless depths of the distant ocean] (383) appear in the tops of trees, carried there by a wind so strong it tears the roofs from poor houses. A heavy rain falls for seven days and seven nights; yellow, thick and sticky, 'como a baba do caracol' (64) [like a snail's slime] (383). Then, in the viscous rain that accumulates on the ground, corpses appear, 'sem nome e rosto' [devoid of face or name], identified by the *curandeiros* as being 'de outros tempos esquecidos' (64–5) [those of other, time-forgotten ages] (384). The day after Damboia dies, following three months of bleeding, the five strongest men in the region wake up permanently impotent (65). There is a new rainfall, and new corpses appear, this time the stillborn babies 'das mulheres que sempre sonharam ter filhos' (72) [of women who had always yearned for children] (388). Finally, in the weeks that follow, chaos and destruction reign as the Portuguese lay siege to the village, causing starvation so severe that 'os homens devoram as mulheres e as mulheres devoram as crianças' (83) [the men devoured the women and the women devoured the children],[15] and ultimately bringing a violent end to Ngungunhane's sovereignty. This escalating upheaval of normality is, in turn, reflected back in the immediate sphere of Damboia's home, as the ground becomes saturated with blood; having nowhere to go, the blood sits on top of the soil, building up until it reaches ankle height (70). Damboia loses her mental faculties, sense of reality and ability to speak, and begins to 'andar de gatas e a trepar as paredes da casa, como um réptil em desespero' (70) [crawl about on all fours and to climb up the walls of the house, like some desperate reptile] (387) and to howl like a dog at night.

With these final corporeal and mental breakdowns, Damboia's body, losing any semblance of cohesion, crosses from its categorization within the everyday grotesque into the realm of the unintelligible abject. But while the abject realm, as Kristeva demonstrates, is usually ever-present but only on the furthest peripheries of consciousness, haunting the subject but only rarely able to truly threaten the subject's stability (1982: 1–2), in Khosa's narrative it comes to displace the subjective realm entirely. The concealed and sublimated threat and fear of menstruation and menstrual blood, manifest in the Tsonga menstrual taboo, are suddenly made excessively, grotesquely palpable. Anxieties over its pollutiveness are realized as the blood becomes ubiquitous, suffocating with its smell, and literally pollutes the village, spilling into its rivers, killing the fish, and turning the water red and undrinkable (71). Distinctions dissolve between land and sea, solid and liquid. Meanwhile, in an outward spiral from Damboia's body's own violent termination of maternal potential, the reproductive continuity on which binary gender identity depends collapses, as men eat women, women eat their own children, and impotence and stillbirth spread, recalling in hyperbolic fashion the gender-troubling power of menstrual blood proposed by Valenzuela. If the abject response reminds us of that which we 'permanently thrust aside in order to live' (Kristeva 1982: 3), then the

15   My translation.

vision of Nguni society presented by Khosa during and after Damboia's demise is one in which what is permanently thrust aside has taken over entirely, erasing individual and collective borders.

With this excessive fulfillment of concealed fears and anxieties, Khosa takes a customarily latent, symbolic and naturalized abject threat and makes it overt and literal. His casting of Damboia as locus of this act, as Owen has demonstrated, represents a radical reversal of the Mãe África figure (2014: 201). Enacting such a reversal allows Khosa to deconstruct this icon of Mozambican collectivity as conceived within the Frelimo nationalist imaginary – and thus to trouble the fabric of that collectivity itself – by exposing and discursively realizing the destructive threat that lies on the flip side of Mãe África's regenerative powers, and is implicit within Frelimo discourse.

This negation of artificial collectivity is underscored by the specific effects of Damboia's illness and death on members of the village both living and dead: the ancient corpses appearing 'sem nome e rosto' (64) [devoid of face or name] (384), and the stillborn babies that later surface, attach a profound and annihilating meaninglessness to the notion of individual and collective identities, while the escalating spread of infertility destroys all hope of collective futurity. In Damboia's narrative, the crushing meaninglessness that constitutes the peripheral presence of the abject realm expands into the subjective sphere, just as her nauseating blood spills from within the private confines of her home into the public space of the village. The precarious symbiotic dependence of Frelimo's imposed collectivity on the illusion of order and constancy, and thus the thorough falsity of its naturalized status, is here brought to the fore. The context of Ngungunhane's dying reign reaffirms this falsity by throwing up a mirror to Frelimo rule, vocalizing the hypocrisy of denouncing tribalism while enforcing a tacitly ethnocentric political sectarianism. By bringing the sublimated threat of the female grotesque into the concrete realm of the subject, Khosa is thus able to exploit the gendered abject to disidentificatory ends.

The End of the Line: 'A Praga'

Like *Ualalapi*, Khosa's short story 'A Praga' [The Plague], from his 1990 collection *Orgia dos Loucos* [*Orgy of the Deranged*] (2nd edn 2008), has the female grotesque at its symbolic core. But while *Ualalapi* relies on a vision of abject non-maternity for its negation of imposed identities, maternity and motherhood themselves provide the foundation for the escalating chaos of 'A Praga'. The story's opening scene describes protagonist Luandle's birth aboard his family's fishing boat, delivered as an urgent interior monologue:

> [...] desde que nascera no meio das águas do mar, por entre as ondas revoltas que acompanhavam o estertor da mãe que se atirava para um e outro lado do barco, a infelicidade abraçara-o de tal modo que o pai sentiu-se dorido a partir do momento em que vira a mãe contorcendo-se de dores, gritando, chorando, e, como todos os homens em tais situações, sentiu-se incapaz de a ajudar, [...] e os olhos esbulgalhados [do pai] [...] viu a mulher de pernas abertas e a criança emergindo por entre as coxas, não com a cabeça primeiro, como milhares de crianças, mas com os pés, como se em terra firme quisesse pisar, e como não houvesse tal espaço sólido a criança esperneou de tal modo que o resto do corpo saiu por si do ventre da mãe que gritava e chorava, suplicando ao marido que a salvasse da dor, coisa que o homem não conseguia fazer, limitando-se a cortar o cordão umbilical que pendeu por entre as coxas da mulher até à morte, e tentar tirar o sangue que cobria o fundo do barco e que trepava pelo mastro, atingindo a vela branca, sem que o homem fosse capaz de limpar [...] (2008: 17–18)

> [[...] ever since he had been born amid the ocean's waters, between the lurching waves that accompanied the death-rattles of his mother who was thrown from one side of the boat to the other, unhappiness had embraced him so thoroughly that his father felt himself stricken from the very moment he saw his son's mother writhing in pain, howling, crying, and, like all men in such situations, felt unable to help her, [...] and his bulging eyes just stared at his wife, open-legged, as the child emerged from between her thighs, not headfirst, like thousands of children do, but with his feet, as if wanting to tread firm ground, and since there was no such solid place the child kicked his way out of his mother's womb as she howled and cried, pleading with her husband to save her from the pain, something he could not do, limiting himself instead to cutting the umbilical cord that would hang between the woman's thighs until her death, and trying to clear out the blood that covered the entire inside of the boat and had crept up to the mast, reaching right up to the white sail, the man unable to clean it up [...]]]

The instability and disorientation evoked by the sea that constitutes the characters' immediate environs is here furthered by Khosa's use of a stream-of-consciousness style and by the characters' anonymity. The focal point of this opening scene, however, is Luandle's unnamed mother's struggle to deliver her baby amidst that unstable landscape, an act that in turn distills the scene's chaos into her maternal body.

As detailed above, childbirth, along with death, is for Bakhtin a process that brings the body's grotesque elements to the fore, forcing acknowledgement of its inherent openness, instability and changeability by exaggerating the body's natural state of perpetual metamorphosis (1984: 25–6). Nancy Christoph expands upon Bakhtin's association between childbirth and the grotesque in her work on Luisa Valenzuela, noting that labour enacts the blurring of the strictly demarcated lines between self and other, since 'the inner becomes the outer when the child traverses the boundaries of the mother's body and is born' (Christoph 1995: 366). Kristeva, meanwhile, suggests that childbirth provokes an abject response in part because it evokes death in its conception as 'a violent act of expulsion through which the nascent body tears itself away from the matter of maternal insides', leaving the postpartum organs in a perceived state of permanent damage (1982: 101–2). The placenta becomes the decaying embodiment of abjection; both an essential organ and waste tissue, part of the maternal body and expelled from it. Viewed through the lens of these theories, Luandle's birth is particularly grotesque, taking all these contributing factors to an excessive level: born in a footling breech position, Luandle only delivers without assistance because he kicks his way out so violently, and after the birth his mother is left with the umbilical cord hanging between her thighs, suggesting a retained placenta.

The dangling umbilical cord, which remains hanging between Luandle's mother's legs until her death fifteen years after her son's birth, provides a visible reminder of a disordered, violent and incomplete labour; furthermore, it suggests that the placenta remains decaying in her body, an abject presence that resists expulsion. If normal childbirth is especially grotesque because it temporarily highlights the body's metamorphic processes and inherent permeability, Luandle's mother's permanently parturient state makes her an inescapable spectre of metamorphosis, permeability and decay. Her body, like Damboia's, becomes the locus of the chaos that spirals out through Khosa's narrative. Having a maternal body serve this role, however, has an important ramification for the text's outcome that distinguishes Khosa's use of the character from that of Damboia in *Ualalapi*. While Damboia's narrative troubles the false collectivity emblematized by the Mãe África trope by confronting the reader with the sublimated threat of non-maternity on the flip side of that trope, Luandle's mother's role attaches disorder, affliction and hopelessness to the concept of maternity itself. Using Luandle's mother's grotesque maternal body as a point of departure, with 'A Praga' Khosa thus enacts a nihilistic negation of the reproductive futurism at the heart of Frelimo's nation-building project.

Following Luandle's mother's eerily quiet and tranquil death (Khosa 2008: 19–20), itself demonstrating a blurring of the lines between life and death that precipitates the breakdown of human boundaries to come, Luandle and his father witness their world's collapse into a state of primordial chaos. Temporal and spatial order become distorted as their attempts to fish yield nothing but the 'restos de naufrágios do tempo de Vasco de Gama que vinham à superfície sem grandes esforços' [remains of shipwrecks from the time of Vasco de Gama, which came to the surface almost effortlessly] (21). Resolving to travel inland in search of survival, they find a stretch of land to cultivate and experience a short-lived period of security; Luandle meets his wife, Nyelete, and she becomes pregnant. Toward the end of her pregnancy, however, the region is devastated by floods, and the family is forced to take refuge in a tree on their land, where Nyelete gives birth exposed to the pouring rain, her blood running down the branches of the trees and mingling with the waters below (23–4). Luandle, Nyelete, and their son are rescued by helicopter, while Luandle's father commits suicide by letting go of the helicopter's ladder, allowing the water to swallow him (25). Luandle's family begins life in a new village, but within years famine strikes and Nyelete succumbs to starvation while searching for food for her son (28). The story closes on Luandle's son, Kufeni, eating the scabs from his own sore-ridden body in an attempt to stave off hunger (29).

Seen through the lens of Frelimo's reliance on a utopic future centred on the imagined image of a symbolic Child, the fate of Luandle's family accrues significance as a disidentificatory narrative. Within Frelimo rhetoric, children were the 'continuadores' of the Revolution, the means by which socialist thought would be perpetuated through future generations to build the ideal, unified Mozambican society. A speech given by Machel at a public rally in July 1975, weeks after independence was finalized, makes the centrality of children to the post-independence project clear: children are 'a seiva da Nação' [the sap of the nation], those who will 'fazer a Revolução' [realize the Revolution] and 'liquidar o imperialismo' [eliminate imperialism] (1975: 27). In his address to the first Frelimo party conference to take place after independence, Machel repeats this sentiment, adding that 'a juventude é a esperança do progresso da nossa revolução, é a continuação da nossa luta' [young people are the beacons of hope for the progress of our revolution, the continuity of our struggle] (*Documentos* 1976: 22). As the post-independence conflict intensifies, so too does the focus on children; in the series of Machel's speeches given in 1983 and referenced earlier in this chapter, children are referred to repeatedly as the 'continuadores da Revolução' [*continuadores* of the Revolution], the 'soldados do 25 de Setembro' [soldiers of 25 September] (iv: 30). Later in the same year, at Machel's fiftieth birthday celebrations, *Tempo* reports that the president dedicated part of his speech to the importance that the Mozambican woman, 'como mãe, desempenha na educação do filho, para consolidar a consciência patriótica e avivar o espírito combativo' [as a mother, plays in the education of the child, consolidating patriotic consciousness and arousing a combative spirit], emphasizing that the nation's first priority must be to 'criar mais continuadores da nossa luta' [create more *continuadores* for our struggle] (Manuel 1983a: 20). Two months later, *Tempo* publishes a full-page photograph of two smiling toddlers, with a one-word caption: 'FUTURO' [FUTURE].

The reproductive futurism and natalism at the foundation of this rhetoric represent, as Lee Edelman proposes, the ultimate grand narrative, an 'ideological Möbius strip' – that is to say, an inevitably formulaic and endlessly circular discourse – that strictly demarcates the limits of political thought within the matrix of compulsory heterosexuality (2004: 2). The symbolic Child that underpins such narratives 'serves to regulate political discourse [...] by compelling such discourse to accede in advance to the reality of a collective future whose figurative status we are never permitted

to acknowledge or even address' (Edelman 2004: 11). As Frelimo's relentless drive toward the creation of 'mais continuadores' [more *continuadores*]
makes clear, however, this symbolic Child remains in a state of permanent deferral, a 'perpetual horizon' (Edelman 2004: 3) that is never fully
embodied and never figures within 'the lived experiences of any historical
children' (11).

In the context of the Mozambican post-independence conflict, this singular focus on future potentialities, embodied by the permanently deferred
Child, seems particularly empty of meaning. As Carolyn Nordstrom demonstrates in her affecting ethnography of the conflict, one of the defining
features of the war was its destruction of futurity: the inextricability of
the 'spectacle of violence' from 'its aftermath, its enduring reality' and its
ability to annihilate 'the very sense of future that gives definition and direction to people's lives' (1997: 130). For Renamo, then, the future Child of
Frelimo nationalism does indeed become very real – as a target for destruction. Meanwhile, in the face of this slow but determined dismantling of
Mozambican futurity by Renamo, enacted in part through the targeting of
children as either the objects or witnesses of violence, Frelimo's blinkered
rhetorical focus on an imagined and idealized future serves only to elide
the lived realities of millions of Mozambicans.

With the character of Kufeni, the last descendent of Luandle's mother,
Khosa exposes this tension between the imagined Child on Frelimo's 'perpetual horizon' and the lived realities of Mozambican children and adults
in the post-independence context. The name 'Kufeni', meaning 'death'
in several Bantu languages including Ronga, already holds within it the
negation of earthly futurity; when Kufeni is seen for the last time, his
teeth red and crusted with the abject waste of his own body, this negation is viscerally confirmed. The line of narrative begun with Luandle's
grotesquely incomplete birth comes to an end in the abrupt and equally
grotesque closed loop of Kufeni's autophagy, fulfilling the threat of disorder and hopelessness attached to Luandle's mother's maternal body as
the boundaries between the subjective and abject realms collapse in on
themselves. The premature deaths of both Luandle's mother and Nyelete
furthermore reveal and emphasize the compulsory female sacrifice inherent
in natalist thought. With the story's end, Khosa thus enacts a wholesale

disavowal of the imposed maternity and reproductive futurity axiomatic to post-independence Frelimo discourse, while casting light on the real lives concealed behind it.

Obliterated Speech: 'O Prémio'

This use of the parturient body as a point of departure for challenging the blinkered discourses of reproductive futurism constitutes the narrative of 'O Prémio' [The Prize], the brief opening story of the *Orgia dos Loucos* collection. In partial contrast to 'A Praga' and to Damboia's narrative in *Ualalapi*, which foreground the externality of the grotesque body – the permeability of its boundaries, the encroachment of the inner on the outer and the distortion of external features – as a means of challenging naturalized collective identities, 'O Prémio' centres around the internality of the body and the interior obliteration of individual subjectivity via the experience of extreme pain. By bringing pain, a deeply private experience, to the page, Khosa is able to evoke a state beyond identity, a state that troubles the construct of subjective integrity upon which political collectivity relies. At the same time, Khosa's writing of pain puts words to the violence that dominated post-independence Mozambique by appealing to an affective response that transcends official narrative and discourse.

'O Prémio' portrays an anonymous woman's desperate attempt to win the prize of the title, a hamper of baby essentials donated by an unmentioned benefactor and given only to babies born on 1 June, Frelimo's 'Dia da Criança' [Day of the Child], by holding back the birth of her son until after midnight – only to give birth five minutes too early.[16] Khosa's descriptions of her agony dominate the narrative:

16   The premise of the story was a real event in Mozambique's capital (taking place at the New Year rather than on the Dia da Criança), at least until 1975; see 'Primeiro Bébé de 1975 em Lourenço Marques: Tradição Johnson & Johnson' (1975: 9). The

Não pode gritar, tem que aguentar. Cerra os dentes, agarra os lençóis com os dedos empapados de suor que escorre pelo corpo como formigas emergindo dos casulos [...]. As formigas percorrem corpo, sobem e descem pelas coxas, trepam as colinas, atingem o cocuruto, descem, dançam, brincam e atiram-se ao rosto. Fecha os olhos. Não suporta a dor, a imagem, não pode gritar. Tem que aguentar. [...] Ela sente o som, o baque contínuo, perpétuo. E imagina, imagina tudo. Vê a menina da infância brincando no campo, alheia a tudo até o momento em que ouve o silvo mortal da serpente que se aproxima, veloz, mortífera. A menina pára, não consegue mexer-se, está paralisada, e nada ouve a não ser o baque contínuo, incessante, do coração. [...] Não, pensa, e foge da imagem, tenta pensar na mãe. Não consegue. A dor nada deixa imaginar. (Khosa 2008: 9–10)

[She cannot cry out, she has to endure this. She grits her teeth, claws at the sheets with her fingers soaked in the sweat that runs over her body like ants coming out of their nest [...]. The ants crawl over her body, up and down her thighs, climb up her spine, reach her head, come back down, dancing, taunting, and throw themselves into her face. She closes her eyes. She cannot withstand this pain, these visions, she cannot cry out. She has to endure this. [...] She feels that sound, the continuous, perpetual thudding. And she imagines, imagines everything. She sees a little girl, an infant, playing in the fields, unaware of everything until suddenly she hears the deadly hissing of a snake that approaches her, fast, lethal. The little girl stops, she cannot move, she is paralyzed, and she hears nothing but the perpetual, incessant thudding of her heart. [...] No, she thinks, and flees from the vision, trying to think about her mother. But she cannot. The pain does not let her imagine anything.]

The woman's pain is unbearable and relentless. Her attempts to dissociate as a means of coping with the pain only serve to lead back to the pain itself, severing her powers of imagination and abstract thought, alienating her from her memories. Reading this description through the lens of Elaine Scarry's work on pain as a psychosocial phenomenon shores up its latent alignment with a specific way in which pain is inflicted and experienced: in the context of torture. As Scarry affirms, the essential aspect of the pain administered during torture is that it deconstructs the victim's subjectivity (1985: 18). It is 'world-destroying' (29), obliterating the capacity for basic thought, memory, affect or feeling of anything other than the

---

1975 prize was awarded to a woman named Albertina Calisto Maculube and her baby girl.

pain itself; when we talk of 'seeing stars', this explosion of consciousness is what is evoked (30). The aim is not to elicit information, but rather to 'deconstruct the prisoner's voice' (20), enacting 'an annihilating negation' of selfhood (36). In service of this objective, the torturer makes a weapon of every external reference point available to the victim, until 'the world is reduced to a single room or set of rooms' (40); then 'there is no wall, no window, no door, no bathtub, no refrigerator, no chair, no bed' (41); ultimately, even the victim's own body is experienced as an agent of pain (47). The boundaries between the external and internal, the self and not-self, are eroded until, in Scarry's words, the pain is experienced 'as either the contraction of the universe down to the immediate vicinity of the body or as the body swelling to fill the universe' (35). The lived experience of identity becomes utterly irrelevant, leaving nothing beyond the body's agony.

This notion of torture as a violent unmaking of the external world is both reflected in and complicated by Nordstrom's work on the atrocities of the Mozambican post-independence conflict, whose prerogatives she identifies as 'attack[ing] the fonts of humanity, sever[ing] person from personhood and individual from identity' by 'destroying wholeness, sabotaging comprehension, violating boundaries, and doing all these in the most excessive ways' (1997: 164). Chief among the contributing factors to these effects is the violation of the domestic sphere, the turning inside-out of the home so that 'the normal and the life sustaining become deadly weapons' (167). Nordstrom cites by way of example a story from Lina Magaia's *Dumba Nengue* (1988), a collection of post-independence wartime testimonies, in which a woman is made to witness her brother being forced to cut her husband's throat (32–4). Her brother is made to use the family's axe as the weapon, while her husband is forced to lie against their mortar, traditionally used to pound grain. All that is familiar and everyday becomes, in an instant, an implement of terror and pain: not only the axe and mortar, but also the woman's brother himself (Nordstrom 1997: 167–8). This grotesque distortion of the quotidian becomes a way of ensuring the devastating pervasiveness of the act of torture, planting the seeds for a trauma that will be renewed 'with each glance at a mortar' (Nordstrom 1997: 168). In partial contrast, then, to Scarry's framework, which relies on a definition of torture limited to one victim and one room, Nordstrom notes that in the context of the public spectacle of pain that defined the Mozambican conflict the world is not 'reduced to a single room', but rather torture and terror '[expand] to the world' (170). Where, for Scarry, 'the obscene and pathetic drama of torture and power is relegated to the prisoner's cell' (Nordstrom 1997: 170), in the Mozambican case 'this drama comes to define the world at large' (170).

The extreme violation of the domestic sphere, identified by Scarry as a means of destroying identity and developed by Nordstrom in the light of Mozambican specificities as a way in which terror comes to constitute everyday reality, is central to Khosa's framing of his protagonist's experience of childbirth. In the opening lines of the story, the woman's bed sheets 'tomam a forma de serpentes na muda interminável, colinas em planícies do fim dos tempos, vales pré-históricas, cordilheiras da idade dos dinossauros' [become endlessly writhing serpents, the peaks and lowlands of an apocalyptic landscape, prehistoric valleys, mountain ranges from the age of the dinosaurs] (2008: 9). The floor becomes '[um] mar de suor que se ligava aos lagos por canais sem margens' [an ocean of sweat fed by lakes through burst channels] (11). Looking to the walls for some illusion of stability, she sees 'rostos de feiticeiros, movimentos de camaleões, serpentes em desespero, gatos miando, pernas de símios gigantes' [the faces of sorcerors, movements of chameleons, desperate serpents, cats screeching, the legs of gigantic apes] (11). Rather than providing her with a sense of anchored familiarity and comfort, her domestic surroundings become utterly alien and frightening, another uncontrollable and unpredictable agent of her torment.

What draws Khosa's descriptions more firmly in line with the points of departure from Scarry's theory identified by Nordstrom, however, is the expansion of his protagonist's pain to increasingly external points of reference. Her attempt to invoke the image of her mother, the embodiment of the domestic sphere, serves to turn her mother into her torturer, with whom she pleads, 'não mais! Não quero mais! Não posso! Não aguento, mãe!' [no more! I don't want this any more! I can't! I can't bear it, mother!] (11). Toward the end of the piece, a further ostensible source of caring and comfort, a hospital nurse, becomes yet another agent of pain, taking on 'o rosto de uma feiticeira' [the face of a sorceror], her smile like that of 'uma torcionária' [a torturer] (13). Just as the woman described in Nordstrom's text comes to associate her brother with torture, murder and trauma, for Khosa's protagonist every affective relation leads only to more pain.

The nature of the relationship between pain and death described by Khosa is a further way in which his writing of the story's protagonist evokes torture while reflecting back on the specificities of Mozambican experience. Khosa's association of extreme pain and death is made clear by his emphasis on the character's psychic erasure and her annihilation of selfhood; indeed, the link is made explicit when she collapses, incapacitated, into '[a] posição da morte' [the position of death] (11). Scarry identifies this psychosocial connection between extreme pain and death as central to the world-destroying experience of torture, noting that both phenomena obliterate meaningful consciousness, representing 'the most intense forms of negation, the purest expressions of the anti-human, of annihilation, of total aversiveness' (1985: 31). Experiencing or witnessing torture, like confronting death, challenges the individual's sense of a private internal self by underscoring the absolute permeability and vulnerability of the borders by which that self is demarcated.

This ability of severe pain to bring the oblivion of death to the fore is strongly manifest in the testimonies of survivors of the post-independence war, in which the lines between confronting and experiencing pain, torture and death become almost indefinable. In her analysis of testimonies from rural Mozambican women refugees, Tina Sideris identifies among them a specific and consistent state of being referred to as *vavisa imoya*, a Tsonga term roughly translatable as 'spirit injury' (2003: 716). Defined by Sideris as a conglomeration of traumatic psychological and somatic symptoms including 'preoccupation with individual violation and social destruction, grief, physical deterioration, bodily distress, loss of vitality, loss of efficacy to sustain life, loss of a sense of continuity of self, feeling lost, and suicidal ideation', one woman describes living with spirit injury as 'worse than those other things of not sleeping, dreaming, being afraid', adding that 'if the spirit is hurt you get thinner and thinner' (716). Another woman says of the atrocities that 'if you hear and see all those kinds of things, you are always in trouble, the spirit will not be okay. To see killing as the Renamo killed, you cannot be ok, you are spiritually dead. [...] Your heart is sore but you are spiritually dead' (716). What is clear from these testimonies is that the Mozambican experience of atrocity and torture, itself far more complex than the definition used by Scarry, also entails a more complex traumatic legacy. Where Scarry emphasizes pain as a means by which death is evoked and brought psychically closer, the witness testimonies cited by Sideris demonstrate a radical and enduring breakdown of the boundaries between life and death, a collapsing of the social taxonomies that define self and other; subject and object; victim, witness and perpetrator.

Khosa's use of labour pain as the frame for his narrative offers a unique means of communicating this context-specific collapse of boundaries, linked back to Bakhtin's characterization of childbirth as a grotesque event: the inherent property of labour as blurring the lines between subject and object, manifest in its lack of a definable agent or perpetrator. Presenting the reader with a torture that has no torturer, no referent, captures the experience of living in a world where torture and terror have expanded to normality; where uncertainty reigns as the individual's life comes to depend on the constant reassessment of an unknowable and diffuse enemy dispersed, as Nordstrom details, over an increasingly complex and ill-defined network of motivations, loyalties and alliances (1997: 46–8). Distilling the terrorizing totality of 'low-intensity' village warfare into the body of one woman, whose experience is narrated by an unknown third person and witnessed by an unknown audience, pushes back against the obstructions to representation inherent within pain and terror. In the process of the narrative, Khosa thus begins to resist the power of terror-warfare: speaking it as a means of exorcism, provoking an affective response as a means of denunciation.

This condemnation of the atrocities at the hands of Renamo is not the only outcome of Khosa's use of the parturient body in 'O Prémio', however. His character's story also serves as a critique of the more subtle and insidious violences inflicted on post-independence Mozambique's citizens by both Frelimo, centred around the reproductive futurism and natalism outlined above, and the neoliberal donor culture that pervaded Mozambique from the late 1980s onward (Arnfred 2011: 130–1), represented here by the absent 'prize' of the story's title. These denunciations are expressed most clearly in the story's bathetic closing lines. While Niyi Afolabi interprets the protagonist's reaction to her newborn son as an indifference that suggests a climate of growing materialism (2010: 92), in the context of the preceding narrative her reaction seems more dysphoric than indifferent: 'Sombras. [...] Névoa. Tudo a desaparecer. [...] O tempo perdido ... A cabeça enterra-se na almofada. [...] É uma criança bonita, ouve uma voz distante, longínqua ... As lágrimas saltam dos olhos, correm pelos lençóis, soluça, desmaia' [Shadows. [...] Fog. Everything is disintegrating. [...] All that wasted time ... She buries her head in the pillow. [...] What a lovely baby, she hears a far-off voice say, in the distance ... The tears fall from her eyes, run down to the sheets; she sobs, collapses] (13). In the face of the protagonist's physical agony and her psychological distress at having failed to win the hamper, her baby, the single potential symbol of hope and futurity in the story, comes to embody nothing more than her profound trauma and the abject hopelessness ahead of her family. Ostensibly the *raison d'être* of Frelimo's nation-building project and certainly a linchpin of their rhetoric, the baby will have no more recourse to collectivity, Khosa implies, than his anonymous mother; neither will he benefit from the empty 'philanthropy' of private corporations. Moreover, the mother herself, having sacrificed her corporeal and psychic integrity to fulfill the duty of procreation imposed on Mozambican women by the Frelimo government, is left materially and discursively abandoned by both socialist state and capitalist institution.

As the embodied locus of intersecting political meanings, the protagonist's parturient body thus provides Khosa with a powerful focal point for a pluralistic condemnation of imposed political violences, identities and imperatives. The author's casting of labour pain as a process of psychosomatic disintegration exposes the collapsing of social and individual boundaries brought about by Renamo's wartime atrocities in a condensed and communicable manner, while the political and economic implications of childbirth itself enable him to use the character to speak to an extreme disillusionment with Frelimo's perpetuation of a discourse of reproductive futurism and at the same time to deny the ethical legitimacy of the party's neoliberal detractors. Evoking a torture that is without direct agent, but that is intensified for its victim by the desperation arising from her economic need, allows the author to resist the interpellation of his narrative into any one system of politics or ideology, even as it imbues the story with a deeply political message. Additionally, just as the grotesque bodies of Damboia and Luandle's mother resist independence-era constructs of femininity and maternity by negating, rather than engendering, political futurities, in 'O Prémio' the protagonist's corporeal manifestation of a specifically gendered pain serves to expose the truth behind the identities imposed on women in the wake of Mozambican independence, while the dysphoric apathy she displays toward her newborn son affectively refuses those social and ideological roles.

No Horizon: 'A Orgia dos Loucos'

'A Orgia dos Loucos' [The Orgy of the Deranged], the climactic centrepiece of the *Orgia dos Loucos* collection, differs from the three texts explored above in that its focal point is not the grotesque female or maternal body *per se*. Rather, the story centres on the non-body: the hopeless and future-less corporealities signified by ghosts, corpses and dismembered body parts. With their abject embodiment of absolute hopelessness, these non-bodies take the private and internal torment of 'O Prémio' and explode it out-wards until, like the terror-warfare of the post-independence conflict, it 'expands to the world' (Nordstrom 1997: 169). Describing the search of one man, Maposse, for his son João following a sudden ambiguous disaster presumed to be a shooting or explosion, the simple narrative of 'A Orgia dos Loucos' leads the reader through a gruesome dystopian landscape of dismembered and decaying cadavers, blood and viscera. Traumatized by the discovery of his wife Maria's naked and mutilated corpse, Maposse comes to believe that he is dead, haunting a post-apocalyptic wasteland. When he finds his son at the end of the story, he believes him to be dead, too: 'Ninguém está vivo. Estamos mortos. Somos espíritos angustiados à procura duma sepultura decente' [Nobody is alive. We are all dead. We are restless spirits in search of a decent burial] (Khosa 2008: 59). Ultimately, the reality of the situation is left uncertain, denying the reader any sense of narrative stability or closure.

The text's central motif is that of the irrevocable loss of physical integrity, made clear by Maposse's discovery of the body of his wife, Maria:

> Maria? ... As mãos ensanguentadas percorrem o corpo, detêm-se nos olhos fora das órbitas, deslizam pelos arranhões sem fim, contornam as contusões dispersas, atêm-se nas coxas dilaceradas; os olhos tremem, a cabeça da mulher resvala pelo tronco nu como uma maçala de dimensões pré-históricas. Estás nua ... tocaram-te ... (Khosa 2008: 54–5)

> [Maria? ... His bloodied hands run over her body, lingering over her hollow eyesockets, sliding over her countless wounds, outlining the bruises spread over her skin, pause on her slashed thighs; his eyes flicker, the head of his wife dangling over her naked torso like a gigantic, grotesque fruit. You're naked ... they touched you ...]

Leaving his wife in order to search for João, Maposse stumbles upon a street filled with dismembered body parts:

> Está no gaveto de uma rua dilacerada e pejada de cadáveres conhecidos e desconhecidos. A rua é um talho de carne humana. Braços sem dono, pernas suspensas em argolas inexistentes, corações em plásticos de areia, fígados amontoados como alforrecas entre os despojos de um naufrágio, pénis suspensos em hastes que proclamam o fim da criação, mãos emergindo de pântanos de sangue, rostos imóveis, distantes, angustiados, aterrorizados, rostos sem vida. O homem afasta-se. Corre. Foge. Grita. Tropeça. Cai. Rebola. Desmaia. João! ... (55)

> [He finds himself on the corner of a blasted street, hung with familiar and unfamiliar corpses. The road is a butcher's shop of human flesh. Disembodied arms, legs hung from nonexistent hooks, hearts in the plasticlike wrapping of dust, livers swaying like jellyfish among the ruins of a shipwreck, penises hoisted up on poles, signalling the end of creation, hands reaching out from swamps of blood; motionless, distant, agonized, terrorized faces, faces devoid of life. The man turns away. Runs, Flees. Howls. Stumbles. Falls. Tumbles. Collapses. João! ...]

With these two encounters, two complex and interrelated outcomes converge to create the story's disidentificatory effect. The first is the dramatic abject response engendered by the presence of corpses and fragmented bodies. As Kristeva affirms, the corpse represents the darkest limit of the abject, its *sine qua non*: that which every other abject element references (1982: 3). Corpses, in themselves, do not 'signify death', but rather evoke it affectively; they '*show me* what I permanently thrust aside in order to live' (3). The corpse is 'the most sickening of wastes, [...] a border that has encroached upon everything. [...] It is death infecting life' (3–4). Completely alone, and immersed in the decaying detritus of mass death, Maposse is left with no means with which to demarcate the boundaries of his physical or psychic self, becoming, to use Kristeva's words, 'without border' (4). As Maposse takes in the spectacle of dismembered limbs, organs and genitals, this loss of physical integrity is both externalized and absorbed. Ultimately, he loses his sense of body schema entirely, becoming, to some extent, a non-body; having corporeality, but unable to integrate it into any sense of subjectivity, and espousing instead the non-identity of a ghost.

The second outcome of Maposse's encounters with the corporeal destruction that surrounds him is the literal and symbolic destruction of futurities, both individual and collective. The possible rape of Maposse's wife represents an extreme violation of her corporeal and psychic integrity, but it also violates the fabric of the family unit; as Sideris demonstrates, in the Mozambican context especially, rape is a trauma that ripples outward, fragmenting interpersonal ties (2003: 721). This specific cultural weight was atrociously exploited by Renamo, who often forced family members to witness rapes in a deliberate bid 'to undermine personal integrity and family relations in their most profound sense' (Nordstrom 1997: 127). Maria's mutilation further deepens this individual and familial damage by distorting the signifiers that constitute her outward identity, violently severing the ties between identity and physicality, a form of individual and familial trauma identified by Nordstrom as widespread in the post-independence conflict and its aftermath (1997: 165). The forcible obliteration of Maria's identity and subjectivity destabilizes, in turn, the identities of both Maposse and João, as the family's collective futurity is traumatically curtailed.

The 'butcher's shop' of mutilated body parts stumbled upon by Maposse presents a further assault on individual and collective futurities, grotesquely externalizing the hopelessness embodied by the protagonist. The dismembered penises are a particularly chilling reminder of this finality, representing in viscerally literal terms the disarmament of the phallocentric family unit and the severance of reproductive futurity. Indeed, Khosa underscores this point with his wording: the penises are 'suspensos em hastes que proclamam o fim da criação' [hoisted up on poles, signalling the end of creation] (55). Physical integrity is no longer a thinkable possibility, and without it both identity and futurity are obliterated. When Maposse and João are finally reunited, the possibility of any future, for Maposse, is already shattered; all that is left is destruction, decay and the flies that darken the sky.

By integrating the most outward expressions of abjection with this absolute destruction of reproductive futurity, Khosa is able to communicate the annihilating horror of the post-independence atrocities while simultaneously denying the legitimacy of Frelimo's utopic discourses of futurity. Like Kufeni from 'A Praga' and the anonymous baby barely featured in 'O Prémio', the character of João exposes the disparity between the permanently deferred Child of Frelimo rhetoric and the real lives of historical Mozambican children, while the pseudo-corporeality that Maposse exhibits makes clear the absolute meaninglessness of dogmatic political collectivity in the face of monolithic national trauma. As in 'O Prémio', in 'A Orgia dos Loucos' Khosa refuses to name a single perpetrator or agent, resisting ideological interpellation. But while *Ualalapi*, 'A Praga', and 'O Prémio' make use of abjective and affective responses to strengthen their impact while retaining an impression of externality, of a spatial or temporal world outside of their narrative limits, 'A Orgia dos Loucos' fulfills its unsettling potential by combining those responses with a sense of expansive and infinite meaninglessness, hinging on the absolute negation of futurity or hope. Mozambique, Khosa implies, can no longer look toward a perpetual horizon, because in the wake of the post-independence conflict, that horizon no longer exists.

Conclusion: Not Yet / That's Not It

This third chapter has sought to elucidate the very different means by which Noémia de Sousa and Ungulani Ba Ka Khosa engage in shared processes of disidentification with the cultural narratives of the colonial and anticolonial, and post-independence periods, respectively. De Sousa's work has frequently been cast, implicitly and sometimes explicitly, as a weak and artistically straightforward imitation of that of her fellow (male) anticolonial poets. Directly challenging that notion, this chapter has shown that reading her work through the concepts of 'disidentification', 'differential consciousness' or 'conciencia de la mestiza', developed in the pioneering works of black, Chicana and Latina/o feminists and queer theorists, reveals the poet's employment of a complex variety of linguistic and symbological strategies in her poems, which serve to resist the racial and sexual politics of the colonial regime while protesting and refusing the gender hegemony within the anticolonial imaginary. De Sousa's work appears to engage with colonial and anticolonial inscriptions on the female body, only to slide out from under that body, resisting corporeal interpellation.

Khosa, on the other hand, presents his readers with bodies that are excessively corporeal, grotesque, damaged and dying as a means of giving voice to the horrors of the post-independence conflict while simultaneously denouncing Frelimo's harmful fiction of national unity and the imposed identities therein. The disidentificatory drive of his work is staked in the gendered female body, which here represents a surface that is both endlessly polysemic and deeply rooted in the embodied realities of the quotidian, allowing him to speak at the levels of symbology and materiality. Mãe África, then, becomes for both de Sousa and Khosa an instrument for inscribing and underscoring Norma Alarcón's resistant epithet of 'not yet/ that's not it' (1996: 129).

Gendered subversion was shown in this chapter to offer a means of challenging cultural narratives more broadly, and it is this concept that will be carried forward in Chapter 4. Rather than examining processes of gender and sexual literary subversion in themselves, this next chapter will instead explore the ways that prose fiction writers Lília Momplé and Suleiman Cassamo have made use in their work of the functions of corporeality in colonial and post-independence narratives of death, life and the body, using Achille Mbembe's theory of necropolitics to inform its analytical approach. In order to properly contextualize this new angle, and to situate necropolitical theory in Mozambican specificities, the chapter will begin by reviewing the symbolic and material roles of death and life in discursive textual flash points from Portuguese imperial and Mozambican histories, from the early expansionist period onward.

CHAPTER 4

States of Exception: Suicide, Hunger and Haunting in Lília Momplé and Suleiman Cassamo

> For those who are haunted, this kind of death becomes a way of life.
> — STUART J. MURRAY, 'Thanatopolitics' (2006: 106)

Africa, as Achille Mbembe affirms, has been implicitly bound up with death in the Western imaginary since the early days of European expansionism, figuring as 'a bottomless abyss where everything is noise, yawning gap, and primordial chaos' (2001: 3). This singular and enduring Western vision of Africa, in all its countless historical and contemporary permutations, has exerted a persistent influence both on the ways that the West has reified and rationalized its imperial presence on the continent, and on the discursive frameworks it has used to understand the processes and events that followed in colonialism's wake. The association of Africa with death contributes heavily to the failure of the Western academy to productively theorize the dynamics of power at work on the continent, a shortcoming outlined in the Introduction to this study, since canonical theories of social and political power structures have tended to centre life as the guiding light of political thought; Michel Foucault's concept of biopolitics is chief among these frameworks. In order to understand the realities of contemporary postcolonial nation-states and occupied territories, Mbembe suggests, we must ask more of theories that centre life in this way, untangling the role played within them by the 'right to kill' (2003: 12), and problematizing the assumed mutual exclusivity of death and life (2003: 21–2). Rather than engaging with a strictly biopolitical framework, then, we must build on it, privileging death in order to develop a methodology that he terms 'necropolitics'.

While Mbembe uses the terms 'necropower' and 'necropolitics' specifically to describe post-millennial political life, in this chapter I will use them in an expanded sense to denote a loosely biopolitical methodology that centres death, in order to examine the roles of life, death and mortality in Mozambican recent history as portrayed in selected short stories and novellas by Lília Momplé (1935–) and Suleiman Cassamo (1962–). While Momplé and Cassamo were born into different generations and employ markedly different literary aesthetics, their respective published corpuses are more or less contemporaneous. This simultaneous intergenerationality and contemporaneity adds a further element of critical interest to comparison of the authors' work, in terms of the impact of their distinct subject positions on their narrative interpretations of lived reality. The chapter will begin with a brief outline of the notion of biopolitics, in order to ground and clarify Mbembe's own postcolonial adaptations. Using Mbembe's question of how 'life, death, and the human body' are 'inscribed in the order of power' (2003: 12) as a theoretical starting point, the study will go on to explore the ways in which the significant historical moments of colonial and post-independence Mozambique can be understood through a necropolitical lens.

By way of tracing the enduring continuity of biopolitical thought in the construction of Mozambique, this section will draw examples from both the recent history that has informed the study thus far, and much earlier discourses from the fifteenth to eighteenth centuries. This wider time span seeks to account for the pivotal role of unknowability in the Portuguese imperial entanglement of sub-Saharan Africa and death, a discursive construct stemming from the very earliest days of Portuguese expansionism. These reflections on key historical flashpoints and themes related to the fluid and uncertain concept of death will be interwoven with analyses of texts by Momplé and Cassamo. Focusing primarily on the writers' portrayals of melancholic suicide, hunger and ghostliness as the affective crystallizations of necropolitical tensions, I will demonstrate that the authors' engagements with necropolitical themes, and the gendered and corporeal meanings tied into them, can be understood as a way of challenging the dehumanizing massification of the Mozambican population enacted during colonialism and selectively perpetuated in its aftermath.

The Necropolitics of Mozambique

Foucault introduced the Western academic community to the twin concepts of biopower and biopolitics in a 1976 lecture at the Collège de France. During the late eighteenth and early nineteenth centuries, he proposed, the nature of Western political life shifted dramatically, and the power to 'take life or let live' that had long represented the bedrock of sovereignty was augmented by 'a new right which [did] not erase the old right but which [did] penetrate it, permeate it': the right to '"make" live and "let" die' (2003: 240–1). Compounding the 'seizure of power' of 'man-as-body' realized via the eighteenth-century emergence of 'anatomo-politics', in the nineteenth century Western governments set their sights on 'man-as-species' (243). As a result, the development of the modern state came to depend upon the use of technologies aimed at negating the aleatory element within a given population in order to 'optimize a state of life' (246). Death, banished from political discourse, thus comes to represent within the modern state 'the term, the limit, or the end of power' (248). Despite this discursive silence, however, the mechanism of killing remains necessary to maintain the illusion of national and societal integrity. For Foucault, it is at this juncture that scientific racism emerged, providing a way to frame killing as necessary for the protection and optimization of life, a means to 'introduc[e] a break into the domain of life that is under power's control: the break between what must live and what must die' (254).

While Foucault's theory has remained highly influential as far as the study of the West is concerned, its shortcomings for the productive analysis of recently colonized states are clear. If death is located at the margins of political discourse, with the right to kill invoked only as a means to reinforce life and justified with scientific racism, then what becomes of death in a society whose very backbone is constituted by that racism? By taking aspects of Foucauldian biopolitics and integrating them with elements of postcolonialism, critical race theory and Black Atlantic studies, Mbembe (2001, 2003) addresses this question, recentring death as fundamental to lived experiences of official and unofficial imperial regimes and their aftermaths. Europe's association of Africa with death did not begin and end at the level of discourse, Mbembe affirms. Rather, it was brought to bear directly on the lived realities of colonized Africans, for whom life was rendered radically precarious and death omnipresent. To die prematurely, 'for nothing, no apparent reason, just like that, without having sought death' has therefore constituted 'the soil of recent memory' on the continent (2001: 199).

Understanding the specific ways in which this brutal circular logic was set in motion in Mozambique requires looking far further back in discursive history than recent memory can account for, however. Central to the imperial construct and deployment of death in the Lusophone African case is the profound sense of *unknowability* that dominates texts of early modern Portuguese expansionism, interwoven with the specific spiritual concerns of that period. It is this unknowability that can be seen as the originating catalyst for the forging of the specifically anxious and affective association between African corporealities and death that would emerge in colonized Mozambique, and which in turn facilitated the Portuguese colonial devaluation of African lives that Momplé and Cassamo reflect and subvert in their respective works. For this reason, the contextual outline featured in the following paragraphs will briefly include texts from some earlier historical moments than have been studied so far, beginning with Gomes Eannes de Azurara's 1453 chronicle of the first Portuguese journey south of Cape Bojador, *Chronica do Descobrimento e Conquista de Guiné* [*The Chronicle of the Discovery and Conquest of Guinea*] (1841, trans. Beazley 1896).

Latent in the introductory chapters of Azurara's seminal text is a consistent sense of mortal danger attached to sub-Saharan Africa's primordiality, a perception itself arising from the region's fundamental unknowability. In his attempt to put words to the uncharted status of the territory south of what is today Western Sahara, the author notes that 'nem per scriptura, nem per memorya de nhuũs homeẽs, nunca foe sabudo determinadamente a callidade da terra que hya a allem do dicto cabo' (1841: 44) [neither by writings, nor by the memory of man, was known with any certainty the nature of the land beyond that Cape] (1896: 27). While these lines alone appear to refer only to the region's unknown cartography, it becomes clear in the pages that follow that those geographical uncertainties are intertwined with more metaphysical anxieties, with one of the reasons for Prince Henry's sponsorship of the voyage south of Bojador described as the 'salvaçom das almas perdidas' (1841: 47) [salvation of lost souls] (1896: 29). Implicit within this evangelical rationale is the spectral fantasy of Africa as a spiritual *tabula rasa*, a space of chaotic negativity. This implication of unknowability, primordiality, and the mortal threat therein is made explicit in the following chapter, which opens with Azurara's description of the dangers of the proposed expedition:

> [E]ra grande duvida qual serya o primeiro que quisesse poer sua vida em semelhante ventuira. Como passaremos, deziam elles, os termos que poserom nossos padres, ou que proveito pode trazer ao iffante a perdiçom de nossas almas, juntamente com os corpos, ca conhecidamente seremos omecidas de nos meesmos? [...] Isto he claro, deziam os mareantes, que despois deste cabo nom hi gente nem povoraçom algũa; a terra nom he menos areosa que os desertos de Libya, onde nom ha augua, nem arvor, nem herva verde [...]. As correntes som tamanhas, que navyo que la passe, jamais nunca podera tornar. (1841: 47)

> [[T]here was great doubt as to who would be the first to risk his life in such a venture. How are we, men said, to pass the bounds that our fathers set up, or what profit can result to the Infant from the perdition of our souls as well as of our bodies – for of a truth by daring any further we shall become wilful murderers of ourselves? [...] For, said the mariners, this much is clear, that beyond this Cape there is no race of men nor place of inhabitants: nor is the land less sandy than the deserts of Libya, where there is no water, no tree, no green herb – and the sea so shallow that a whole league from land it is only a fathom deep, while the currents are so terrible that no ship having once passed the Cape, will ever be able to return.] (1896: 259)

As Josiah Blackmore proposes, this passage encapsulates the Portuguese affective vision of the Bojador as 'a border of spiritual and corporal danger', a perilous gateway to the 'arena of blankness' that lies beyond (2009: 47). This foundational premise of mortal danger underpins the rest of the text as a rationale for the summary killing and enslavement of Africans, exemplified by one passage in which slave-trader Álvaro Fernandes is described as coming to shore, encountering 'homeẽs que mostravam que queryam defender suas casas' (1841: 407) [men who showed they had a will to defend their houses] (1896: 259), and immediately killing one, taking his shield and spear, and enslaving a woman, an adolescent girl, and an infant boy assumed to be members of his village (407–8).

While the more pragmatic geographical fears demonstrated in Azurara's text are largely diminished in later imperial writings, the affective entanglement of sub-Saharan Africa with the mortal threat of chaotic meaninglessness persists in their portrayals of indigenous Africans. Inácio Caetano Xavier, secretary to the Mozambican government, writes in 1758 that the indigenous people of Mozambique are 'cafres inimigos do trabalho e cultura' [kaffirs, enemies of work and culture] (1955: 144). Those that are not childishly docile are 'barbaramente belicosos' [barbarously bellicose] and often bound in bloody conflict with neighbouring groups (145). They engage in the trafficking of their own children, which Xavier offers as an explanation for why, 'em todos os seos idiomas [...] não se articula palavra que diga *amor*' [in all their languages [...] there is no word spoken that means *love*] (146–7). In another eighteenth-century chronicle, António Pinto de Miranda says of coastal southern Africa's indigenous inhabitants that 'mais se lhe podem chamar feras do que homens' [are more beasts than they are men] (1955: 248). They have no concept of law, engage in bestiality, and commit suicide by burying themselves alive with their dead superiors (249). The implication of both texts is clear: that for Africans, life is cheap, morality absent and death ubiquitous.

At the time that both Xavier and Miranda were putting their impressions to paper, the slave trade out of Mozambique was on the brink of exponential growth. In the decades between the 1760s and the 1820s, the number of slaves exported from Portuguese southeast African territories each year rose, albeit inconsistently, from fewer than 1,000 to over 30,000 (Newitt 1995: 250). Though information on how such great numbers of slaves were acquired is sparse, as Malyn Newitt notes, it appears that imperial and tribal exploitation of the unsurvivable living conditions created by warfare or natural disaster might have generated the majority (1995: 252). Slavery, as expounded by Orlando Patterson, represents 'one of the most extreme forms of the relation of domination' (1982: 1), an amalgamation of violent gestures of disempowerment, centred around the enacting of the slave's natal alienation, that come to constitute him or her as 'a socially dead person' (5). The slave, stripped of all independent power, experiences a 'secular excommunication' (5), becoming 'the ultimate tool, as imprintable and as disposable as the master wished' (7). His or her master thus becomes a 'mediat[or] between the socially dead and the socially alive', and is in this way rendered 'godlike' (46).

Mbembe, expanding on Patterson's characterization of the slave system, concludes that 'the slave is therefore kept alive but in a *state of injury*, in a phantom-like world of horror and intense cruelty and profanity', experienced as 'a form of death in life' (2003: 20). The construction in the Portuguese imaginary of African life as arbitrary and precarious, reflected in texts like those of Azurara, Xavier and Miranda, thus becomes a self-fulfilling fantasy, crystallized in the Mozambican slave trade. The selected works by Momplé and Cassamo are set many decades or centuries after the ostensible end of the Mozambican slave trade; nonetheless, this notion of 'death in life' as an existential imposition on the oppressed subject, arising from a continually perpetuated characterization of African life as radically precarious, is a recurrent motif of both writers and a key point of departure for this chapter's literary analyses.

The totalized domination of colonized subjects signified here by the slave trade persisted long into the post-1884 period described in Chapter 1 of this study. These final decades of the nineteenth century saw Portugal's colonial grip on southern Africa tighten significantly, with a proliferation of fiscal laws and labour regulations, and increased militarization of areas resistant to colonial control. With the advent and enforcement of these codes and strategies, the instrumentalization of indigenous Mozambican lives and bodies in service of those of the metropolitan and colonial Portuguese, imposed during the slave trade, was able to persist long after abolition; meanwhile, the protection and optimization of Portuguese lives became officially construed as dependent upon the absolute domination and control of the Mozambican native population. Indeed, the perpetuation of the power relations instituted during the slave trade is an explicit objective of António Ennes's 1893 report on the Mozambican colony, examined from a different angle in Chapter 1. Ennes's treatise proposes that despite the abolition of slavery and its attendant 'crimes e horrores' [crimes and horrors], it would be economically beneficial to 'aproveitar e conservar os hábitos de trabalho que [a escravidão] impunha aos negros' [preserve and take advantage of the working habits that [slavery] imposed on the blacks] (70). This suggestion follows a detailed rationale for the augmentation of Portugal's commercial intervention in Mozambique, beginning with a reminder of the ways in which the economic exploitation of Angola is bettering Portuguese lives: 'está, neste moment, socorrendo tão munificentemente a crise comercial da Metrópole!' [it is, in this very moment, so generousaly alleviating the economic crisis of the Metropolis!] (20).

Ennes's treatise plainly illustrates how early imperial perceptions of indigenous Africans were written into legislative discourse as a means of rationalizing their instrumentalization as essential for the advancement and bettering of the Portuguese Empire. Having first warned that the Vatua, in particular, are the '*fidalgo* da selvageria, para quem o trabalho é desdouro, glória o assassínio e a rapina direito' [*noblemen* of savagery, for whom work means dishonour, murder glory, and pillaging right of force] (1893: 23), he goes on to reveal that the situation elsewhere in the country is hardly better: 'em muitas regiões o carácter e os costumes dos habitantes não permitem à civilização contar com eles para seus instrumentos, e é certo que os negros, todos os negros de todas as partes da África, consideram a ociosidade como o estado mais perfeito de beatitude depois da embriaguez' [in many regions, the character and customs of the inhabitants prevent civilization from counting them among its tools, and it is certain that the blacks, like the blacks from all over Africa, consider leisureliness to be the second most perfect and beatific state after drunkenness] (23–4).

This initial outline by Ennes clearly recalls the above-cited characterizations of Africans as existing in a chaotic state of amorality and thus living lives of inferior intrinsic value. Proposing later in his report that the solution to Mozambique's problems is a system enforcing compulsory work for the country's indigenous inhabitants, Ennes warns that 'se a administração pública não mudar de doutrinas e de práticas relativamente aos direitos e deveres dos indígenas, dentro de poucos anos serão eles que pretenderão fazer trabalhar os Europeus, muito embora em países estranhos se sujeitam a andar adiante a chicote' [if the administration does not change its doctrine and practice regarding the rights and duties of the indigenous, within a few years it will be them that are ordering Europeans to work, even as in other countries they are forced to walk in front of the whip] (1893: 69).

The subjugation of Mozambique's native populations, then, becomes essential for the protection of Portuguese interests both economic and social. While Ennes repeatedly decries the means of the slave trade, the list of proposed regulations that follows clearly reflects the objective of reviving its ends: aside from his motion that all indigenous men between fourteen and seventy years old must be engaged in work (495–513), his suggestions include the expansion and increased enforcement of the head tax system (303–5); the substitution of prison terms for forced labour, including in penal colonies away from the condemned subject's place of residence (482–6); and a list of ill-defined infractions for which such a sentence might be imposed, which includes the failure to follow labour regulations in the first place (483). As Allen Isaacman notes, the partial implementation of Ennes's labour requirement failed to meet local workforce demands due to the competitive salaries available for migrant workers in South Africa and Rhodesia, meaning that it was quickly supplanted by a system known locally as *xibalo* or *chibalo*, wherein colonial administrators would simply round up poor indigenous men and women and hand them over to employers for periods of forced manual labour regardless of their legal or working status (1992: 491–2). The *xibalo* system, which emerges as a key plot point in two of the works studied in this chapter, namely Momplé's short story 'Aconteceu em Saua-Saua' and Cassamo's novel *Palestra para um Morto*, was so widespread that forced labour ultimately constituted the bulk of the colonial administration's main workforce (Newitt 1995: 410).

Written shortly after Ennes's highly influential endorsement of indigenous instrumentalization, cavalry officer and imperial hero Joaquim Augusto Mousinho d'Albuquerque's account of his 1895 campaign against Gazan chief Ngungunhane provides further evidence of the depreciation of Mozambican lives for the putative purpose of bolstering those of the Portuguese. In the opening lines of his 1896 report on the campaign, Albuquerque affirms that its purpose is to 'iniciar as medidas mais urgentes para estabelecer a ordem' [initiate the most urgent measures with which to establish order] in the Gaza region, implicitly conflating security and peace with Mozambican subjugation (5). He makes clear that the continued servility of local Mozambicans, brought about by means of several successful battles with indigenous forces, hinges on

his killing or capture of Ngungunhane (11). Later, following the summary execution of two indigenous men accused of being enemy spies,
he observes the enhanced sense of motivation among his black troops,
and concludes that 'elles confundem perfeitamente a força e coragem
com a crueldade, e que é absolutamente necessário d'estes exemplos para
os dominar e fazer-m'o-nos respeitar' [they precisely confound strength
and courage with cruelty, which is thus absolutely necessary to dominate
[the indigenous] and make ourselves respected] (19). With this assertion,
the imperial logic born of the early days of expansionism emerges in full
circle: Africa is a chaotic and lawless abyss, and indigenous Africans
are thus innately prone to senseless cruelty; ergo, the enforcement of a
state of exception, including the repeated deployment of arbitrary and
lethal violence and the threat thereof, is both justified and necessary for
Portugal's continued sovereignty.

This discursive enforcement of a racialized state of exception, based
around the instrumentalization of indigenous Mozambicans and the depreciation of their lives, continued throughout the first half of the twentieth
century, albeit couched in less explicitly violent terms. The *Estatuto Político,
Civil e Criminal dos Indígenas de Angola e Moçambique* [Indigenous Statute],
first introduced following the installation of the Military Dictatorship in
1926 and revised in 1954 under the title of *Estatuto dos Indígenas Portuguesas
das Províncias da Guiné, Angola e Moçambique*, excluded from Portuguese
citizenship all 'indivíduos de raça negra ou dela descendentes que, pela sua
ilustração e costumes, se não distingam do comum daquela raça' [individuals
of the black race or descendants of the same, who, judging by their presentation and customs, are not readily distinguishable from what is common
among that race] (1926: 153). The latter qualifier hinged on an individual's
ability to prove to an administrative official that they met certain 'condições especiais' [special conditions] (153), left unspecified in the original
Statute but outlined in the 1954 revision to include financial independence, no criminal history, a good command of Portuguese, and a sufficient
espousal of certain nebulously defined 'habits' (1954: 21–2). Indigenous
women, meanwhile, had no recourse to citizenship at all. Expelled from
the privileges of civil life, Mozambicans classified as 'indígenas' were also
subject to distinct punitive measures for criminal transgressions, including,

following Ennes, the punishment of minor and major legal infractions with minimally paid compulsory labour (*Regulamento dos Tribunais* 1933: 6–7); the *xibalo* system, meanwhile, became ever more pervasive and brutal (Isaacman 1992: 493–503). With this deliberate and violent alienation of the colonized from civil society and independent power, echoes of Patterson's notion of the 'social death' or 'secular excommunication' imposed upon slave subjects (1982: 5) ring through clearly.

Charting the evolution of Portuguese colonialism in Mozambique as a reiterative series of devaluations of African lives, set in motion by the *a priori* imagining of Africa as an unknowable space of spiritual and moral negation, reveals the progressive encroachment on Mozambique of biopolitical thought as explicated by Foucault, manifest in the increasing massification and instrumentalization of native Mozambicans' bodies in service of the advancement of Portuguese socioeconomic interests. At the same time, however, studying colonial Mozambican discursive history from this starting point makes clear that while Foucauldian biopolitical theory may facilitate analysis of Portuguese imperial thought, it falls short of allowing us to parse the Mozambican experience of the same. It is at this point that Mbembe's work, building on biopolitical theory but focusing on subjects whose lives have been excluded from the narratives of protection and optimization that biopolitical discourse engenders, can provide us with the tools necessary to reach a fuller understanding of both sides of the Portuguese imperial project. If the depreciation of indigenous lives has held strong at the heart of Portuguese colonial endeavour since its earliest days, then death, in its many guises, images and metaphorical renderings, must also be located at the centre of any framework that aims to understand Mozambican colonial and post-independence experiences.

Though Mbembe does not give his foregrounding of the role of death in colonial, post-independence and neocolonial political life a specific name until the publication of his essay 'Necropolitics' in 2003, his earlier monograph *On the Postcolony* (2001) uses colonialism in Africa as a starting point for many of the ideas that would form the basis for the later text. *On the Postcolony* proposes that *commandement* – the exercise and upholding of colonial sovereignty – depended upon three types of violence, all of which find clear analogies in the examples of Portuguese colonial implementation given above. The first is 'founding violence', which 'helped to create the space over which it was exercised' and thus 'underpinned not only the right of conquest but all the prerogatives flowing from that right' (2001: 25). Azurara's 1453 chronicle of the Portuguese arrival in Guinea, with its framing of the killing and enslavement of native Africans as both justified by the expansionist mission and proving the necessity for it, provides a textual encapsulation of this founding violence in the Lusophone African context, while later texts dealing with the subjugation of resistant regions, including Mousinho's, reiterate it.

The second type of violence is the legitimation of conquest, which can be produced before, during or after the fact and which 'provide[s] self-interpreting language and models for the colonial order, to give this order meaning, to justify its necessity and universalizing mission' in order to '[convert] the founding violence into authorizing authority' (2001: 25); we see this legitimating violence perpetuated from the early encounters of 'salvation' described by Azurara right into the days of the Portuguese New State's 'civilizing mission'. The third violence encompasses the everyday subjugation that ensured the 'maintenance, spread, and permanence' of the authority arising from the legitimation of conquest (2001: 25), perhaps most transparently represented by the treatises and codes proposed and instituted during Mozambique's nineteenth and early twentieth centuries.

For Mbembe, it is through the colonial state's seamless and reiterative deployment of these three types of violence, in a process that 'eliminate[s] all distinction between ends and means', that the indigenous subject is fully interpellated into colonial discourse as 'the property and *thing* of power' (2001: 26). Under such a system, the colonized subject could be seen as 'belong[ing] to the *sphere of objects*', reduced to a 'body-thing' that 'could be destroyed, as one may kill an animal' (27). At the same time, however, the colonial system required indigenous Africans to be rendered tools in the state's 'quest for productivity' (28). In order to achieve this end while upholding generalized colonial control over indigenous populations, the colonial state 'introduced extensive surveillance machinery and an impressive array of punishments and fines for a host of offences' (31). The nineteenth- and twentieth-century proliferation of regulations and codes governing both private and public life in Mozambique, and in particular the imposition of laws requiring indigenous subjects to be engaged in work and encouraging the use of forced labour as a punitive measure, clearly reflect this dual-purpose strategy. The colonial subject embroiled in this system, in Mbembe's words, 'had no rights against the state', and was 'bound to the power structure like a slave to a master' (31). With the introduction of the 1926 Indigenous Statue in Portuguese Africa, this construction of the colonial subject as being at once precluded from civil rights and unconditionally obligated to the state became an explicit cornerstone of the Portuguese colonial system. Forced into the margins not just of social life but of the domain of life itself, the indigenous subject's own life was rendered utterly precarious, at the mercy of the 'arbitrariness of desire and whim' that, for Mbembe, constituted the colonization of Africa (2001: 189). Hence, as the author concludes, 'to have been colonized is, somehow, to have dwelt close to death' (189). The precariousness of African lives, an invented justification for the earliest colonial endeavours on the continent, is thus again reiterated as a lived reality.

Self-Destruction as Subjectivity: 'Aconteceu em Saua-Saua' (Momplé 1988) and 'Ngilina, Tu Vai Morrer' (Cassamo 1989)

If the indigenous subject is excluded from the domain of human life in this way, Mbembe asks (2001: 174), then what does it actually mean for him or her to be killed? This chapter's first pair of literary analyses will expand upon this question in the light of themes shared by Momplé and Cassamo to ask what it means, in the colonial environment of near-absolute domination and control, for the indigenous subject to desire death, to take comfort in its proximity, or even to kill her or himself. Momplé's short story 'Aconteceu em Saua-Saua' [It Happened in Saua-Saua], part of a collection of stories set during the late colonial period entitled *Ninguém Matou Suhura* [*Nobody Killed Suhura*] (1988; 5th edn 2009), raises this last inquiry. Set in 1935, Momplé's year of birth, the story narrates the final evening and night of the life of Mussa Racua, a worker on a colonial rice plantation in rural northeastern Mozambique, as he struggles in vain to meet the quota of rice demanded by the Portuguese administrator. Facing *xibalo* on a sisal plantation as punishment for this failure, he returns home to spend one last night with his pregnant wife Maiassa. In the morning, Maiassa finds her husband hanged from a mango tree, with a buried sack of rice serving as his counterweight. When the administrator is informed of Mussa Racua's suicide, his response is to demand that the six bags of rice the worker did manage to accumulate are retrieved. The story's final lines are spoken by the administrator: 'Estes cães, assim que lhes cheira a trabalho, arranjam sempre chatices. Ou fogem ou suicidam-se. Maldita raça!' [These dogs – as soon as they catch a whiff of work, they manage to wriggle out of it. Either they run off, or they kill themselves. Damned race!] (21).

Mussa Racua embodies the situation of colonized subjects as theorized by Mbembe, while his characterization additionally bears the hallmarks of the specific psychoanalytical concept of melancholia. The text opens on his desperate meeting with a friend, Abudo, from whom he intends to beg any surplus rice in order to meet his quota. On his approach to Abudo's home, Mussa Racua is shown at the end of a day 'de caminhadas infrutíferas' [fruitless wanderings], with exhaustion evident 'no olhar, cuja melancólica serenidade reflecte uma tristeza sem esperança' [in his gaze, whose melancholic serenity speaks of hopeless despair] (9). His countenance reflects 'a conformada lassidão do jogador que tudo perdeu' [the resigned fatigue of the player that has lost everything] (9). When Abudo informs him that he has no spare rice to give, Mussa Racua speaks 'em frases curtas como soluços' [in phrases short as sobs] (11). Despite the burgeoning intensity of his anguish, however, he knows to 'escondê-[la] dentro de si' [hide it within himself] (9). He loses his appetite; he cannot speak to his wife, whom he is resigned to losing (15). Every muscle in his body is 'um foco de dor' [a point of pain] (16). Lying in bed with Maiassa at his side, he sees nothing ahead but hopelessness, and reaches a grim conclusion: 'Não, não posso aguentar outra vez tanto sofrimento [...]. É melhor morrer. Não acordar nunca mais' [No, I cannot endure such suffering again. [...] Better to die. To never wake up again] (18).

These descriptions speak to the profundity of melancholia as described by Julia Kristeva, for whom this psychological-somatic mode of being manifests as 'an abyss of sorrow, a noncommunicable grief' (1989: 3). Kristeva's melancholic subject exists in a state of 'living death', faced with 'the impossible meaning of a life whose burden constantly seems unbearable', and in possession of a body whose 'flesh is wounded, bleeding, cadaverized' (4). He or she is 'witness to the meaninglessness of Being' (4). This characterization of melancholia, denoted by the symbol of the 'black sun', matches closely with Mbembe's figuring of the colonized subject as experiencing a 'nameless eclipse' that is 'accompanied by a proliferation of a metaphysics of sorrow' (2001: 199).

However, while for Kristeva this deep sense of grief, the readiness 'at any moment for a plunge into death', is experienced as organic, arising from some unplaceable 'eerie galaxy' (1989: 3–4), the melancholia of the colonized subject, metonymized in Momplé's story by Mussa Racua, is deliberately and transparently inflicted by the almost omnipotent other of the colonial state. The somatic, affective and psycholinguistic manifestations of melancholia that for Kristeva appear to be spontaneous, lacking an agent outside of the subject's own body and mind, thus emerge in Momplé's text as the manifold effects of abuse and oppression. The Kristevan melancholic's psychosomatic experience of the body as 'wounded, bleeding, cadaverized' (1989: 4) is a corporeal reality for Mussa Racua, whose body bears the painful burden of excessive manual labour in service of the Portuguese Empire, and the physical scars from the whippings, beatings and mosquito infestations that dominated his most recent term of *xibalo* (16–17). Kristeva's notion of the depressed subject as remembering or pre-empting the inevitable loss of lovers and loved ones and thus remaining in a perpetual state of mourning (1989: 5–6) likewise takes on a far more instrumentalized cast in Mussa Racua's case, as Momplé describes how he returned home from his last period of *xibalo* to find that his first wife Anifa, unable to subsist in her husband's absence, had left him for another man (17–18). Kristeva's melancholic is caught in a 'living death', confronted with a burgeoning expanse of meaninglessness centred on the empty arbitrariness of life (1989: 4); Mussa Racua exists under the 'pure terror of desire or whim' that constitutes colonization (Mbembe 2001: 189), and is rendered socially dead by virtue of his lack of civil recourse.

Furthermore, while for Kristeva the melancholic subject suffers alienation from their mother tongue as a result of failing to fully accept language as a substitute for the pre-linguistic maternal figure (1989: 41–2),
in Momplé's text Mussa Racua is deliberately alienated from his mother
tongue, Makhuwa. The Portuguese language, meanwhile, is used against
him and his fellow workers by the colonial state, represented by the administrator, as a tool of this alienation (2009: 19–20). Phillip Rothwell, using
Kristeva's theory on melancholia to examine 'Stress', a story from Momplé's
later collection of post-independence stories *Os Olhos da Cobra Verde*
(1997), notes the significance of this linguistic alienation for the (post)
colonial melancholic:

> In post-independence Mozambique, the psychic replacement for mother, language,
> always bears the scars of a double alienation. Not only does it distance its users from
> the pre-linguistic realm of the maternal, it also haunts them with a colonial past
> because the principle cultural mechanism used to define and replace the mother
> hinges [...] on the tongue of Portugal. (2002: 188)

If language in post-independence Mozambique 'bears the scars' of the country's colonial past, as Rothwell suggests, then in the environs of Momplé's
story, set long before independence, language is the tool used to inflict the
originating wounds beneath.

Momplé's writing of the colonial subject's melancholia bears witness to the cumulative effects of colonial abuse as producing an untenable
and traumatic psychological burden the 'proliferation of a metaphysics
of sorrow, of thoughts of final things and days' that Mbembe identifies
as central to the end point of colonized subjectivity (2001: 199). It also
carries more profound implications, however. Mussa Racua's melancholic
state serves to communicate not only the direct psychological effects of
colonial subjugation, but also the all-encompassing, senseless and arbitrary nature of colonization as a concatenation of multifaceted violences.
For the colonized worker, Mbembe affirms, there is no meaning outside
of domination; colonial violence is both means and end, discourse and
praxis, 'insinuat[ing] itself into the economy, domestic life, language, consciousness' and 'pursu[ing] the colonized even in sleep and dream' (2001:
175). Likewise, for Patterson, the colonizer is 'godlike', the socially dead

indentured worker's only discursive gateway to the world of the socially alive (1982: 45). Momplé's transposition of the classically organic and spontaneous state of melancholia onto the deliberately abused body of the colonized serves to communicate this imposition of a boundless state of negation, while simultaneously reclaiming the colonized subject from his dehumanized state by underscoring his interior subjectivity.

To Be an Animal No Longer

Mussa Racua's suicide provides the logical conclusion of this imposed state of melancholia: the corporeal manifestation of the colonized subject's social death. In addition, this act of ultimate self-destruction reveals the complexity attached to notions of agency and resistance in Mozambique's late colonial era. As Foucault demonstrates, both the abstract notion of suicide and the act itself emerge as fissures in the imagined coherence of the biopolitical state, speaking 'to the individual and private right to die, at the borders and in the interstices of power that was exercized over life' and coming to represent 'one of the first astonishments of a society in which political power had assigned itself the task of administering life' (1998: 138–9). Margaret Higonnet expands on Foucault's point, stating that '[s]uicide is a scandal' that 'ruptures the social order and defies sovereign power over life and death' (2000: 229). The person that commits suicide confounds comprehension by 'break[ing] the frames that society relies on to produce meaning', and pointing toward 'an understanding that resides beyond the social maxim, and perhaps beyond narrative itself' (Higgonet 2000: 229–30).

The Foucauldian notion of suicide is complicated by the necropolitical context of the colonial state, wherein, as Mbembe notes, 'death and freedom are irrevocably interwoven' (2003: 38). Paul Gilroy's *The Black Atlantic* (1993), cited by Mbembe, provides a compelling example of this interconnectedness centred around archival documentations of Middle Passage slaves committing suicide by throwing themselves into the Atlantic (63). For

Gilroy, this 'turn towards death as a release from terror and bondage and a chance to find substantive freedom accords perfectly with [Patterson's] celebrated notion of slavery as a state of "social death", thus making clear that 'the order of authority on which the slave plantation relied cannot be undone without recourse to the counter-violence of the oppressed' (63). Analysing African-American writer Toni Morrison's literary depictions of such suicides, Katy Ryan characterizes the self-destructive act as a 'leap to freedom, and death' that does not tell 'a history of capitulation to dominant powers' but rather 'comprises one part of a larger multivalent narrative of black survival in North America', demonstrating 'a dual impulse toward erasure and survival' (2000: 389–90). In this ambiguous way, Mbembe concludes, death becomes 'represented as agency', while 'the lines between resistance and suicide, sacrifice and redemption, martyrdom and freedom are blurred' (2003: 39–40).

This double-edged imagining of the act of suicide is revealed, in Momplé's story, in one brief but significant fragment of Mussa Racua's internal monologue: 'Não, não posso aguentar outra vez tanto sofrimento [...]. É melhor morrer. Não acordar nunca mais. *Não mais ser um animal*' [No, I cannot endure such suffering again. [...] Better to die. To never wake up. *To be an animal no longer*] (2009: 18, emphasis mine). For Mussa Racua, death offers the chance to escape the dehumanizing colonial system that reduces indigenous workers to the status of animals. By biologically negating himself, he reclaims power over his own body, withdrawing it from use as the inscriptive surface of colonial necropower. At the same moment that this reclamation is achieved, however, he will cease to exist, becoming literally 'an animal no longer'. The character's use of a buried sack of rice as his counterweight further underscores this ultimate ambiguity: the image of the rice as evidently heavier than him shores up his lack of discursive meaning under the biopolitical order of the colony, while at the same precise instant becoming the means by which he removes himself from that oppressive order. This suicidal use of the rice furthermore provides Momplé with an implicit means of condemning the imposition of cash crop cultivation by the imperial regime, and particularly the colonial administration's notorious manipulation of the scales used to measure the output of colonized subjects and thereby determine their payments, a practice further referenced in the author's 1997 story 'Era uma Outra Guerra' [That Was Another War]. The protagonist's distorted appropriation of this manipulation of weights and measures here becomes the grotesque method of his own resistant gesture, revealing the horrifying end point of these seemingly minor acts of colonial oppression.

Mussa Racua's fleeting enactment of resistance and seizure of agency comes at a price beyond his own biological death, however. It is here that Momplé uses the character's pregnant wife Maiassa to point to the gendered implications of workers' resistance to colonialism. Suicide, as Stuart Murray affirms, is paradoxically never an act inflicted only on oneself; rather, 'it is an act of cruelty that has far-reaching social and historical valences. It is a wound that never closes. [...] [O]ur suicide is never entirely our own, never merely our own death' (2006: 205). Maiassa is the first person to find her husband's body following his death, a trauma that causes her to collapse and lose consciousness (Momplé 2009: 19), physically experiencing the outward ripples of his violent act of self-destruction. Mussa Racua thus produces a trauma that will become generational, passed down from Maiassa to their unborn child. Furthermore, by killing himself, Mussa Racua has put the ongoing survival of his wife and child perilously at risk; the reader here recalls Anifa's inability to survive alone during Mussa Racua's deportation. Resistance, Momplé appears to imply, even in its most desperate and impossible circumstances remains a man's game, with women the permanent losers.

Unwitnessed Resistance

Momplé's choice to set 'Aconteceu em Saua-Saua' in 1935, her own year of birth, suggests that the urge reflected in the story to resolve colonial dehumanization through self-destruction is itself the 'black sun' eclipsing the lives of her generation: a burden of meaninglessness from which they must construct their identities. Less anchored in historical specificities, but nonetheless reflecting this same paradoxical drive toward both meaningfulness and oblivion, is Suleiman Cassamo's brief short story 'Ngilina, Tu Vai Morrer' [Ngilina, You're Going to Die], from his 1989 collection *O Regresso do Morto* (2nd edn 1997), which like 'Aconteceu em Saua-Saua' ends with the protagonist's suicide. Cassamo's framing of the act, however, is distinct from that of Momplé; it also carries far more explicitly gendered implications. Written in Cassamo's characteristic linguistic style, which combines Ronga vocabulary and syntax with those of Portuguese to produce a dialect that is both restrained and – for the outsider at least – densely complex, 'Ngilina, Tu Vai Morrer' tells the story of a woman *lobolada* at sixteen to a man the same age as her father.[1] Ngilina is exploited and abused by her mother-in-law, who burdens her with the lion's share of domestic chores, and by her husband, who rapes and beats her '[c]om cinto que tem ferro, com paus, com socos, com pontapés, com tudo' [with belt that has buckle, with sticks, with punches, with kicks, with everything]: a level of abuse that increases when she does not bear him a child (1997: 17). Reduced to a state of despair, one morning Ngilina wakes early, walks into the forest, and hangs herself from a tree (18).

Like Momplé's Mussa Racua, Ngilina embodies a deep sense of melancholia as conceived by Kristeva. Her body bears the wounds of beatings and overwork, an externalized manifestation of the psychosomatic degeneration experienced by the Kristevan melancholic; her face is marked with '[c]haga na bochecha, boca inchada, nariz arranhado, dentes partido' [wound on her cheek, swollen mouth, skinned nose, broken teeth] (Cassamo 1997: 15) and she wakes with 'dores na coluna, nas ancas, na cabeça, todo o corpo' [pain in her spine, in her hips, in her head, all through her body] (17). She vacillates between trying to find meaning in her pain and attempting to resign herself to it, telling herself that 'é assim vida de mulher' [the life of a woman is like this] (15). She is alienated from language and from those around her by virtue of having no one with whom she can safely share her anguish. She is drawn toward death, reminding herself repeatedly that 'é melhor morrer. Morrer é mesmo bom' [it's better to die. Dying is really

---

1   *Lobolo* translates roughly as 'bride price', that is, goods or money paid by a groom or his family to that of a bride. *Lobolada*, therefore, is the state of having been exchanged for *lobolo*.

good] (15). Furthermore, like Mussa Racua, she is explicitly dehumanized and instrumentalized, appearing to herself as 'burro de puxar nholo'
[donkey for pulling cart], 'boi de puxar charrua' [ox for pulling plough] and
'máquina de moer farinha' [machine for grinding flour] (15). In contrast
to 'Aconteceu em Saua-Saua', however, in 'Ngilina, Tu Vai Morrer' there
is no indication of an overarching state apparatus. The reader is unable to
deduce any sense of temporality from the text, meaning that it is devoid
of even a latent or implied sense of political context; the story could take
place at any moment in Mozambique's history.

It is against the backdrop of this timelessness that the gendered implications of Ngilina's life and death are able to emerge, speaking to the double
colonization of indigenous Mozambican women under the colonial system
and their ongoing biopolitical instrumentalization in its aftermath. Ngilina,
like Mbembe's colonial subject, lives 'under the pure terror of desire or
whim' (2001: 189), an example of 'the person who, everywhere and always,
possesses life, property, and body as if they were alien things' (2001: 235).
She may or may not exist under the racialized state of exception represented
by late Portuguese colonial administration, but she lives, nonetheless, in an
exceptional state; like Patterson's slave, she is socially dead, natally alienated
and violently dominated (1982: 13). And, in line with Mbembe's expansion on Patterson's concept, her social death does not preclude her value
as property and instrument of labour, represented here by the *lobolo* that
her husband explicitly cites as justification for her being kept, in Mbembe's
words, 'alive but in a *state of injury*, in a phantom-like world of horror and
intense cruelty and profanity' (2003: 20).

In this way, Cassamo is able to evoke the social and physical violences
of colonialism without ever referencing them, in a literary sleight of hand
that uses Ngilina's melancholia to reveal the mechanisms of dehumanization underlying gendered oppression *and* the colonial system itself, as well
as the ways in which the two systems are intertwined. The individual and
systemic sexual subjugations of women, the original gestures of phallic
power represented here by Ngilina's sale by her father into a life of rape
and abuse by another man, bring into relief the phallic nature of colonization: the gestures and discourses that worked together to figure Africa and
its inhabitants as irrational, chaotic and in need of penetrative conquest.

For Mbembe, this phallocentrism lies at the foundations of colonial sovereignty and violence, with the colonizer 'think[ing] and express[ing] himself through his phallus' in a 'sadistic gesture' that 'accomplish[es] a sort of sparky clean act of coitus, with the characteristic feature of making horror and pleasure coincide' (2001: 175). Conversely, the covert evocation of colonial abuse underscores the subjugation of women as an insidious act of colonization in itself. The story's timeless setting, meanwhile, implies that indigenous women occupy the interstices of these two mirror images, where imperial colonization and gendered subjugation by their indigenous male counterparts not only share features, but are often indistinguishable.

Cassamo's latent alignment of female subjugation and colonization in Ngilina's story furthermore serves to shore up the limited recourse of subaltern women to resistant gestures, an outcome that becomes particularly clear when Ngilina's suicide is compared to that of Momplé's Mussa Racua. While the suicide of Momplé's protagonist is barely acknowledged by colonial representatives, the figure of Maiassa and her unborn child imply that his act will persist as a gesture of resistance to biopolitical instrumentalization that will be passed on: a generational trauma that will serve, in some way, to enshrine colonial abuse in Mozambican collective memory. Cassamo's story, on the other hand, closes abruptly on the image of Ngilina's hanged body, still narrated in her own patterns of speech, suggesting that there is no one to grieve for her, or to pass her story on. His focus on her body as 'a lengalengar' [dangling], her throat 'na corda tesa' [on the tight rope] and her eyes as remaining 'muinto abertos' [wide open] (1997: 18) further reminds the reader of the horrific violence of her death, and emphasizes that suicide, for Ngilina, is no safe refuge. The implication with this final, graphic scene is that the most marginalized women are barred from participation in even the most desperate and abject expressions of resistance. Ngilina's suicide represents a final act of resistance – both to her violent gendered oppression, and by symbolic extension to colonization – but by virtue of going unheard, unseen and unrooted in historical context, her gesture is ultimately meaningless.

The authors' invocations of suicidality in these two stories make clear the role of death as both a disciplining mechanism and a final means of resistance within colonial society, and in Cassamo's case within gendered oppression as a symbiotic metaphor for colonization. The image of suicide, in revealing these seemingly contradictory meanings for death and life, thus uses the oppressed body as a surface for communicating the complex directions, distributions and instabilities of power in colonial states, undermining the power dichotomies implied by the literal and discursive massification of indigenous Mozambicans during the colonial period. The following section explores Momplé's and Cassamo's shared engagement with a second necropolitical image that uses the gendered body in this manner, this time in the specific setting of the aftermath of independence: that of food. A brief review of Frelimo's nation-building discourse from this particular perspective is here useful to ground the literary analyses that follow.

Consuming Chaos, Consuming Conformity: 'Laurinda, Tu Vai Mbunhar' (Cassamo 1989) and *Neighbours* (Momplé 1995)

With the advent of post-independence rule in Mozambique came Frelimo's enthusiastic espousal of a nation-building project rooted firmly in the biopolitical drive toward optimal life. Politicized investment and intervention in life became, in line with Murray's interpretation of biopolitics, 'the moral mission of a "secular sacred"' (2006: 193): the essential discursive foundation of Mozambican socialist endeavour. From within this framework, food emerged alongside the emotive symbol of the Child examined in Chapter 3 to form a second touchstone of Frelimo's biopolitical thinking. Representing both engagement with the wider Soviet focus on national production and the new government's ability to optimize the lives of its subjects, food appears to encapsulate post-independence success and prosperity in Mozambican state discourse. Indeed, an ear of corn still features in the foreground of the Frelimo logo, posters of which cover buildings all over Maputo (see Figure 3).

Figure 3: The current logo of the Frelimo Party.

Hunger, meanwhile, was discursively cast as fundamentally attached to colonialism, a planned outcome of imperial capitalist exploitation of Mozambican land for the purpose of engagement with industrial agriculture. In Samora Machel's July 1975 victory speech, this association is made clear:

> Nas zonas libertadas produzíamos amendoim, produzíamos milho, gergelim, rícino, feijão, produzíamos agrupados em cooperativas.
>
> Mas, em Lourenço Marques, temos ouvido dizer que esta parte do sul, até ao centro, importa amendoim para alimentar o Povo. Vocês vivem do amendoim que vem do exterior. Vocês vivem do milhos que vem do exterior. [...]

Podem responder: 'Mas a fome foi planificada pelo colonialismo em Moçambique, porque as terras pertenciam aos senhores da terra. Como é que sairemos deste sistema?' Temos uma solução para o problema da terra, pois pensamos que ela pertence ao Povo e agora é controlada pelo Estado. (Machel 1975: 17)

[In the liberated zones we produced peanuts, we produced corn, sesame, castor, beans, we produced all of this in our cooperatives.

But in Lourenço Marques, we have been hearing that in these southern parts, up to the central regions, peanuts are imported to feed the People. You live off peanuts that come from elsewhere. You live off corn that comes from elsewhere. [...]

You might rightly respond: 'But hunger was planned deliberately during colonialism in Mozambique, because the land belonged to its owners. How can we escape this system?' We have a solution to this land problem: we believe that the land belongs to the People, and is now, therefore, controlled by the State.]

This framing of hunger as the deliberate consequence of capitalist domination or interference, rooted in Mozambican collective memory of colonial agricultural commodification and use of food as a method of popular control, is reinforced in a 1976 *Tempo* article on malnutrition, which is described as 'a medida exacta da exploração internacional' [the precise measure of global exploitation] ('Nutrição' 1976: 33). The same article explains that 'a sub-nutrição é na verdade um mal dos povos explorados' [malnutrition is a malaise of the exploited] (33), and that:

nas nações que lutaram e lutam contra a dominação colonial-capitalista e imperialista e que saem vitoriosas dessa guerra, criam as condições para liquidar as raízes da exploração e deste modo partirem para um tipo de produção que sirva o povo do seu tudo, perspectivando e concretizando o fim das causas da sub-nutrição. (33)

[in the nations that fought and continue to fight against colonial-capitalist and imperialist domination, the conditions have been created to destroy the roots of exploitation, and in this way they begin the type of production that serves the people as a whole, creating and consolidating the end of the causes of malnutrition.]

The catastrophic then-recent famine in communist China is not mentioned. The solution to hunger, *Tempo* maintains, is the 'organização política das massas para uma correcta produção' [political organization of the masses to enable the right kind of production] (37).

Within this understanding of hunger and malnutrition, women's labour, and indeed women's bodies themselves, are imagined as the key tools for alimentary optimization. As Kathleen Sheldon demonstrates, Frelimo's association of women and food was nothing new; food supply and preparation had been gendered activities across Mozambique long before the imposition of European cultural practices, and were often strongly correlated with social control over women's reproductive capacities, indicated in southern regions by the synchronization of female fertility rites with important points in the agricultural year (2002: 24–5). Familial food supply remained a primarily female-coded task during the colonial era, a responsibility greatly hindered by the instrumentalization of indigenous women in service of centralized cash crop production (Sheldon 2002: 49–53). The post-independence reiteration of this relationship, however, is accompanied by a distinct discursive shift toward the massification of women's labour. Where women's ability to acquire food for the consumption of their families or wider kinship groups was once for the tangible and immediate purpose of assuring the continuity of that group, in post-independence state media it becomes discursively construed as serving the more nebulous objective of nation-building. Indeed, the above-cited article on malnourishment is replete with images of women with children (while images of adult men, apart from one photograph of a white UN official, are absent); one such image, showing a woman caring for several young children, is captioned '[c]rianças terão de ter uma nutrição correcta, pois de contrário 20 anos depois serão homens incapazes de contribuir com todas as potencialidades físicas e mentais para a construção do país' [children must be nourished properly, otherwise in 20 years' time, as men, they will be unable to contribute all their physical and mental potential to the construction of the country] ('Nutrição' 1976: 32).

In close tandem with this shift toward massification under the vague rubric of nation-building comes the interpellation of women's bodies into a specifically medico-biological ideology in which the ongoing health of the nation is predicated on women obeying certain rules around somatic conduct. In terms of food and hunger politics, this movement is perhaps best illustrated by Frelimo's increasing promotion of breastfeeding in the years following independence. *Tempo*'s above-cited 1976 article includes a large image of a woman breastfeeding a young baby, adjacent to a separate image of another woman bottle-feeding an older infant (36–7). The text alongside explains that '[n]os problemas inerentes à sub-nutrição há que ter um cuidado especial com as crianças [porque] uma criança mal alimentada é um futuro cidadão incapaz de reconstruir um país com plena rentabilidade física e mental' [when facing the problems inherent in malnutrition, we must be particularly careful when it comes to children, [because] a poorly fed child is a future citizen incapable of rebuilding a country with their full physical and mental potential] (37). The article then lists ten ways in which adequate nutrition can be ensured, three of which refer explicitly to breastfeeding: 'Amamentar pelo peito é melhor; [...] A amamentação de peito deve terminar lentamente; [...] O "biberón" é mau' [Breastfeeding is better; [...] Breastfeeding must be tapered off slowly; [...] Bottle-feeding is bad] (37).

This discursive triangulation of nutrition, women's bodies and nation-building emerges as a particularly frequent motif in Mozambican pro-state media during the early 1980s, as food shortages, brought about by the coincidence of increasing civil instability and drought, became a part of everyday life for many Mozambicans. A 1981 *Tempo* inquiry into Mozambique's high infant mortality rate blames poor child nutrition, resulting in the starvation-related conditions of marasmus or kwashiorkor, on women's failure to breastfeed for a sufficient period after birth due to their tendency to have several children in quick succession (Marmelo 1981: 20–2). The article ends with a lengthy reminder that breast milk is superior to infant formula, but offers very little in the way of acknowledging potential nutritional issues among women themselves, or the interpersonal and cultural pressures on them to have children in rapid succession (24). A February 1983 Machel speech attributing famine to natural disaster and colonialism is illustrated by the image of an emaciated woman with her baby, who carries the swollen stomach and oedematous extremities typical of kwashiorkor (Machel 1983b: 17). A *Tempo* front cover from June of the same year features a background of parched, cracked earth, while a superimposed image shows a woman breastfeeding; the cover is captioned 'SECA: A TERRA TEM SEDE' [DROUGHT: THE EARTH IS THIRSTY]. In the last six weeks of 1983, *Tempo* ran no fewer than three full-length features on the importance of breastfeeding (Albuquerque 1983a, 1983b; Manuel 1983b), in addition to several shorter articles ('Em Defesa do Leite'; 'Leite Materno'; Ribas 1983), the latest of which describes the tendency among Maputo women to bottle-feed their babies as 'uma psicose nas zones urbanas' [a psychosis in urban regions] (Albuquerque 1983a: 23).

As food shortages intensified in both frequency and severity during the post-independence conflict as a result of Renamo's targeting of small- and large-scale agricultural development, women were often left unable to procure sufficient food to feed themselves or their children. A 1990 UNICEF/OMM report makes clear that household food insecurity during these years affected women and children most severely, the result of a complex amalgamation of factors which included, significantly, women's reluctance to reduce overall familial food supply by eating enough to meet their increased caloric demands at times of excessive work, pregnancy and lactation (31–5). The symbolic interconnection of women and food provision reinforced by pro-Frelimo media was thus grimly reflected in the lives and bodies of individual women.

Examining this biopolitical association of food, gender and nationalism from the Mbembian starting point of negation, death and affect raises the interrelated questions of what role gender plays in affective discourses of hunger, and what meaning the hungry body holds in the post-independence Mozambican context. Yet affective readings of hunger in non-Western contexts are notably absent from the fields of literary and cultural studies; instead, such readings remain largely confined to the disciplines of physiology and psychology, which first identified the intimate clinical links between hunger and affect during studies such as Ancel Keys's infamous 1945 starvation experiment.[2] As Kirsten Hastrup has demonstrated, hunger

2   Dubbed the Minnesota Experiment, Keys's project recruited thirty-six conscientious objectors who were voluntarily subjected to semi-starvation conditions for a period of six months in order that the medical community might improve refeeding strategies in the wake of World War II's famines. The study is still frequently used to understand the physiological and psychological presentations of famine victims and restrictive eating disorder patients (Kalm and Semba 2005).

as both cause and manifestation of individual suffering in non-Western societies has been neglected even by the social sciences, contributing to the Western tendency to '[reduce] the starving populations of the world to anonymity', which itself casts the members of those populations 'as having basically undifferentiated emotional lives' (1993: 732).

Contemporary Kenyan writer Binyavanga Wainaina's scathing satirical essay 'How to Write About Africa' (2006) summarizes this massifying tendency in Western media with the parodical instruction that '[a]mong your characters you must always include The Starving African, who wanders the refugee camp nearly naked, and waits for the benevolence of the West. [...] She must look utterly helpless. She can have no past, no history; such diversions ruin the dramatic moment.' Within these homogeneous Western discourses on African hunger, centred around the catastrophe of famine, Africans themselves become once again subsumed, and their lives thus depreciated, under the age-old colonial notion of the continent as 'a vast dark cave where every benchmark and distinction come together in total confusion, and the rifts of a tragic and unhappy human history stand revealed' (Mbembe 2001: 3).

Rehumanizing Hunger

Cassamo's short story 'Laurinda, Tu Vai Mbunhar' [Laurinda, You're Going to Fail] can be read as an attempt to reappropriate the portrayal of hunger, casting it as a means of uncovering the realities behind both the massifying triangulation of women, food and nationhood promoted by pro-Frelimo Mozambican media and the anonymizing tendencies inherent in Western representations of African food insecurity. Narrating the titular character's struggle to buy bread for herself and her family, the story's precise time setting is unclear, though its mention of 'meticagi' indicates that it takes place in 1980 or later.[3] Laurinda is seen queuing overnight outside a bakery; being offered bread in exchange for sex, a transaction she vociferously refuses; and finally collapsing against a wall with exhaustion and hunger just as she reaches the counter. Ultimately, however, the baker does sell her some bread.

The narrative focuses throughout on the protagonist's interior experience of severe hunger, driving home the grinding pain, literal and figurative tunnel vision, and encroaching listlessness and despondency that starvation entails. It opens on Laurinda walking barefoot along a street to join the bakery queue. Her hunger is such that she does not feel the hot tarmac burning her feet. The narrator asks, directly addressing the text's readers, '[c]omo querem que ela sinta o alcatrão se a cabeça dela está cheia de pão?' [how do you suppose she's going to feel the tarmac if her head is full of bread?] (Cassamo 2009: 21). Bread is all she can think of; it fills her thoughts, 'rouba força nos joelhos, cega os olhos, gira o juízo' [steals the strength from her knees, blinds her, clouds her judgement] (21). When the bread does not appear, rage 'aperta a garganta da Laurinda, sobe na cabeça, desce nos braços' [tightens Laurinda's throat, rises up in her head, coarses down her arms] (22), but when she hears a false rumour that the bakery has no more bread, she grows despondent: 'quer cair, [...] ficou vazia como saco de pão sem pão. Não tem força nenhuma, não tem cansaço, nada lhe dói, nada quer a não ser uma parede, uma árvore para se encostar. E ficar' [she just wants to collapse, [...] she has become empty like a bag of bread with no bread. She has no strength left, nor exhaustion, nothing hurts any more, she doesn't want anything except a wall, a tree to rest against. And to stay there] (24). Hunger 'gera estrelas nos olhos, racha a cabeça' [makes her see stars, splits open her head] (24) and she begins to lose touch with reality, unable to discern whether her basket is empty or heavy with bread, or whether the movement she feels is the queue moving or her own head spinning. She hears her own heartbeat as 'Pão! Pão! Pão!' [Bread! Bread! Bread!] (24).

This focus on Laurinda's interiority serves here to root both Western and pro-state Mozambican rhetoric on hunger in the corporeal and affective

3   *Meticagi* is a colloquial pluralization of 'metical', the currency introduced in Mozambique in June 1980.

everyday life of the individual. The intense and detailed descriptions of her physical and psychological suffering interrupt the discontinuity and anonymity that Michael Watts has identified as the defining characteristics of the image-based Western discourse on African catastrophe, reminding the reader that suffering is always-already an embodied phenomena (1991: 10–11). Similarly, the author's framing of Laurinda's children as the driving force behind her struggle – 'Laurinda, tu vai mbunhar. [...] E se mbunhar? Teus filhos não vai comer nada' [Laurinda, you're going to fail. [...] And if you fail? Your children will have nothing to eat] (24) – and yet absent from the narrative action, along with her husband, brings the embodied reality of the food supply burden placed on Mozambican women, and the concomitant depreciation of their own nutritional needs, into relief. The concept of nationhood, meanwhile, melts into the background, hinted at only in ambiguous references to unknown 'milícias' [militiamen]. This negation-by-omission of the nation-building project underlines the ultimate insignificance of its grand utopian promises in the everyday lives of poor Mozambican women, so often used as talking-points in pro-Frelimo rhetoric on nationhood and yet afforded no more than a symbolic role in nation-building itself.

The images evoked by Laurinda's internal monologue underscore the dehumanizing effects of severe hunger; she comes to see herself as part of 'um cortejo de caranguejos' [a bunch of crabs], while her fingernails become 'garras de caranguejo' [crab claws] that 'mordem as ancas' [bite into the hips] of the woman next in line (22); later, as she collapses, she is 'um caranguejo já sem força para agarrar' [a crab without any strength to claw and grab] (25). At the same time, however, Laurinda is shown to persistently assert her autonomy in the face of this adversity. When offered bread in exchange for sexual favours, she explodes with anger, mixing Portuguese and Ronga vocabulary in a brief but pointed speech that forces acknowledgement of her individuality, her belief system, the history and culture behind her: 'Sacana! Eu não me vende com pãozinho! Eu não é puta, ouviu? Tem marido, tem filhos, eu. [...] Eu não é cadela, ouviu! Você és moluene! Vai-te subir, moluene! Mbuianguana! [...] Não tem virgonha!' [You bastard! I don't sell myself for a bread roll! I'm not a whore, you hear me? I've got a husband, I've got children, me. [...] I'm not just some bitch, you hear!

You're nothing but a deadbeat! Go fuck yourself, deadbeat! Motherfucker! You've got no shame!] (23). Such expressions of agency work to reaffirm Laurinda's three-dimensional subjectivity and humanity, challenging the Western tendency to extrapolate individual dehumanization arising from hunger to populations as a whole, and to thus characterize such groups as being at once powerless victims and somehow subhuman. As noted in the Introduction to this study, Mbembe has proposed that Western writing on Africa has historically failed 'to account for *time as lived*, not synchronically or diachronically, but in its multiplicities and simultaneities, its presence and absences' (2001: 8). With the character of Laurinda, Cassamo uses hunger as a means of articulating the multivalent and often contradictory modalities intrinsic to post-independence Mozambican life, an expression of ambiguity encapsulated by the double negative of the story's last line, 'Laurinda não mbunhou o pão' [Laurinda did not fail to get the bread], in which the Ronga-rooted verb 'mbunhar' [to not get/find/achieve] is further negated with the Portuguese 'não' [no/not] (25).

Feast, Famine, Freedom

This problematization of Mozambican and Western grand narratives around food, hunger and the relationship of African women to them is reflected from a very different perspective, namely one of wealth and abundance, in Momplé's 1995 novella *Neighbours*, which tells the story of three Maputo families in the hours leading up to a South African-led Renamo raid on a flat in the city. The events in *Neighbours* are based on the very real killing of an innocent young couple and a security guard by anti-ANC[4] South African terrorists, assisted by Mozambicans, in the early hours of 29 May 1987, at the height of the post-independence war (Owen 2007a: 146–7).

---

4   'ANC' refers to the African National Conference, which at the time in which Momplé's novel was set was South Africa's main national anti-apartheid movement.

The targeting of a couple with no discernible involvement in anti-apartheid causes was interpreted by Mozambican police as an accident (Owen 2007a: 146); Momplé, by contrast, casts it as a deliberate 'mistake' designed to spread panic and to discourage popular support of the ANC (1995: 86). As an interview given by Momplé to Owen and Claire Williams makes clear, one of the murdered victims of the real-life attack, Suzana Pinto, was Momplé's colleague, and is portrayed in the text by the character of Leia (2004: 177–87).

The text spans one evening and three homes, describing events and conversations in each home at 7 pm, 9 pm, 11 pm, 1 am, and 8 am, and explaining the backstory of each character as the main narrative progresses. The first house is occupied by Narguiss and her daughters, a relatively wealthy middle-class Islamic family of Indian descent, who are preparing to celebrate Eid al-Fitr in the absence of Narguiss's husband Abdul; the second by Leia and Januário, a poor young couple with an infant daughter, Íris, and another baby on the way; and the third by Mena, a Mozambican woman, and her Mauritian husband Dupont, who has become involved with South African factions seeking to destabilize the Frelimo government, with whom he plans to orchestrate an attack that night. In the text's last ten pages the three families become dramatically intertwined as the targets of the attack are revealed to be Leia and Januário, who are shot to death on their balcony. Narguiss witnesses the attack shortly before being killed herself, shot in the chest and throat.

Owen has interpreted Momplé's use of food in *Neighbours* as a means of demonstrating the three families' relative wealth or poverty along class and racial lines (2007a: 148). This metonymical association is certainly evident throughout the text, with Narguiss's comfortable lifestyle reflected in her preparation of a lavish Eid feast – a result of her husband's machinations – despite the ongoing food shortages gripping much of the country, while Leia and Januário endure the monotony of everyday *ushua* (maize porridge) and cabbage. Yet Momplé's engagement with the symbology of food, eating and appetite surpasses this association with wealth, poverty and class, becoming a means of putting voice to the often-silent ways in which women attempt to negotiate some level of agency or power within the confines of a hierarchical gender structure. In this way, her women

characters' relationships with food and consumption act to subvert the
biopolitical depreciation of women's lives enacted through their discursive
equation with food supply, while at the same time emphasizing the fluidity and ambiguity of the power relations underlying post-independence
Mozambican society.

Momplé's characterization of Narguiss and her daughter Muntaz provides the clearest example of this use of food symbology for subversive
ends. Momplé immediately defines Narguiss in terms of her exceptional
relationship with food by describing her as having a 'corpo imenso' (1995: 11)
[huge body] (2001: 2),⁵ and her obesity is cited throughout the novel as
a grotesque deformity, including as her corpse lies in a morgue awaiting
autopsy (101). Moreover, when the reader first meets Narguiss she is preparing a feast to celebrate the end of the Ramadan fasting period, furthering
her latent association with extremes of consumption. When her backstory
is clarified later in the text we learn that Narguiss was initially married at
sixteen, to a wealthy man of Indian descent. Her memories of the wedding
are restricted to ones of its ostentatious abundance of luxury food items,
and her feelings of being suffocated by her red bridal veil. Her groom
instantly despised her and was compulsively unfaithful (75). Her shame
and humiliation at the marriage's failure was too great to tell her parents,
who nonetheless learned of her situation and agreed with her husband
that she be brought home; she recalls waiting between her father and her
husband, 'em silêncio, [...] vendo-os decidir o seu destino como se este não
lhe pertencesse' (76) [in silence, [...] watching them decide on her destiny
as if it didn't belong to her] (89).

Narguiss met Abdul at the funeral of a brother-in-law, and accepted
his advances and ultimately his marriage proposal 'apenas para cumprir o
seu destino de mulher' (76) [only to fulfil her destiny as a woman] (90),
but was surprised to find that she enjoyed partaking in physical intimacy
with him. On learning that Abdul, like her first husband, was frequently
unfaithful, she attempted to resign herself to the situation and to 'amá-lo

5   All translations of *Neighbours* are from Richard Bartlett and Isaura de Oliveira's 2001
     version. Bartlett and de Oliveira's translations are indicated by the page numbers in
     parentheses after the square brackets.

apesar de tudo' (76) [lov[e] him, despite everything] (90). Following the birth of her second daughter, Narguiss gained a large amount of weight, and continuing to love Abdul in spite of his numerous infidelities thus became a way for her to compensate for her obesity; his frequent absences, however, exacerbated this bodily shame, causing her to 'compensar-se com guloseimas que a fazem inchar cada vez mais' (77) [look for compensation in sweet delicacies [...] [that] made her a little fatter with each mouthful] (90). In response to this vicious cycle, Narguiss endured futile cycles of 'dietas de fome' (76) [starvation diets] (90), and subsequently developed chronic bulimia.

While Momplé primarily frames Narguiss's disordered eating as a way of attempting to keep her weight down, the cyclical patterns of self-destruction associated with bulimia nervosa – self-imposed starvation followed by uncontrollable binge-eating followed by self-induced vomiting or other purging, and back to starvation – signal the presence of deeper and more complex desires attached to consumption and the body, particularly when viewed in the context of Narguiss's personal narrative. Feasting on the luxury foods provided for her by Abdul suggests a temporary acceptance of the food as compensation for his infidelity, a literal and figurative swallowing of what he offers materially in place of emotional provision. By inducing vomiting, however, Narguiss refuses to assimilate the food, to take nourishment from it: in short, to allow it to physically constitute her. Unable to prevent Abdul from seeking gratification through the bodies of other women, Narguiss retreats inside her own body and casts out the limited gratification he offers to her, in a violent attempt to demarcate her own corporeal boundaries and thus to assert some form of power and control over her place in their marriage through the communicative medium of her body.

Like the suicidal characters in 'Aconteceu em Saua-Saua' and 'Ngilina, Tu Vai Morrer', then, Narguiss's only means of speaking through her body is through self-destruction. And ultimately, like Cassamo's Ngilina, her corporeal speech goes unheard by those it addresses. The last time Narguiss's body is shown, it is lying on a morgue table, ravaged by bullet wounds, awaiting a persistently delayed autopsy itself symbolic of this permanent bodily silence (Momplé 1995: 101). If Cassamo's Laurinda embodies both imposed negation and the dogged assertion of the desire to survive, Narguiss's self-destruction illustrates a drive toward negating desire altogether, which ironically serves only to intensify it. Her dead body, rendered grotesque by Momplé's descriptions of her obesity, thus encompasses abundance and lack, feast and famine, self-protection and self-destruction, murder and suicide, speaking to both the violent excesses and the chronic scarcities of the post-independence era. Both women's bodies, meanwhile, symbolically manifest the realities behind women's association with food, representing two extreme polarities on the same spectrum.

While Narguiss's attempt to utilize food and eating as a means of accruing a limited level of power and agency is ultimately futile, her youngest daughter Muntaz's similar pursuit, mentioned in the text only in passing, ends very differently. To the disappointment of her mother, for whom the exclusive acceptable female objective is 'agarrar marido' (1995: 14) [grabbing a husband] (2001: 7), Muntaz insists on staying in education and away from anything that might impede her, including romantic relationships. When her parents resist her desire to finish secondary education, Muntaz launches a series of protests, beginning with 'rogos e silêncios acusatórios' (14) [begging [and] accusatory silence] (7) and escalating to a refusal to eat. This realization of a hunger strike of sorts is, in the end, successful, resulting in Muntaz finishing her secondary schooling, which in turn leads to her enrolment in medical school. By deliberately engaging in self-starvation, Muntaz thus frees herself from the confines of the domestic sphere. In this way, she effectively subverts the discursive synonymity of women and food by withdrawing from food altogether, symbolically negating her espousal of a maternal role. Recalling a long, worldwide tradition of hunger striking as a method of passive resistance, Muntaz's refusal of food here signals a direct seizure of corporeal subjectivity.

Reading this brief anecdote from Muntaz's past in the immediate narrative context of her family's preparation for a festival marking the end of Ramadan reinforces this interpretation: Muntaz has taken fasting, an activity intended to represent an ascetic prostration before God, and reappropriated it as a means of resisting patriarchal obligations. With the character of Muntaz, Momplé indicates that the biopolitical instrumentalization of women may carry within it the keys to its own undoing; what she also implies, however, is that the ability to utilize those keys may rely on a background of privilege granted to few women. The complexities, ambiguities and contradictions of post-independence Mozambican power structures are thus, once again, pulled into the foreground.

Mortal Transgressions: 'Xirove' (Momplé 1997) and *Palestra para um Morto* (Cassamo 2000)

Suicidality and hunger, then, emerge in the works of Momplé and Cassamo as two 'exceptional states' within the 'states of exception' that dominated Mozambican political life in the long twentieth century, working to complicate the flows and hierarchies of power and agency attached to the biopolitical machinations of both the colonial and post-independence regimes. A third such state, evident in the work of both writers, is that of ghostliness. The metaphoric notion of haunting has often been deployed by postcolonial theorists as a way to envision the relationship between the metropole and the colony during both colonial occupation itself and the post-independence aftermath: to name but a few examples pertinent to this chapter, Mbembe writes of the 'phantom-like world' inhabited by the colonized, wherein 'relations between life and death [...] are blurred' (2003: 20–2); Gilroy perceives the postcolonial 'enthusiasm for tradition' as 'the fallout from modernity's protracted ambivalence towards the blacks that haunt its dreams' (1993: 191); and Paulo de Medeiros (2009) characterizes the postimperial nationalist discourse of both colonizer and colonized as always having been 'foremost a spectral one, with the necessary holding on to some ghostly figure of the past as guarantee for the vitality of the nation'. In her work on Momplé specifically, Owen describes the writer's narratives as '[s]taged as a series of literary "hauntings"', which represent the 'shifting experiences of national alienation, allegiance, and self-exile in the conflicted home spaces of colony and postcolony' and ultimately indicate 'the resurgence of neocolonial power working through paternalist family relations' (2007a: 132–3). Yet the literary trope of ghostliness – that is to say, the image, whether figurative or literal, of the (un)dead ghost or phantom itself – in postcolonial literature has remained relatively unexamined. This final section will explore the implications of Cassamo's and Momplé's textual renderings of ghostliness for the questions that started this chapter, asked by Mbembe (2003: 12): 'What place is given to life, death, and the human body', and 'how are they inscribed in the order of power?'

Closing Death's Door

Momplé's short story 'Xirove', originally published in her 1997 collection *Os Olhos da Cobra Verde* and reproduced in her 2012 anthology of selected works, describes the return of a Renamo soldier, Salimo, to his natal village in rural northern Mozambique at the end of the post-independence war. During his eleven years of absence, the members of the village have endured both the acute brutality of Renamo attacks and the more chronic dread of their reoccurrence, and are thus reluctant to accept his return; his own brother, Atumane, is no exception (2012: 122). Atumane's wife Rafa, however, experiences an instant spark of attraction to Salimo upon meeting him for the first time, a feeling reciprocated by Salimo and immediately noticed by his mother (122–3). Following Salimo's first, strained encounter with the villagers, his family arrange for him to undergo the *xirove* of the story's title, an old Makhuwa ritual intended to initiate the reintegration of disgraced village members back into the group (126–7). In the days that follow, as he waits for the ceremony to take place, Salimo becomes increasingly drawn to Rafa, and she to him (128). One hot night, she leaves her marital bed and walks out naked into the family orchard, watched by Salimo, who in turn is watched by his mother. As Salimo observes Rafa from a distance, his mother approaches, warning him against hurting his family again (130). In the final pages of the story, the time comes for Salimo to undergo the *xirove*. The day after the ritual, however, in place of attending the *batuque* that marks his full reintegration into village life, Salimo announces that he is going to find work in the city of Nampula, and leaves his family, this time implicitly for good (130–1).

Salimo's return to the village is framed as a haunting almost gothic in quality, a supernatural return from the unknown by a restless entity transgressing the boundary between life and death. When he arrives at his family's home, it is as if he has appeared out of nowhere; he seems to have 'brotado da própria tempestade que se abatera sobre toda a região' [sprouted from the storm itself, which had battered the entire region] (121). The electrical storm, alongside the 'energia electrizante' [electrifying energy] (121) Salimo appears to emanate, suggests a disturbance in the atmosphere, an upset in the normal order of things that coincides with his homecoming. His demeanour is not quite human: he has 'uma cor argilosa' [the colour of clay]; his smile is 'retorcida' [twisted]; his teeth appear 'precocemente corroídos' [prematurely corroded] and his eyes 'raiados de sangue' [streaked with blood]; and his smell is that of 'animais da selva' [jungle animals] (121). His arrival scares his brother's children, who hide in their mother's *capulana* as he stands, 'infestando o ar com o seu fedor' [polluting the air with his stench] (121–2). Momplé does not specify the events that Salimo has witnessed in the last eleven years, attributing his appearance only to 'anos e anos de deambulação pela mata' [years and years of wandering through the wilderness] (121) – an aimless activity suggestive of ghostly restlessness – but his presence provokes an expansive feeling of dread in his mother: 'a impressão de que ele trazia ainda, aderente ao corpo, resquícios de sangue das vítimas da guerra' [the impression that he still carried, clinging to his body, remnants of the blood of his war victims] (122).

As the narrative continues, this sense of ghostliness is intensified by Momplé's descriptions of Salimo's behaviour in the village, which make clear that both Salimo's family and the other villagers do indeed experience his presence in their midst as a haunting. He seems to 'mover-se ainda num mundo onírico' [still move through a dreamlike world] despite the 'aspecto mais humanizado' [more humanlike appearance] he attains having washed and changed clothes (Momplé 2012: 125). In the period between his arrival in the village and the realization of the *xirove*, he is excluded from social gatherings or rites, spending the days sleeping and only leaving the house 'a coberto da noite' [under cover of night] (128). It is during these nights that he begins to watch Rafa, silently and from afar, remaining in the shadows, as she too begins to take on ghostly characteristics, suffering from insomnia, wandering aimlessly in the night, and entering into silent communion with the moon. Salimo's ghostliness, it seems, is contagious. Meanwhile, through his connection with Rafa, Salimo begins to reassume elements of human desire, 'vibrando intimamente, mesmo à distância, com o som da sua voz, o roçar das capulanas, o odor chamativo do seu corpo' [quivering inwardly, even from afar, with the sound of her voice, the rustling of her *capulanas*, the beckoning scent of her body] (128). Rafa's body thus becomes the means by which Salimo might enter back into the domain of life, a consummation his mother ultimately prevents.

Salimo's exclusion from the domain of full humanity can be read as a form of social death, as understood by Patterson and Mbembe: a 'secular excommunication' (Patterson 1982: 5) enacted through imposed marginality. His ghostly demeanour functions as a literal embodiment of this liminal state; he is, to borrow Mbembe's phrasing, 'a perfect figure of a shadow', existing in the borderlands of life and death (2003: 21). Yet while social death as defined by Patterson and Mbembe is a form of violence carried out by the colonial state, a means of deliberately alienating colonized persons from their subjectivities, in 'Xirove' it becomes an instrument for collective healing and regeneration that seeks to delegitimize the sources of violence in place of allowing them to take root once again.

In her ethnography of the Mozambican post-independence war, Carolyn Nordstrom describes a discussion that reinforces this interpretation of Salimo as the ghostly embodiment of a state of social death, collectively imposed as a means of cauterizing violence. Noting the central role of 'phantoms and the phantasmagorical' in certain African belief systems, she relays the following statement given to her by a Mozambican man during a conversation about the war:

> Do you know why, when you meet a phantom on the path at night, you run back the way you came, and never look behind the phantom? Because if you pass him and turn around to look back, you will see there is nothing there. This war, it is a lot like that phantom. (1997: 132)

For Nordstrom, the phantom in this story finds physicality in the figure of the Renamo soldier. One does not pass the phantom because 'to do so means the phantom is aware of you and can then interact with you'; likewise, one does not risk being noticed by a Renamo soldier, with whom even the most passing of encounters could result in injury or death (133). She furthermore interprets the dangerous 'nothingness' behind the phantom as signifying the 'violent meaninglessness' and 'existential absurdity' of the conflict itself (133).

Read through the critical lens of Nordstrom's testimony, Salimo can be seen as personifying this proverbial phantom, carrying with him the weight of meaningless violence that defined the post-independence war. When he interacts with Rafa, she is drawn toward the meaninglessness behind him, taking on the characteristics of a phantom herself, while Salimo begins to recover his humanity. Rather than allowing Salimo to consolidate his humanity through the body of Rafa, however, Salimo's mother asks that he turn back. In doing so, she sacrifices the child she conceived, denying his humanity in order that the village may begin to regenerate. The cleansing ritual of the *xirove* thus becomes funereal, assuring Salimo's safe passage while marking his exclusion from the domain of the living. Salimo's social death, for those still haunted by the violent meaninglessness he embodies, becomes a way of renewing life.

A Ghost and a Machine

This implication of haunting with regeneration and sacrifice is a pivotal theme in Cassamo's 2000 novella *Palestra para um Morto* [*Speech to a Dead Man*], a short but densely enigmatic and ambiguous work with a narrative spanning the late colonial and post-independence eras. The text, as the title suggests, is addressed to a dead man and written mostly in the second person, and is narrated by the person who finds the dead man's body: a shepherd's young nephew, tending his uncle's herd of goats. The dead man's ghost appears to the narrator immediately after his discovery, troubling the boundaries between life and death in a way that persists throughout the novella. As a result of this initial encounter, the narrator loses his uncle's goats, and runs away in fear of reprisal, becoming lost in the wilderness (38).[6]

The narrator is rescued by a young man on a bicycle, en route to inform his mother of 'más novas' [bad news]; as they arrive in the 'Xilunguini',[7] the young man explains that the bad news is his own death in the mines of Johannesburg, and then vanishes and is replaced by a cage of hummingbirds (39–42). The narrator takes refuge in the city with priests, and learns how to read and write, thereafter making a living by writing letters for women whose husbands work in the Johannesburg mines (82–3). As he reaches adulthood and then enters old age, his encounters with the dead man become more frequent, accompanied by visions of a mysterious and unfamiliar machine (79–80). He begins to sketch the visions, building the resulting design (87–90). The machine is ultimately revealed to be a coffin that allows for self-burial. The narrator understands that he must sacrifice and bury himself, along with a wooden statue of a priest, in order to put the dead man to rest (91). The text ends, ambiguously, with an ecstatic monologue looking back on the narrator's life (93–5).

Cassamo's narration of the dead man's final months clearly evokes the processes of social death at the heart of the Portuguese colonial project. From within this theme, however, a further possibility emerges that reflects the notion of self-destruction as the means to freedom: that of social suicide. In a chapter that begins with the grotesque image of his unclaimed cadaver, '[c]heio de bichos, unhas de fera, e mais desses cabelos crescidos do estrume do próprio corpo' [covered in bugs, the claws of wild animals, and thread-like growths sprouting from the mulch of your own body] (2012: 27), the

6   Neither the dead man nor the boy that finds him (who is, by the end of the novel, an old man) are given names; in order to maintain clarity, I will refer to them as the 'dead man' and 'narrator' respectively, despite the former being alive in some parts of the text and the narrative voice being ambiguous at certain points.

7   *Xilunguini* refers to Lourenço Marques/Maputo and translates as 'where the whites live' ['el lugar donde viven los blancos'], as an *El País* interview with Mia Couto makes clear (Machado 2013).

narrator describes finding the man's home, 'uma cabana despachada tipo ninho de rola' [a ramshackle cabin like a a dove's nest] (28) containing the entrance to a deep tunnel, and pieces together the circumstances leading up to his demise, describing them as follows: the man is a fugitive, living undercover having escaped *xibalo* on the colonial railway (28–9). Hearing a knock on the door one day, the man glimpses a *cipaio*'s[8] hat through his doorway, and, assuming that he has been denounced to colonial authorities, hides in the cabin, watching the doorway (29). The *cipaio* does not leave, and in desperation the man begins to dig an escape route beneath the house, 'a cavar parece bicho, com todas as patas possíveis, dias, meses, anos' [digging like some creature, with all the paws you had, days, months, years] (29). Eventually he meets with fresh air, and leaves the tunnel to hunt, but always returns to it, out of fear or force of habit. One day, his tunnel begins to shake, and he realizes that it is the train. Reminded of his labour on the railway, and that of his fellow forced workers, he is overwhelmed by rage, and tunnels back to the cabin to confront the *cipaio* (30). When he opens the door, he realizes that the '*cipaio*' is merely a hat on a stick. The train whistles suddenly, shocking him into cardiac arrest, and he dies (31).

By fleeing first the *xibalo* and later his improvised cabin, the dead man temporarily removes himself from the biopolitical order of the colony. In doing so, he deliberately espouses the social death imposed on the colonized subject in a way that can be seen as a figurative suicide, alienating himself from both his original and affective homes. His tunnelling beneath the cabin thus comes to represent a form of self-burial, wherein he becomes assimilated with the earth, a dehumanized 'bicho' [creature] surviving, the narrator speculates, on '[t]oupeiras, minhocas, raízes, os próprios excrementos em ciclo fechado' [moles, earthworms, roots, your own excrement in a closed loop] (29). As with Mussa Racua's literal suicide in Momplé's 'Aconteceu em Saua-Saua', then, self-destruction here comes to figure as a means of asserting resistance to the biopolitical instrumentalization of the colonized subject.

8   A *cipaio* was roughly equivalent to the English 'sepoy', that is, an indigenous policeman in the colonial administration.

The Makalanhana, the name given to the steam train whose whistle stops the dead man's heart, is here symbolic of the totalization of power identified by Mbembe as the desired end point of the biopolitical colonial project, representing in concrete form the 'crystallization of the state as a technology of domination' (2001: 42). The dead man's attempt to reclaim somatic agency through social suicide is initially successful, exempting his body as instrument for the construction of the railway, but the train literally catches up with him, 'exhuming' him from his self-burial in the tunnel and commandeering his body, life and death in an ironic act of reappropriation. The 'longos alfinetes do apito desse comboio que veio ter o nome de Makalanhana' [long needles of the whistle of that train that came to have the name of Makalanhana] (31) that drive through the dead man's heart thus come to signify the industrialized violence of the colonial regime, which 'penetrate[s] almost everywhere' to the point where 'it pursues the colonized even in sleep and dream', or, in this case, even in pseudo-death (Mbembe 2001: 173–5).

Following this interpretation, the dead man's phantom embodies both the ultimate resistance to biopolitical instrumentalization and the persistent, haunting presence of its violence. The haunting enacts a stubborn drive toward meaning, pushing back against the colonial construction of the indigenous subject as, in Mbembe's terms, the 'perfect figure of a shadow' (2003: 21): that which 'is, but only insofar as it is nothing' (2001: 187). The narrator's discovery of the dead man's corpse, meanwhile, serves to represent the former's interpellation into the apparatus of the colonial regime, an initiation that proves to be inescapable. It is here that the relationship between haunting, sacrifice and regeneration reflected in Momplé's 'Xirove' comes to the fore, as the narrator's inability to escape the figurative apparatus of colonial violence embodied by the phantom ultimately culminates in his construction of the literal apparatus for his own death. Just as Salimo's mother becomes aware that she must sacrifice her son in order that her village might regenerate following the atrocities of the post-independence war, the narrator arrives at the understanding that he must sacrifice himself in order that the ghostly presence of colonial violence might be put to rest. His meticulous construction of the machine for his own suicide, described in the following quotation, figures as a reenactment of the dead man's labour on the railway, which in turn is a metonym for the colonial labour system's instrumentalization of the colonized subject in service of his or her own destruction:

> Suada labuta, obrigação feita sedução, cada traço do esboço a dizer quero ser objecto, pau, ripa de chanfuta, músculo de bambu, corda de sisal, pele de antílope, fibra de ulolo e eticetra e eticetra e mais a boca escura da cova, até o esboço virar palpável objecto, pomposo aparato, e, quiçá, o meu foguetão na Lua. (Cassamo 2012: 87)

> [Sweaty drudgery, obligation turned seduction, each line of the sketch saying I want to be an object, wood, bamboo muscle, sisal rope, antelope hide, fibrous twine and etcetera and etcetera and again the dark mouth of the pit, until sketch becomes palpable object, grandiose apparatus, and, perhaps, my rocket on the Moon.]

This reenactment of colonial labour for the purpose of putting the ghost of imperial violence to rest can here be seen as effectively reversing the flow of power through the colonial labour system, displacing the use of physical labour as a means of consolidating colonial authority and reappropriating it as a means of unmaking colonial violence as a whole.

The narrator's lack of children, recalled as he succumbs to the suicide machine, suggests that his suicide enacts the sacrifice not only of himself, but also of any notion of futurity. This sense of the narrator's annihilation of his own futurity is furthered when he unwraps what he believes to be the wooden statue of a priest to accompany him into his tomb, which turns out instead to be a carving of his first love, Biana. Rather than signifying the possibility of afterlife, the carving embodies the past; the narrator's suicide thus collapses past into future, destroying the possibility of further haunting. This negation of the future self, reflecting the alienation from futurity imposed on the colonized subject, provides further evidence that the narrator's final deeds mimic the colonization process, representing a ritualized reenactment that serves to disempower the original. As he draws nearer death, the narrator reaches a state of existential ecstasy, transcending his physicality while simultaneously embracing it, indicating a true detachment from the machinations of biopower. The analogy of the suicide machine as the narrator's 'foguetão na Lua' [rocket on the Moon] underscores this framing of his suicidal sacrifice as a sublime act, functioning outside the reach of power; an attainment of absolute freedom. As in

'Xirove', death again provides a means to life, shoring up the complex and often contradictory entanglement of biopower, death and freedom in the (post)colonial context.

Conclusion: Biopower at the Brink

With its blurring of the lines between life and death, embodiment and transcendence, the social and the individual, suicide and the attainment of freedom, and self-destruction and sacrifice, *Palestra para um Morto* brings together many of the prevailing themes from this chapter, providing a non-linear metanarrative of necropolitics in colonial and post-independence Mozambique. As this final chapter has sought to demonstrate, a necropolitical focus on the evolution of Portuguese imperial endeavour in Africa underscores the centrality of death to the country's colonial presence on the continent, first reflected prior to sub-Saharan expansion through the association of unknowability with nothingness and chaos. Encounters with indigenous Africans cemented this association, with Africans construed as amoral and putting little value on life, an impression of arbitrariness later used as a circular justification for rendering African lives precariously depreciated. The proliferation of laws and treatises in colonial Mozambique in the later nineteenth and early twentieth centuries institutionalized these notions, forcing native populations into a state of social death.

Biopolitical thought, and its concomitant depreciation of certain lives, furthermore emerged as fundamental to the post-independence ideology of Frelimo, whose triangulation of women, food and national unity and progress held women responsible for the optimization of the independent nation while simultaneously excluding them from the same. Meanwhile, death persisted – and continues to persist – as the primary signifier for Africa in Western discourses on the continent, portrayed as 'a headless figure threatened with madness and quite innocent of any notion of center, hierarchy, or stability' (Mbembe 2001: 3), a void of negation in opposition to which the West might shape its own self-image. Within this conception,

Africans themselves become either barbaric despots or helpless victims, a racially charged imagining that brings the West's lack of critical thought on the complexities and contradictions of power relations on the continent into relief.

The selected works by Momplé and Cassamo, with their subversive interpretations of the polyvalent meanings of death, life and self-destruction, serve to deconstruct both the archaic colonial and contemporary Western entanglements of Africa and death, while also challenging the post-independence fetishization of life and futurity. Momplé's 'Aconteceu em Saua-Saua' and Cassamo's 'Ngilina, Tu Vai Morrer' both narrate the stories of characters ultimately driven to suicide by a profound melancholia imposed on them by external entities. For both characters, suicide is presented as a means of asserting somatic agency in the face of instrumentalization, whether as part of the colonial regime or by an abusive spouse; at the precise moment that such agency is achieved, however, the subject ceases to be. Mussa Racua's story is anchored in a specific time and place, and the text emphasizes the affective implications of his suicide for those around him, indicating a sense of futurity for his narrative. Ngilina's story, by contrast, is free of temporal markers, and this timelessness serves to shore up the parallels between colonial subjugation and the enduring oppression of Mozambican women. Both characters attempt to speak through their bodies, but while Mussa Racua's final protest lives on, Ngilina's goes unheard.

This notion of bodily protest, or of making the body speak, also features in Cassamo's 'Laurinda, Tu Vai Mbunhar' and Momplé's *Neighbours*, here focused on the state of hunger. With the character of Laurinda, Cassamo gives voice to the interior affective experience of hunger, a state neglected by discourses on food insecurity. Meanwhile, by foregrounding Laurinda's grasp on moral agency, the narrative displaces the Western notion of populations undergoing starvation as driven to a subhuman state of helplessness. Momplé's portrayal of Narguiss in *Neighbours* diverges sharply from Laurinda's narrative, showing her living amidst an abundance of food that she nonetheless deliberately abuses in silent protest of her husband's betrayal and neglect. Beyond a straightforward attempt to regain control over her own body, Narguiss's bulimia also represents a desire to speak through her body by refusing to assimilate her husband's material compensations for his absence. Yet her body, like Ngilina's, ultimately remains silent, outwardly inscribed only with the arbitrary violence of the post-independence conflict. Within the same narrative, however, her daughter Muntaz's similar attempt to glean agency by refusing nourishment is successful, suggesting that female resistance via the means of their oppression is possible, if only from the springboard of privilege granted to women like Muntaz.

Haunting and ghostliness represent a final state in the work of both writers in which necropolitical tensions come to the fore, bringing together the complexities around self-destruction, social death and the body reflected in the writers' other texts. Momplé's 'Xirove' presents the chance for rehumanization following a period of social death, with the female body figured as the catalyst. In order that Salimo's mother might ensure collective regeneration, however, his possibility of social resurrection is refused. Social death, historically both method and outcome of colonial instrumentalization, is thus removed from this subjugative role and reappropriated as a means of post-traumatic healing. Cassamo's *Palestra para um Morto* also figures social death as presenting a possibility of freedom, but here it is one that is displaced by the encroachment of colonial control. The narrator's subsequent encounter with death serves to interpellate him into the framework of colonial violence, whose phantom exerts a haunting presence until he understands that he must unmake the futurity of imperial violence through a sublime reenactment of the colonial process that ultimately ends his own life.

These six texts evoke exceptional states as a way of demonstrating their characters' drive toward a sense of meaning lost in the centuries of violence and subjugation that defined both the colonial rule of Mozambique and its uncertain aftermath. By speaking for those whose lives have all-too-often been excluded from the biopolitical optimization of life, and indeed whose lives have been sacrificed and instrumentalized in service of it, Momplé and Cassamo reverse the biopolitical orders of the colony and postcolony while simultaneously challenging the West's ongoing construction of Africa as the embodiment of meaninglessness. Far from remaining simply a symptom of the negation of Africa and African lives, death and self-destruction are thus reclaimed as expressive signifiers for the continent's mercurial and sometimes contradictory flows of power.

Firing Lines

On 1 July 2015, a new Mozambican penal code was brought into effect. With it came the reminder that Mozambique's previous legal framework, a grim inheritance from Portugal, had been in force since 1886. A change that received little attention in the Mozambican press itself was the removal of a law prohibiting 'vícios contra a natureza' [unnatural vices], a reform that Western media outlets were quick to interpret and endorse as decriminalizing homosexuality (Smith 2015; Associated Press 2015). The flag of Mozambique was flown at the London LGBT+ Pride Parade on 27 June of that year, alongside those of the USA and Ireland, 'in recognition of [the countries'] recent advances in LGBT+ equality' ('Parade Flagbearers' 2015).

While this change could indeed be seen as breaking the steadfast silence of Frelimo on the subject of homosexuality, and as going some way toward delegitimizing the compulsory heterosexuality underpinning the country's gendered and sexual history and politics, the reactions of both Mozambican periodicals and Mozambique's only LGBT rights organization Lambda were more subdued. The national dailies *Verdade* and *Jornal Notícias* were at pains to point out that the law in question had not been used to punish 'homosexual acts' since independence (Lusa 2015), with the latter publication emphasizing that 'não há aqui espaço para falar-se de descriminalização do homossexualismo, porque se trata de uma conduta que nem sequer chegou a ser criminalizada no nosso país' [there is insufficient space here to talk about the decriminalization of homosexuality, since this is a behaviour that has never even been criminalized in our country] ('Editorial' 2015). A spokesperson from Lambda, meanwhile, was reported as urging caution, stating that the organization welcomed the reform but did not 'actually see it as something that will bring a change for how LGBT people live in Mozambique' (Smith 2015).

It is this brief but meaningful final comment on the intransigence of sexual politics in Mozambique's recent history, in tandem with the conflicting ways that these judicial changes have been reported in and outside of Mozambique, that brings us back to where this study began, at the contested intersection of official discourse, tacit implication and lived reality. The aim of this study has been to situate the gendered body within Mozambican narratives as a battleground: a site where power relations are produced, enforced and, most significantly, contested, via close readings of literary works by José Craveirinha, Paulina Chiziane, Noémia de Sousa, Ungulani Ba Ka Khosa, Lília Momplé and Suleiman Cassamo. The study has furthermore sought to illustrate the value of consciously ahistorical, intergenerational and inter-aesthetic comparisons, and a flexible and dynamic 'toolbox' approach to critical theory, as methods for producing new perspectives on the representation of the sexed body in Mozambican literature.

Chapter 1's initial examination of the latent presence of gender and sexuality in colonial, anticolonial and post-independence Mozambican official discourses, beginning with the intensification of Portuguese colonial endeavour following the Berlin Conference in 1884–5 and ending with the peak of the Frelimo-Renamo post-independence conflict in the late 1980s and early 1990s, revealed their foundational role in the construction of sociopolitical and affective meaning-making throughout the long twentieth century. Gendered and sexual meanings were shown to be inextricably bound up with Mozambique's contested territorial borders, with gendered and territorial anxieties in a persistent state of symbiosis. Reinscribing and enforcing gendered power hierarchies, both in terms of the gender binary and within genders, thus represented for both the colonial and post-independence regimes a way of soothing unease around the permeability of national borders and the unworkable fiction of national unity.

The reification of white Portuguese masculinity as occupying a position of naturalized superiority in relation to black masculinity was shown to be pivotal to the Portuguese imperial regime's reinforcement of gender hierarchies, and the emasculation of black men on which it relied was a key mechanism in colonial discourses from the late nineteenth century through to the New State's promotion of Lusotropicalist mythology in the

1950s and 1960s. In Chapter 2, José Craveirinha's (1964) use of a mythic black male 'hero' as the recurrent subject of his early poetry was seen as a direct counternarrative to this facet of Portuguese colonial control, reflecting both the romanticized imagining of black masculinity typical of the negritude aesthetic and its stoic reworking in the anticolonial writing of Frantz Fanon. This revindication of black masculinity was shown to be realized in Craveirinha's early poems, namely 'Xigubo', 'África' and 'Manifesto', through the identification of the black male hero with virility, strength, resilience and a uniquely regenerative relationship with the Mozambican terrain, poetically embodied by the Mãe África trope and affirmed through a semiotics of sexual penetration and insemination.

Engaging this sexual symbology with the theories of compulsory heterosexuality principally developed by Judith Butler (1990, 1993), however, revealed the objectification of black femininity and reinforcement of the hierarchical gender binary on the flipside of this consolidation of black masculinity. In this way, anticolonial subjectivity as imagined by Craveirinha was shown to be essentially masculine, predicated on reiterated sexual dominance over women and thus ultimately serving to perpetuate the Lusotropicalist discourses of gender that posited black women as in a permanent state of sexual availability. While Craveirinha does recast the emasculated male body as a site of resistance to colonial ideology as a whole, then, the underlying gendered meanings on which that resistance relies remain, for women in particular, oppressively consistent with those of colonial discourse. Divested of agency and subjectivity of their own, women become in these poems merely the telluric vessels of an imagined authenticity.

Paulina Chiziane's 2000 novel *O Sétimo Juramento* was seen in the second half of this first chapter as a satirical response to masculinist anticolonial narratives like that of Craveirinha. The corrupt protagonist David's attempt to reinforce his fragile sense of masculinity through the Faustian espousal of exaggerated precolonial Tsonga rituals was interpreted as a parody of the 'return' to authentic African origins poetically endorsed by Craveirinha, with its farcical drive made clear through the author's deployment of the language of excess. Identified by Butler as a means of destabilizing gendered boundaries by emphasizing the performative aspects of gender, and thus bringing into relief the performative nature of all gender, this engagement with the hyperbolic is especially evident in the novel's lurid portrayals of David's orgiastic sexual behaviour, and his subsequent reimagining of himself as a hypermasculine warrior figure. Meanwhile, Chiziane's parallel use of unflinching realism, exemplified most clearly in her depictions of David's acts of sexual violence against child prostitute Mimi and his incestuous rape of his own daughter Suzy, was seen to root this hyperbolic parody firmly in the lived realities of Mozambican women and girls, exposing the violent logical conclusion of the anticolonial poetics of Mãe África typified by Craveirinha's early work. The masculine body as an instrument of oppression is thus reimagined as a surface for the author's inscription of cartoonish parody, while the female body as naturalized site of hegemonic enforcement becomes a means of exposing the ultimate abject violence of that naturalized role.

While Chapter 2 thus explored Craveirinha's identification of his male subjects with a regenerative meaning for black male corporeality, and Chiziane's troubling of that identification through the strategic use of satire, parody and realism, Chapter 3 sought to examine the writing of poet Noémia de Sousa (1948–51) and prose fiction writer Ungulani Ba Ka Khosa (1987, 1990) in terms of the works' shared capacity for enacting a radical *dis*identification with colonial, anticolonial and post-independence restrictions on black female corporeality, despite the authors' wholly different literary styles and techniques. The chapter was underpinned by queer Latino theorist José Esteban Muñoz's theory of 'disidentification' (1999), which itself builds on the notions of 'differential consciousness', 'determinate negation', and 'conciencia de la mestiza' developed respectively by Chicana feminists Chela Sandoval (1991), Norma Alarcón (1996) and Gloria Anzaldúa (1987), and brings them into dialogue with poststructuralist frameworks of gender subversion like that of Butler. Common to all these theories is the value placed on the disavowal of fixed subjecthood in favour of an identity of slippage that resists clear definition or categorization.

De Sousa was seen as embracing this slippage through the use of three poetic strategies, which included the avoidance of specific gendered grammatical agreement in favour of the first-person plural form, the playful switching of male–female/subject–object positionalities, and the identification with a masculine poetic voice. The first strategy, seen most clearly in poems 'Passe' and 'Nossa Voz' was shown to have a refractive effect on the author's subject positionality, allowing her to resist the notion of identificatory affiliation. The second, exemplified by 'Poema para um Amor Futuro' and 'Se Me Quiseres Conhecer', was interpreted as affirming anticolonial solidarity while simultaneously sliding out from the gendered body, thereby disavowing the reinforcement of gender hierarchies that the mainstream anticolonial struggle entailed. The latter strategy, meanwhile, was seen particularly clearly in de Sousa's lesser-studied poem 'Zampungana', in which the poet combines masculine identification with an aesthetics of abjection, as understood by Julia Kristeva (1982) and Elizabeth Grosz (1994). This use of an at once masculine and abject poetic persona was seen as resisting imposed femininity while simultaneously challenging the naturalized position of masculinity at the apex of gender hierarchy, speaking powerfully to J. Halberstam's work on female drag (1998). The gendered body thus becomes a site for resistance in de Sousa's work insofar as it is disavowed and rejected.

The use of abjection as a means of disidentification was carried forward as a primary point of analysis for the second half of the chapter, which focused on Khosa's novel *Ualalapi* (1987), particularly the character Damboia, and short stories from his *Orgia dos Loucos* (1990) collection. The use of disidentificatory strategies in Khosa's work was explored as a means of exposing the atrocities committed by Renamo during the post-independence conflict, while simultaneously speaking to a profound disillusionment with the nation-building project as conceived by Frelimo. In contrast to de Sousa, whose enactment of disidentification was shown to hinge primarily on her disavowal of fixed corporealities through the ludic manipulation of language, Khosa's work was shown to be firmly staked in corporeality itself, and specifically in the excessively visceral portrayal of damaged, dying or dead bodies.

Theories of the grotesque, originating in the work of Mikhail Bakhtin (1968) and developed by Mary Russo (1994), were here used to parse the unsettling potential of damaged and excessive female corporeality as embodied by *Ualalapi*'s Damboia, aunt of chief Ngungunhane, who dies after three months of unending menstruation and whose death unleashes a wave of chaos across Ngungunhane's kingdom. Damboia's troubling presence was interpreted as expressing disidentification with the Mãe África figure in line with that of de Sousa. Additionally, however, the grotesque corporeal focus of Damboia's characterization was seen to speak to the latent abjectification of the female body inherent in Frelimo's characterization of it as the maternal site of imagined national unity, thus rejecting the validity of the unity itself.

The parturient bodies of the female characters of Khosa's short stories 'A Praga' and 'O Prémio' were likewise seen as the catalysts for disidentification with Frelimo's narrative of nationhood, this time specifically in terms of the party's promotion of a discourse of reproductive futurism, a concept taken from the work of queer theorist Lee Edelman (2004). The grotesquely delayed placental expulsion of protagonist Luandle's anonymous mother in the former story was interpreted as a graphic corporealization of the permanent deferral of the symbolic Child of Frelimo's reproductive futurism, an omen ultimately fulfilled by the starved desperation of Luandle's son Kufeni. In 'O Prémio', meanwhile, the relentless labour pains of the parturient main character were understood through the lens of Elaine Scarry's pain theory (1985) as evoking the subjectivity-destroying distortion of the domestic sphere consistent with the infliction of torture. Using Carolyn Nordstrom's interarticulation of Scarry's theories with the specific acts of torture committed during the Mozambican post-independence conflict (1997), the protagonist of 'O Prémio' was thus interpreted as embodying both the atrocities committed by Renamo and the oppressive implications of Frelimo's reproductive futurism, while her damaged corporeality expressed Khosa's disavowal of both. This doubled disavowal was also seen as the central message of 'A Orgia dos Loucos', in which Khosa's use of abjection converges with his negation of reproductive futurity to produce a depiction of a family unit utterly destroyed by rape, torture and the lasting trauma of war. While the troubling of gendered boundaries via the rejection of corporeality was seen in de Sousa's work as a powerful means of resistance to gendered oppression, in Khosa's work it is the focus on corporeality that allows the gendered body to becomes a site of disidentification with broader political grand narratives.

This mapping of gendered resistance onto wider discourses of disavowal provided the starting point for the study's fourth and final chapter, which used Achille Mbembe's concept of necropolitics (2003), a reworking of of Michel Foucault's theory of biopolitics (1975–6), to explore the corporeal 'exceptional states' of suicidality, hunger and ghostliness in works by prose fiction writers Lília Momplé (1988, 1995) and Suleiman Cassamo (1989, 2000). An examination of early modern Portuguese expansionist documents and a revision of later colonial texts showed death to be bound up in Portuguese imperial thought on Africa along the same anxious lines as gender and sexuality, used in circular fashion as both a disciplining mechanism for the colonized population and as a justification for colonial subjugation. For Frelimo, meanwhile, death was seen to appear as the implicit counterpart to the party's aggressive emphasis on the attainment of optimal life, an objective rooted firmly in the female body. In Lília Momplé's 'Aconteceu em Saua-Saua' the impact of the colonial use of social death was seen as manifest in the protagonist Mussa Racua's melancholia. In contrast to the organic melancholia extensively theorized by Kristeva (1989), Mussa Racua's deep despair and psychosomatic disintegration are shown by Momplé to be deliberately imposed by colonial power structures. Though the character's suicide is on one level the ultimate fulfillment of this imposed state of social death, it was read here as a final, fleeting gesture of agency, signifying a purposeful removal of the colonized self from the biopolitical order of the colony. Even this self-destructive grasping of agency, however, was shown to be a male prerogative, as Momplé's spotlighting of its impact on Mussa Racua's wife and unborn child makes clear.

In Cassamo's 'Ngilina, Tu Vai Morrer', whose eponymous protagonist's life also ends in suicide, the gendered implications of the act were shown to be more central to the story. Despite Ngilina's display of a melancholic state, her story is not contextualized under any one external state apparatus; the piece could be set during any point in recent Mozambican history. Instead, colonial social death was here shown to be evoked by Cassamo through his depiction of gendered oppression, shoring up both the fundamentally gendered and phallocentric nature of colonial endeavour as explicated by Mbembe (2001), and the colonization of women's bodies that characterizes patriarchal gender structures. Ngilina's suicide was furthermore shown to point toward the voicelessness of subaltern women when compared with the death of Momplé's protagonist: whereas Mussa Racua's suicide is shown by the author to carry within it an expansive and potentially intergenerational longevity, Ngilina's violent death belongs to nobody except her silent self. While Mussa Racua's body was thus shown to become a site of ongoing resistance – albeit in the most violent and self-destructive fashion – thanks to his fulfillment of procreational imperatives, Ngilina's hanged body was seen to represent only her deep and inescapable silence.

The biopolitical power systems underpinning both Portuguese imperial thought and patriarchal subjugation were shown to persist throughout the Mozambican post-independence period, clearly emerging in Frelimo's triangulation of female body, food and nation. Within the post-independence nation-building project the optimization of food supply was construed as a key necessity for national unity, with the result that women, as the traditional bearers of responsibility for familial food supply, now discursively bore the burden of feeding the entire nation. The importance of breastfeeding was shown to have been promoted in a particularly aggressive fashion, with women who failed to breastfeed for a sufficient duration implicitly – and sometimes explicitly – blamed for high infant mortality rates. The interconnection of women and food supply was seen to engender an acutely negative impact on women during 1980s food shortages, which saw women sacrificing their own caloric needs in order to maintain a consistent food supply for their families. Women's lives thus became implicitly disposable. During this same decade, Africa as a massified whole became embroiled with starvation in the Western imaginary, homogenizing Africans themselves under the familiar imperialistic notions of the continent as a monolith of hopeless tragedy.

Cassamo's 'Laurinda, Tu Vai Mbunhar' was shown to expose the lived reality behind Frelimo's triangulation of women, food and nation, while simultaneously challenging this specific massification of Africans in late twentieth- and early twenty-first-century Western discourses, by focusing on the eponymous protagonist's hunger as a deeply affective and physically devastating individual experience. The author was seen to subtly acknowledge the role of family and nation in Laurinda's hunger through vague, brief references, while at the same time pushing them into the textual background in favour of the protagonist's interior monologue. Similarly, her sense of dehumanization and sexual objectification is made clear, but Cassamo's emphasis is consistently on the expressions of autonomy and subjectivity with which she responds to these oppressive barriers. Laurinda's hungry gendered body was thus shown to be used by Cassamo as a way to manifest the multifaceted, fluid and dynamic lived experiences of power in post-independence Mozambican life.

This use of embodied and gendered hunger as a means of emphasizing the ambiguous and inconsistent modalities of post-independence Mozambique was additionally identified in Momplé's *Neighbours*. Food was here seen to be utilized metonymically, representing wealth and poverty, but also as a way for women to acquire limited forms of agency within patriarchal power systems. The protagonist Narguiss was seen as a compelling example of this symbology thanks to Momplé's reference to her bulimia, a disorder associated with a cycle of starvation, bingeing and purging via self-induced vomiting. Narguiss's implicit engagement with these self-destructive behaviours was interpreted as expressing a refusal to assimilate the luxury foods her unfaithful husband provided to her in lieu of fidelity, thus gleaning a form of agency and power from her marriage through her hungry body. Like Ngilina's suicide, however, Narguiss's attempt to speak through her body was ultimately shown to be futile, with her dead body, displayed on a morgue table at the close of the novella, encapsulating the contradictions of the post-independence period while remaining irrevocably silenced. Narguiss's daughter Muntaz, by contrast, was seen to use self-induced starvation in the form of hunger strikes as a successful way of expressing her refusal to subscribe to the sexist obligations imposed upon her. Her outright withdrawal from food was thus read as disrupting her interpellation into the maternal role by subverting the interconnection of women and food. As with Cassamo's Laurinda, then, the hungry bodies of both Narguiss and Muntaz were interpreted as the corporeal manifestations of gendered protest; the behaviours and successes of all three women, however, remain wildly dissimilar, itself indicative of the ambiguities and contradictions of the post-independence period.

The final 'exceptional state' explored in the final chapter was that of ghostliness, which was shown to have been used as an analytical metaphor within postcolonial studies, while remaining relatively unexplored as a post-colonial literary trope. In Momplé's 'Xirove', the author's portrayal of the return of a former Renamo soldier, Salimo, to his rural family home after eleven years was identified as a gothic haunting spreading disorder and dis-trust through his family and village, who impose upon him a state of social death comparable to that inflicted on colonized subjects. Salimo's mother's warning that her son must leave the village for good in order to prevent the destruction of familial and community integrity was interpreted as a reit-eration of this social death. In contrast to oppressive colonial uses of this status, however, in the hands of Salimo's mother it is a way of resisting the power seized by Renamo through the exercise of violence, thus becoming a means of collective healing, an interpretation that speaks to Nordstrom's work on the phantom as symbolic of meaningless violence within rural popular culture during the post-independence war (1997). The meaningless violence – and violent meaninglessness – that Salimo embodies is thus cast out from the domain of the living, rendering his social death a way for the village to ensure the renewal of meaningful life. His 'dead' body becomes a site of a contestation and resistance, but one that does not belong to him.

Cassamo's novel *Palestra para um Morto* (2000) was seen to revisit this interconnection between ghostliness, sacrifice and regeneration through the characters of the dead man and narrator. The author's framing of the dead man's final activities was interpreted as indicating a form of social suicide, wherein the character removes himself from the biopolitical order of the colony while deliberately adopting the status of social death. Like Momplé's Mussa Racua, the dead man was here seen as utilizing self-destruction as a means of corporealizing resistance to colonial instrumentalization, a resistance that is ultimately disrupted with the sudden arrival of the steam train as a concrete manifestation of industrialized colonial biopolitics. The dead man's haunting of the narrator was shown to represent a further form of determined resistance to imposed social death, a spectral reminder that colonial subjugation must not be forgotten. Meanwhile, the narrator's realization that the only way to free himself from the haunting is to kill and bury himself was understood as an acceptance of self-sacrifice for the purpose of resolving that subjugation, with his machinated suicide and self-burial a reappropriative reenactment of colonial instrumentalization.

This ritualized mimicry of the colonial process was shown to allow the narrator to reach a state of transcendent freedom while exorcizing the imperial ghost of Mozambique's past, with his body the enigmatic means to making and unmaking imperial violence.

The disparities and contradictions between the ways that these six authors have attempted to reappropriate the gendered body for subversive means, with some achieving similar and others very different ends, have made the diachronic structure and flexible approach to theory used throughout this book both necessary and highly productive. The approach has allowed the study to find differences and similarities in unexpected places, casting new light on the continuities, junctures and disjunctions in twentieth-century Mozambican gender discourse and the literature that has reimagined it, while working against the conventional structures of comparative literary analysis that have hitherto characterized Mozambican cultural studies. In the work of Craveirinha, the reproductive potency and capacity of the black male and female bodies is a way of challenging the imperial emasculation of black men, but its reliance on the passive subjugation of women serves ultimately to reaffirm imperial gender discourses as a whole. For Khosa and Chiziane, on the other hand, the juxtaposition of images of reproductive capacity with ones that disrupt anatomical presence and integrity, through the use of grotesquery or parody, forestall the power of biological essentialism to reinforce social power structures, gendered and otherwise. The subversive power of de Sousa's work also lies in this troubling of anatomical presence, though for her this disordering practice is latent and concealed within linguistic nuance; Momplé and Cassamo, by contrast, take the opposite path, making notions of survival and suffering literal and deeply corporeal where they might have thus far remained discursive, rhetorical or symbolic outside of individual lived realities.

The central and frequently homogeneous status of gendered meaning in the visions of nationhood constructed by each iteration of state control in Mozambique has made gendered oppression a constant throughout the country's long twentieth century. It is this very constancy, however, that has simultaneously reified the gendered and sexual body as a site upon which the fundamental discourses of state power and control might be challenged, pushed against and ultimately destabilized. And it is in the most basic, essential and constant aspects of the gendered body – reproductive and sexual capacity, anatomical presence and integrity, resistance to pain and suffering, the drive toward survival – that Mozambique's authors have found the means to deconstruct the naturalized power frameworks upholding oppressive mechanisms of social control both local and global. On the very battleground on which power is produced, displayed and violently maintained, the writers of Mozambique have found the weapons to contest it.

Bibliography

Aboim, Sofia, 'Masculinidades na encruzilhada: hegemonia, dominação e hibridismo em Maputo', *Análise Social* 43/187 (2008), 273–95.

Afolabi, Niyi, ed., *Emerging Perspectives on Ungulani Ba Ka Khosa: Prophet, Trickster and Provocateur* (Trenton, NJ: Africa World Press, 2010).

——, 'Ungulani Ba Ka Khosa: A Rebellious Voice of Mozambican Regeneration', in Niyi Afolabi, ed., *Emerging Perspectives on Ungulani Ba Ka Khosa: Prophet, Trickster and Provocateur* (Trenton, NJ: Africa World Press, 2010), 59–103.

Ahmed, Sara, 'Brick Walls: Racism and Other Hard Histories', paper given at Manchester Metropolitan University, 11 March 2015.

——, 'Declarations of Whiteness: The Non-Performativity of Anti-Racism', *Borderlands E-journal* 3/2 (2004) <http://www.borderlands.net.au/vol3no2_2004/ahmed_declarations.htm> [accessed 28 June 2016].

Alarcón, Norma, 'Conjugating Subjects in the Age of Multiculturalism', in Avery F. Gordon and Christopher Newfield, eds, *Mapping Multiculturalism* (Minneapolis: University of Minnesota Press, 1996), 127–48.

Albuquerque, Fátima, 'Crianças Mais Sadias com Leite Materno', *Tempo*, 25 December 1983, 20–3.

——, 'Leite da Mãe é o Ideal para o Bebé: Amamentar é Garantir Saúde das Crianças', *Tempo*, 18 December 1983, 9–11.

Albuquerque, Joaquim Mousinho d', *A Prisão do Gungunhana* (Lourenço Marques [Maputo]: Sampaio e Carvalho, 1896).

Amadiume, Ifi, *Male Daughters, Female Husbands: Gender and Sex in an African Society* (London: Zed Books, 1987).

Andrade, António Alberto de, ed., *Relações de Moçambique Setecentista* (Lisbon: Agência Geral do Ultramar, 1955).

Anzaldúa, Gloria, *Borderlands/La Frontera: The New Mestiza* (San Francisco: Aunt Lute Books, 1987; 4th edn 2012).

——, 'Speaking in Tongues: A Letter to 3rd World Women Writers', in *This Bridge Called My Back: Writings by Radical Women of Color*, ed. Cherríe Moraga and Gloria Anzaldúa (Watertown, MA: Persephone Press, 1981; 2nd edn: Latham: Kitchen Table Women of Color Press, 1983), 165–73.

Apusigah, Agnes Atia, 'Is Gender Yet Another Colonial Project?: A Critique of Oyeronke Oyewumi's Proposal', *Quest: An African Journal of Philosophy* 20 (2006), 23–44.

Arnfred, Signe, *Sexuality and Gender Politics in Mozambique: Rethinking Gender in Africa* (Woodbridge: James Currey, 2011).

Azevedo, Licínio, dir., *Virgem Margarida* (Ébano Multimédia, Ukbar Filmes, and JBA Productions, 2012).

Azurara, Gomes Eannes de, *Chronica do Descobrimento e Conquista de Guiné* (Paris: J. P. Aillaud, [1453] 1841).

——, *The Chronicle of the Discovery and Conquest of Guinea*, trans. Charles Raymond Beazley, 2 vols (London: Hakluyt Society, 1896–9), vol. 1 (1896).

Bakhtin, Mikhail, *Rabelais and his World*, trans. Helene Iswolsky (Bloomington: Indiana University Press, 1984).

Banks, Jared, 'Violence and the (Re)Writing of History: A Reading of *Ualalapi*', in Niyi Afolabi, ed., *Emerging Perspectives on Ungulani Ba Ka Khosa: Prophet, Trickster and Provocateur* (Trenton, NJ: Africa World Press, 2010), 173–91.

Bergner, Gwen, 'Who Is That Masked Woman? Or, the Role of Gender in Fanon's *Black Skin, White Masks*', *PMLA* 110/1 (1995), 75–88.

Blackmore, Josiah, *Manifest Perdition: Shipwreck Narrative and the Disruption of Empire* (Minneapolis: University of Minnesota Press, 2002).

——, *Moorings: Portuguese Expansion and the Writing of Africa* (Minneapolis: University of Minnesota Press, 2009).

Bozzoli, Belinda, 'Marxism, Feminism and South African Studies', *Journal of Southern African Studies* 9/2 (1983), 139–71.

Briggs, Philip, 'Maputo: A View from our Expert Author', *Bradt Travel Guides* <http://www.bradtguides.com/destinations/africa/mozambique/maputo.html> [accessed 28 June 2016].

Brod, Harry, 'Some Thoughts on Some Histories of Some Masculinities: Jews and Other Others', in Harry Brod and Michael Kauffman, eds, *Theorizing Masculinities* (Thousand Oaks: Sage, 1994), 82–96.

——, and Michael Kauffman, eds, *Theorizing Masculinities* (Thousand Oaks, CA: Sage, 1994).

Butler, Judith, *Bodies that Matter: On the Discursive Limits of 'Sex'* (New York: Routledge, 1993; repr. 2011).

——, *Gender Trouble: Feminism and the Subversion of Identity* (New York: Routledge, 1990; repr. 2007).

Campos, Sandra, 'Corporeal Identity: Representations of Female Sexuality and the Body in the Novels of Paulina Chiziane', in Hilary Owen and Phillip Rothwell, eds, *Sexual/Textual Empires: Gender and Marginality in Lusophone African Literature* (Bristol: Bristol University Press, 2004) 137–54.

Cassamo, Suleiman, *Palestra para um Morto* (Maputo: Ndjira, 2000).

——, *O Regresso do Morto* (Maputo: Associação dos Escritores Moçambicanos, 1989; 2nd edn: Lisbon: Caminho, 1997).

Castanheira, Narciso, 'Viver por Dentro a "Operação Produção"', *Tempo*, 21 August 1983, 20–2.

Castelo, Cláudia, *O Modo Português de Estar no Mundo: O Luso-tropicalismo e a Ideologia Colonial Portuguesa (1933–1961)* (Porto: Edições Afrontamento, 1998).

Chabal, Patrick, *Vozes Moçambicanas: Literatura e Nacionalidade* (Lisbon: Vega, 1994).

——, ed., *The Postcolonial Literature of Lusophone Africa* (London: Hurst, 1996).

Chan, Stephen, and Moisés Venâncio, eds, *War and Peace in Mozambique* (Basingstoke: Macmillan, 1998).

Chiziane, Paulina, *Balada de Amor ao Vento* (Maputo: Associação dos Escritores Moçambicanos, 1990).

——, 'Eu, Mulher ... Por uma Nova Visão do Mundo', in Ana Elisa de Santana Afonso, ed., *Eu Mulher em Moçambique* (Maputo: Associação dos Escritores Moçambicanos, 1994), 11–18.

——, *O Sétimo Juramento* (Lisbon: Caminho, 2000; 3rd edn 2008).

——, *Ventos do Apocalipse* (Maputo: the author, 1993).

Christoph, Nancy, 'Bodily Matters: The Female Grotesque in Luisa Valenzuela's *Cola de lagartija*', *Revista Hispánica Moderna* 48/2 (1995), 365–80.

'Código Penal Moçambicana que Substitui Texto Colonial Entra em Vigor na Quarta-Feira', *Verdade* <http://www.verdade.co.mz/newsflash/53799-codigo-penal-mocambicano-que-substitui-texto-colonial-entra-em-vigor-na-quarta-feira> [accessed 28 June 2016].

Collins, Patricia Hill, *Black Feminist Thought: Knowledge, Consciousness, and the Politics of Empowerment* (New York: Routledge, 1991).

Coltrane, Scott, 'Theorizing Masculinities in Contemporary Social Science', in Harry Brod and Michael Kauffman, eds, *Theorizing Masculinities* (Thousand Oaks, CA: Sage, 1994), 39–60.

Connell, R. W., *Gender and Power* (Cambridge: Polity, 1987).

'Constituição Política da República Portuguesa', *Diário do Governo*, 22 February 1933, 227–36.

Craveirinha, José, *Xigubo* (Maputo: Alcance Editores, 2008). First pub. as *Chigubo* (Lisbon: Casa dos Estudantes do Império, 1964).

Decreto n.º 951: Regulamento Geral do Trabalho dos Indígenas nas Colónias Portuguesas (Lisbon: Imprensa Nacional, 1914).

Dinerman, Alice, *Revolution, Counter-Revolution and Revisionism in Postcolonial Africa: The Case of Mozambique, 1975–1994* (New York: Routledge, 2006).

Documentos da 8a Sessão da Comité Central Frelimo (Maputo: Departamento de Informação e Propaganda, 1976).

Dworkin, Andrea, *Intercourse* (New York: Basic Books, 2007).

Edelman, Lee, *No Future: Queer Theory and the Death Drive* (Durham, NC: Duke University Press, 2004).

'Editorial', *Jornal Noticias*, 3 July 2015 <http://www.jornalnoticias.co.mz/index.php/editorial/39127-edit702> [accessed 28 June 2016].

'Em Defesa do Leite Materno: Opinião de Especialistas da Cidade de Nampula', *Tempo*, 18 December 1983, 14–15.

Ennes, António, *Moçambique: Relatório Apresentado ao Governo* (Lisbon: Imprensa Nacional, 1893; 4th edn 1971).

'Entrevista do Presidente Salazar: Concedida à Revista Norte-Americana *U.S. News and World Report*', *Boletim Geral do Ultramar* 38/445 (1962), 3–20.

Estatuto dos Indígenas Portugueses das Províncias da Guiné, Angola e Moçambique (Lisbon: Agência Geral do Ultramar, 1954).

'Estatuto político, civil e criminal dos indígenas de Angola e Moçambique', *Boletim Geral das Colónias* 2/17 (1926), 152–6.

Fanon, Frantz, *Black Skin, White Masks*, trans. Charles Lam Markmann (London: Pluto Press, 1986). First pub.: London: Grove Press, 1967.

Ferreira, Ana Paula, 'Caliban's Travels', in Sheila Khan, Ana Margarida Dias Martins, Hilary Owen and Carmen Ramos Villar, eds, *The Lusotropical Tempest: Postcolonial Debates in Portuguese* (Bristol: Bristol University Press, 2012), 307–22.

——, 'Home Bound: The Construct of Femininity in the Estado Novo', *Portuguese Studies* 12 (1996), 133–44.

——, 'Specificity without Exceptionalism: Towards a Critical Lusophone Postcoloniality', in Paulo de Medeiros, ed., *Postcolonial Theory and Lusophone Literatures* (Utrecht: Universiteit Utrecht, 2007), 21–40.

Fitzpatrick, Mary, et al., *Lonely Planet: Zambia, Mozambique and Malawi* (London: Lonely Planet, 2013).

Foucault, Michel, *The History of Sexuality I: The Will to Knowledge*, trans. Robert Hurley (London: Penguin, 1998).

——, *Society Must Be Defended: Lectures at the Collège de France, 1975–76*, ed. Arnold I. Davidson, trans. David Macey (New York: Picador, 2003).

Frelick, Bill, 'RENAMO: The Khmer Rouge of Africa; Mozambique, its Killing Field', testimony before the House Subcommittee on Foreign Operations (Washington, DC: 1989).

Freyre, Gilberto, *Casa-Grande e Senzala: Formação da Família Brasileira sob o Regime da Economia Patriarcal* (São Paulo: Global Editora, 1933; 19th edn: Rio de Janeiro: José Olympio, 1978).

——, *The Masters and the Slaves: A Study in the Development of Brazilian Civilization*, trans. Samuel Putnam (New York: Alfred A. Knopf, 1946).

Ganho, Ana Sofia, 'Sex in the Shadow of the Nation: Angola in the Voices of Lopito Feijóo and Paula Tavares', in Hilary Owen and Phillip Rothwell, eds, *Sexual/ Textual Empires: Gender and Marginality in Lusophone African Literature* (Bristol: Bristol University Press, 2004), 155–75.

Gengenbach, Heidi, 'Boundaries of Beauty: Tattooed Secrets of Women's History in Magude District, Southern Mozambique', *Journal of Women's History* 14/4 (2003), 106–41.

Gersony, Robert, 'Summary of Mozambican Refugee Accounts of Principally Conflict-Related Experience in Mozambique', report submitted to Ambassador Jonathan Moore and Dr Chester Crocker (Washington, DC: 1988).

Gilroy, Paul, *The Black Atlantic: Modernity and Double Consciousness* (Cambridge, MA: Harvard University Press, 1993).

Grosz, Elizabeth, *Volatile Bodies: Toward a Corporeal Feminism* (Bloomington: Indiana University Press, 1994).

Guedes, Pedro Paulo d'Alpoim, *Iron in Building, 1750–1855: Innovation and Cultural Resistance*, unpublished doctoral thesis (University of Queensland, 2010).

Halberstam, Jack, 'On Pronouns' <http://www.jackhalberstam.com/on-pronouns/> [accessed 28 June 2016].

Halberstam, Judith, *Female Masculinity* (Durham, NC: Duke University Press, 1998).

Hamilton, Russell G., *Voices from an Empire: A History of Afro-Portuguese Literature* (Minneapolis: University of Minnesota Press, 1975).

Hamner, Jalna, 'Men, Power and the Exploitation of Women', in Jeff Hearn and David Morgan, eds, *Men, Masculinities and Social Theory* (London: Unwin Hyman, 1990), 21–42.

Hastrup, Kirsten, 'Hunger and the Hardness of Facts', *Man* 28/4 (1993), 727–39.

Hearn, Jeff, and David Morgan, eds, *Men, Masculinities and Social Theory* (London: Unwin Hyman, 1990).

Higonnet, Margaret, 'Frames of Female Suicide', *Studies in the Novel* 32/2 (2000), 229–42.

Honwana, Luís Bernardo, *Nós Matámos o Cão-Tinhoso* (Lourenço Marques [Maputo]: Sociedade de Imprensa de Moçambique, 1964; 7th edn: São Paulo: Ática, 1980).

hooks, bell, *Ain't I a Woman?: Black Women and Feminism* (Cambridge, MA: South End Press, 1981).

——, *Feminist Theory: From Margin to Center* (Boston, MA: South End Press, 1984).

Igreja, Victor, 'Memories as Weapons: The Politics of Peace and Silence in Post-Civil War Mozambique', *Journal of Southern African Studies* 34/3 (2008), 539–56.

Isaacman, Allen, 'Coercion, Paternalism and the Labour Process: The Mozambican Cotton Regime 1938–1961', *Journal of Southern African Studies* 18/3 (1992), 487–526.

Jones, Eleanor K., 'Diminished Returns: Mozambican Masculinities in José Craveirinha's *Xigubo* and Paulina Chiziane's *O Sétimo Juramento*', *Forum for Modern
Language Studies* 52/1 (2016), 81–99.

——, 'Discipline, Disease, Dissent: The Pathologized Body in Mozambican Post-
Independence Discourse', *Journal of Lusophone Studies* 1/2 (2016), 205–29.

Kalm, Leah M., and Richard D. Semba, 'They Starved So That Others Be Better Fed:
Remembering Ancel Keys and the Minnesota Experiment', *Journal of Nutrition*
135/6 (2005), 1347–52.

Khosa, Ungulani Ba Ka, '"Damboia" from *Ualalapi*', trans. David Brookshaw, in Niyi
Afolabi, ed., *Emerging Perspectives on Ungulani Ba Ka Khosa: Prophet, Trickster,
and Provocateur* (Trenton, NJ: Africa World Press, 2010), 381–8.

——, *Entre as Memórias Silenciadas* (Maputo: Alcance Editoras, 2013).

——, *Orgia dos Loucos* (Maputo: Alcance Editores, 2008). First pub.: Maputo: Associação dos Escritores Moçambicanos, 1990.

——, *Ualalapi* (Maputo: Associação dos Escritores Moçambicanos, 1987; 2nd edn:
Lisbon: Caminho, 1990).

Kimmel, Michael S., 'Masculinity as Homophobia: Fear, Shame, and Silence in the
Construction of Gender Identity', in Harry Brod and Michael Kauffman, eds,
Theorizing Masculinities (Thousand Oaks, CA: Sage, 1994), 119–41.

Klobucka, Anna, 'Lusotropical Romance: Camões, Gilberto Freyre, and the Isle of
Love', *Portuguese Literary and Cultural Studies* 9 (2002), 121–38.

Kristeva, Julia, *Black Sun: Depression and Melancholia*, trans. Leon S. Roudiez (New
York: Columbia University Press, 1989).

——, *Powers of Horror: An Essay on Abjection*, trans. Leon S. Roudiez (New York:
Columbia University Press, 1982).

Laranjeira, Pires, *A Negritude Africana de Língua Portuguesa* (Porto: Edições Afrontamento, 1995).

Leite, Ana Mafalda, *A Poética de José Craveirinha* (Lisbon: Vega, 1991).

'Leite Materno é o Melhor: Comunicado do GOAM', *Tempo*, 18 December 1983, 12–13.

'LIFEMO', *A Voz da Revolução: Edição Especial*, October 1966, n. p.

Lima, Alfredo Pereira de, *Casas que Fizeram Lourenço Marques* (Lisbon: Chiado
Editora, 1968; 2nd edn 2013).

——, *Edifícios Históricos de Lourenço Marques* (Lourenço Marques: Tip. Académica,
1966).

Lindsay, Lisa A., and Stephen Miescher, eds, *Men and Masculinities in Modern Africa*
(Portsmouth, NH: Heinemann, 2003).

Lisboa, Eugénio, 'Nota Muito Sumária a Propósito da Poesia em Moçambique', in Rui
Knopfli, *Mangas Verdes com Sal* (Mem Martins: Publicações Europa-América,
1969), 7–13.

Lopes, Arliado, 'Um Dia Inesquecível para Moçambique e Portugal', *Notícias*, 17 June 1985, 1.

Lopes, Mário, 'Mia Couto entre os Finalistas do Man Booker International Prize', *Público*, 24 March 2015 <http://www.publico.pt/culturaipsilon/noticia/mia-couto-entre-os-finalistas-do-man-booker-international-prize-1690175> [accessed 28 June 2016].

Lorde, Audre, *The Collected Poems of Audre Lorde* (New York: W. W. Norton, 1997).

——, *Sister Outsider: Essays and Speeches* (Freedom, CA: The Crossing Press, 1984).

Mac an Ghaill, Máirtín, 'The Making of Black English Masculinities', in Harry Brod and Michael Kauffman, eds, *Theorizing Masculinities* (Thousand Oaks, CA: Sage, 1994), 183–200.

McClintock, Anne, *Imperial Leather: Race, Gender and Sexuality in the Colonial Contest* (New York: Routledge, 1995).

Macêdo, Tania, and Vera Maquêa, eds, *Literaturas de Língua Portuguesa: Marcos e Marcas. Moçambique* (São Paulo: Arte e Ciência, 2007).

Machado, Lola Huete, 'Mia Couto: "En África no es que se vive un realismo mágico, es realismo real"', *El País*, 30 September 2013 <http://elpais.com/elpais/2013/09/27/eps/1380282368_900161.html> [accessed 28 June 2016].

Machel, Samora Moisés, *A Libertação da Mulher é uma Necessidade da Revolução, Garantia da sua Continuidade, Condição do seu Triunfo* (Porto: Textos da Revolução, 1974).

——, 'Ngungunyane Viveu e Morreu como Grande Herói do Povo', *Notícias*, 17 June 1985, 1.

——, *A Nossa Força Está na UNIDADE*, 4 vols (Maputo: Instituto Nacional do Livro e do Disco, 1983).

——, 'Povo é Construtor da Paz', *Tempo*, 27 February 1983, 14–23.

——, *Revolução: Transformação Profunda das Estruturas, Transformação Profunda da Nossa Vida* (Lourenço Marques [Maputo]: Imprensa Nacional, 1975).

Madureira, Luís, *Imaginary Geographies in Portuguese and Lusophone-African Literature: Narratives of Discovery and Empire* (Lampeter: Edwin Mellen Press, 2006).

——, 'Tropical Sex Fantasies and the Ambassador's Other Death: The Difference in Portuguese Colonialism', *Cultural Critique* 28 (1994), 149–73.

Magaia, Albino, 'Prostituição: Tráfico Sexual Mata a Fome', *Tempo*, 13 October 1974, 18–25.

Magaia, Lina, *Dumba Nengue – Run for Your Life: Peasant Tales of Tragedy in Mozambique* (Trenton, NJ: Africa World Press, 1988).

Manuel, Fernando, '50º Aniversário do Presidente Samora Machel', *Tempo*, 9 October 1983, 17–21.

——, 'Leite e Derivados: Vem Longe a Fartura', *Tempo*, 13 November 1983, 18–23.

Marmelo, António, 'Fracturas que a Revolução Vai Cimentar', *Tempo*, 31 May 1981, 18–24.

Martins, Ana Margarida, 'Gender and the "Postcolonial Exotic"', *Journal of Commonwealth Literature* 48/1 (2013), 145–58.

——, *Magic Stones and Flying Snakes: Gender and the 'Postcolonial Exotic' in the Work of Paulina Chiziane and Lídia Jorge* (Oxford: Peter Lang, 2012).

Mata, Inocência, 'O Sétimo Juramento, de Paulina Chiziane – uma alegoria sobre o preço de poder', *Scripta* 4/8 (2001), 187–91.

Mbembe, Achille, 'Necropolitics', trans. Libby Meintjes, *Public Culture* 15/1 (2003), 11–40.

——, *On the Postcolony* (Berkeley: University of California Press, 2001).

Medeiros, Paulo de, 'Ghosts and Hosts: Inheritance and the Postimperial Condition', paper given at the VI Congresso Nacional Associação Portuguesa de Literatura Comparada (2009) <http://ceh.ilch.uminho.pt/publicacoes/Pub_Medeiros. pdf> [accessed 28 June 2016].

Minter, William, 'The Mozambican National Resistance (Renamo) as Described by Ex-participants', report submitted to Ford Foundation and Swedish National Development Agency (Washington, DC: 1989).

Miranda, António Pinto de, 'Memória sobre a Costa de África (c. 1766)', in António Alberto de Andrade, ed., *Relações de Moçambique Setecentista* (Lisbon: Agência Geral do Ultramar, 1955), 231–302.

'Mixed Reaction to Scrapping of Anti-Gay Law in Mozambique', *LGBTQ Nation*, 4 July 2015 <http://www.lgbtqnation.com/2015/07/mixed-reaction-to-scrapping-of-anti-gay-law-in-mozambique/> [accessed 28 June 2016].

Mohanty, Chandra Talpade, 'Under Western Eyes: Feminist Scholarship and Colonial Discourse', *Boundary 2* 12/3–13/1 (1984), 333–58.

Momplé, Lília, *Antologia de Contos* (Maputo: the author, 2012).

——, *Neighbours* (Maputo: Associação dos Escritores Moçambicanos, 1995).

——, *Neighbours: The Story of a Murder*, trans. Richard Bartlett and Isaura de Oliveira (Cape Town: Penguin, 2009).

——, *Ninguém Matou Suhura* (Maputo: Associação dos Escritores Moçambicanos, 1988; 5th edn: Maputo: the author, 2009).

——, *Os Olhos da Cobra Verde* (Maputo: Associação dos Escritores Moçambicanos, 1997).

Morrell, Robert, *Changing Men in Southern Africa* (Natal: University of Natal Press, 2001).

——, 'Of Boys and Men: Masculinity and Gender in Southern African Studies', *Southern Africa Studies* 24/2 (1998), 605–30.

'Mozambican Priest at the UN, A', *Mozambican Revolution*, October–November 1967, 9–11.

Muiuane, Armando Pedro, ed., *Datas e Documentos da História da Frelimo* (Maputo: Frelimo, 3rd edn 2006).

'Mulher: Futuro do Homem', *Tempo*, 30 October 1983, front cover.

Mulvey, Laura, 'A Phantasmagoria of the Female Body: The Work of Cindy Sherman', *New Left Review* 188 (1991), 136–50.

Muñoz, José Esteban, *Disidentifications: Queers of Color and the Performance of Politics* (Minneapolis: University of Minnesota Press, 1999).

Murray, Stuart J., 'Thanatopolitics: On the Use of Death for Mobilizing Political Life', *Polygraph* 18 (2006), 191–215.

Naroromele, Albano, 'Ngungunyane Regressou à Pátria: Povo Recebeu Herói da Resistência', *Notícias*, 17 June 1985, 1.

Newitt, Malyn, *A History of Mozambique* (London: Hurst, 1995).

——, 'Mozambique', in Patrick Chabal, ed., *A History of Postcolonial Lusophone Africa* (London: Hurst, 2002), 185–235.

'Ngungunhane: Herói da Luta Anticolonial', *Tempo*, 11 December 1983, 27–35.

Nordstrom, Carolyn, *A Different Kind of War Story* (Philadelphia: University of Pennsylvania Press, 1997).

Noronha, Eduardo de, *O Districto de Lourenço Marques e a África do Sul* (Lisbon: Imprensa Nacional, 1895).

'Nutrição e Sub-nutrição', *Tempo*, 29 February 1976, 30–9.

'Organised Civil Oppression', *Mozambican Revolution*, June 1964, 5.

'Organização da Mulher Moçambicana', *Tempo*, 23 February 1975, 34–7.

Owen, Hilary, *Mother Africa, Father Marx: Women's Writing of Mozambique, 1948–2002* (Lewisburg, PA: Bucknell University Press, 2007).

——, 'Third World/Third Sex: Gender, Orality and a Tale of Two Marias in Mia Couto and Paulina Chiziane', *Bulletin of Hispanic Studies* 84/4 (2007), 475–88.

——, 'Women on the Edge of a Nervous Empire in Paulina Chiziane and Ungulani Ba Ka Khosa', in Ana Mafalda Leite, Hilary Owen, Rita Chaves and Livia Apa, eds, *Narrating the Postcolonial Nation: Mapping Angola and Mozambique* (Oxford: Peter Lang, 2014), 199–211.

——, and Claire Williams, 'Interview with Lília Momplé', in Hilary Owen and Phillip Rothwell, eds, *Sexual/Textual Empires: Gender and Marginality in Lusophone African Literature* (Bristol: Bristol University Press, 2004), 177–87.

——, and Phillip Rothwell, eds, *Sexual/Textual Empires: Gender and Marginality in Lusophone African Literature* (Bristol: Bristol University Press, 2004).

Oyěwùmí, Oyèrónké, *The Invention of Women: Making an African Sense of Western Gender Discourses* (Minneapolis: University of Minnesota Press, 1997).

Padilha, Laura Cavalcante, 'Silêncios Rompidos: A Produção Textual de Mulheres Africanas', *Ellipsis* 1 (1999), 63–79.

'Para Onde Foram as Prostitutas?', *Tempo*, 31 August 1975, 27–9.

'Parade Flagbearers', *Pride in London* <http://web.archive.org/web/20150823021900/http://prideinlondon.org/flagbearers/> [accessed 28 June 2016].

Patterson, Orlando, *Slavery and Social Death: A Comparative Study* (Cambridge, MA: Harvard University Press, 1982).

Pazos-Alonso, Cláudia, 'The Wind of Change in *Nós Matámos o Cão-Tinhoso*', *Ellipsis* 5 (2007), 67–85.

'Primeira Conferência da Mulher Moçambicana: Comunicado Final', *A Voz da Revolução*, March 1973, 5–7.

'Primeiro Bébé de 1975 em Lourenço Marques: Tradição Johnson & Johnson', *Tempo*, 12 January 1975, 9.

'Problemas Portugueses em África: Entrevista Concedida pelo Presidente do Conselho, Prof. Dr. Oliveira Salazar, à Revista Norte-Americana *Life*', *Boletim Geral do Ultramar* 38/443 (1962), 3–15.

'Problemas Sociais – Aspectos Gerais', *Tempo*, 23 February 1975, 37–8.

'Regulamento do Trabalho dos Indígenas', *Diário do Governo*, 9 November 1899, 647–54.

Regulamento dos Tribunais Privativos dos Indígenas (Lourenço Marques [Maputo]: Imprensa Nacional, 1933).

Ribas, Filipe, 'Em Nome da Ciência', *Tempo*, 13 November 1983, 23.

Rich, Adrienne, 'Compulsory Heterosexuality and Lesbian Existence (1980)', in Barbara Charlesworth Gelphi and Albert Gelphi, eds, *Adrienne Rich's Poetry and Prose* (New York: Norton, 1993), 203–24.

Rodrigues, Isabel Fêo P. B., and Kathleen Sheldon, 'Cape Verdean and Mozambican Women's Literature: Liberating the National and Seizing the Intimate', *African Studies Review* 53/3 (2010), 77–99.

'Role of Poetry in the Mozambican Revolution, The', *Mozambican Revolution*, 25 April 1969, 17–32.

Rothwell, Phillip, 'Momplé's Melancholia: Mourning for Mozambique', *Portuguese Studies Review* 10/1 (2002), 185–93.

——, 'Perverse Prosperos and Cruel Calibans', in Clara Sarmento, ed., *From Here to Diversity: Globalization and Intercultural Dialogues* (Newcastle-upon-Tyne: Cambridge Scholars Publishing, 2010), 307–22.

——, 'The Phylomorphic Linguistic Tradition: Or, the Siege of (the) Portuguese in Mozambique', *Hispanic Research Journal* 2/2 (2001), 165–76.

——, *A Postmodern Nationalist: Truth, Orality, and Gender in the Work of Mia Couto* (Lewisburg, PA: Bucknell University Press, 2004).

Russo, Mary, *The Female Grotesque: Risk, Excess and Modernity* (New York: Routledge, 1994).

Ryan, Katy, 'Revolutionary Suicide in Toni Morrison's Fiction', *African American Review* 34/3 (2000), 389–412.

Sabine, Mark, 'Gender, Race, and Violence in Luís Bernardo Honwana's *Nós Matámos o Cão-Tinhoso*: The Emasculation of the African Patriarch', in Hilary Owen and Phillip Rothwell, eds, *Sexual/Textual Empires: Gender and Marginality in Lusophone African Literature* (Bristol: Bristol University Press, 2004), 23–44.

Sandoval, Chela, 'U.S. Third World Feminism: The Theory and Method of Oppositional Consciousness in the Postmodern World', *Genders* 10 (1991), 1–24.

Santos, Boaventura de Sousa, 'Between Prospero and Caliban: Colonialism, Postcolonialism, and Inter-identity', *Luso-Brazilian Review* 39/2 (2002), 9–43.

Saúte, Nelson, 'A Mãe dos Poetas Moçambicanos', in Nelson Saúte, ed., *Sangue Negro* (Maputo: Marimbique, 2011), 125–31.

——, *Maputo: Desenrascar a Vida* (Maputo: Ndjira, 1997).

Scarry, Elaine, *The Body in Pain: The Making and Unmaking of the World* (Oxford: Oxford University Press, 1985).

Scott, Catherine V., 'Men in Our Country Behave Like Chiefs: Women and the Angolan Revolution', in Mary Ann Trétault, ed., *Women and Revolution in Africa, Asia, and the New World* (Columbia, SC: University of South Carolina Press, 1994).

'Seca: A Terra Tem Sede', *Tempo*, 19 June 1983, front cover.

Sedgwick, Eve Kosofsky, *Between Men: English Literature and Male Homosocial Desire* (Chichester, NY: Columbia University Press, 1985).

Segal, Lynne, *Slow Motion: Changing Masculinities, Changing Men* (London: Virago, 1990).

Sexsmith, Sinclair, 'Jack Halberstam: Queers Create Better Models of Success', *Lambda Literary* (2012) <http://www.lambdaliterary.org/interviews/02/01/jack-halberstam-queers-create-better-models-of-success> [accessed 28 June 2016].

Shapira, Yael, 'Hairball Speaks: Margaret Atwood and the Narrative Legacy of the Female Grotesque', *Narrative* 18/1 (2010), 51–72.

Sheldon, Kathleen, 'Markets and Gardens: Placing Women in the History of Urban Mozambique', *Canadian Journal of African Studies* 37/2–3 (2003), 358–95.

——, *Pounders of Grain: A History of Women, Work, and Politics in Mozambique* (Portsmouth, NH: Heinemann, 2002).

Sideris, Tina, 'War, Gender and Culture: Mozambican Women Refugees', *Social Science & Medicine* 56 (2003), 713–24.

Silva, Calane da, 'Prostituição: Primeiros e Decisivos Golpes', *Tempo*, 17 November 1974, 64.

Silva, Teresa Cruz e, 'The Influence of the Swiss Mission on Eduardo Mondlane (1930–1961)', *Journal of Religion in Africa* 28/2 (1998), 187–209.

'Sister Selina Simango in China', *Mozambican Revolution*, June 1964, 5–6.

Slater, Mike, *Globetrotter Travel Guide: Mozambique* (London: New Holland, 2013).

Smith, David, 'Mozambique LGBT Activists Move on to Next Battle after Anti-Gay Law Scrapped', *The Guardian*, 30 June 2015 <http://www.theguardian.com/world/2015/jun/30/mozambique-lgbt-activists-anti-gay-law-scrapped> [accessed 28 June 2016].

Sousa, Noémia de, *Sangue Negro*, ed. Nelson Saúte (Maputo: Associação dos Escritores Moçambicanos, 2001; 2nd edn: Maputo: Marimbique, 2011).

UNICEF/OMM, *The Situation of Children and Women in Mozambique* (Maputo: Ministry of Co-operation, 1990).

Valenzuela, Luisa, 'Mis brujas favoritas', in Gabriela Mora and Karen S. Van Hooft, eds, *Theory and Practice of Feminist Literary Criticism* (Ypsilanti: Bilingual Press, 1982), 88–95.

Wainaina, Binyavanga, 'How to Write About Africa', *Granta* 92 (2006) <http://granta.com/How-to-Write-about-Africa/> [accessed 28 June 2016].

Watts, Michael, 'Entitlements or Empowerment? Famine and Starvation in Africa', *Review of African Political Economy* 18/51 (1991), 9–26.

Westwood, Sallie, 'Racism, Black Masculinity and the Politics of Space', in Jeff Hearn and David Morgan, eds, *Men, Masculinities and Social Theory* (London: Unwin Hyman, 1990), 55–72.

Wheeler, Douglas L., 'Gungunyane the Negotiator: A Study in African Diplomacy', *Journal of African History* 9/4 (1968), 585–602.

Williams, Claire, 'Maidens, Matriarchs and Martyrs: Mozambican Women in the Works of Lília Momplé', in Hilary Owen and Phillip Rothwell, eds, *Sexual/Textual Empires: Gender and Marginality in Lusophone African Literature* (Bristol: Bristol University Press, 2004) 117–35.

Xavier, Inácio Caetano, 'Notícias dos Domínios Portuguezes na Costa de África Oriental', in António Alberto de Andrade, ed., *Relações de Moçambique Setecentista* (Lisbon: Agência Geral do Ultramar, 1955), 139–88.

Yekani, Elahe Haschemi, *The Privilege of Crisis: Narratives of Masculinity in Colonial and Postcolonial Literature, Photography and Film* (Frankfurt a.M.: Campus, 2011).

Zimba, Benigna, *A Mulher Moçambicana na Luta de Libertação Nacional: Memórias do Destacamento Feminino* (Maputo: Organização da Mulher Moçambicana, 2013).

Index

RECONFIGURING IDENTITIES IN THE PORTUGUESE-SPEAKING WORLD

Edited by

Paulo de Medeiros and Cláudia Pazos-Alonso

The series publishes studies across the entire spectrum of Lusophone literature, culture and intellectual history, from the Middle Ages to the present day, with particular emphasis on figurations and reconfigurations of identity, broadly understood. It is especially interested in work which interrogates national identity and cultural memory, or which offers fresh insights into Portuguese-speaking cultural and literary traditions, in diverse historical contexts and geographical locations. It is open to a wide variety of approaches and methodologies as well as to interdisciplinary fields: from literary criticism and comparative literature to cultural and gender studies, to film and media studies. It also seeks to encourage critical dialogue among scholarship originating from different continents.

Proposals are welcome for either single-author monographs or edited collections (in English and/or Portuguese). Those interested in contributing to the series should send a detailed project outline to oxford@peterlang.com.

VOL. 1   Ana Margarida Martins: Magic Stones and Flying Snakes: Gender and the 'Postcolonial Exotic' in the Work of Paulina Chiziane and Lídia Jorge.
ISBN 978-3-0343-0828-1. 2012